CREATIVE
HOMEOWNER®

ULTIMATE GUIDE TO

Bathrooms

CREATIVE
HOMEOWNER®

ULTIMATE GUIDE TO

Bathrooms

PLAN ■ REMODEL ■ BUILD

CREATIVE HOMEOWNER®, Upper Saddle River, New Jersey

ULTIMATE GUIDE TO BATHROOMS

MANAGING EDITOR	Fran J. Donegan
SENIOR GRAPHIC DESIGN COORDINATOR	Glee Barre
PHOTO RESEARCHER	Robyn Poplasky
EDITORIAL ASSISTANT	Jennifer Calvert
INDEXER	Schroeder Indexing Services
COVER DESIGN	David Geer
ILLUSTRATIONS	Ian Warpole; Glee Barre
FRONT COVER PHOTOGRAPHY	Randall Perry
BACK COVER PHOTOGRAPHY	*Top* Beth Singer, architect: Dominick Tringali Associates, builder: Custom Homes by DeRocher, Inc.; *bottom row left to right* Freeze Frame Studios; Mark Lohman; Freeze Frame Studios

CREATIVE HOMEOWNER

VICE PRESIDENT AND PUBLISHER	Timothy O. Bakke
PRODUCTION DIRECTOR	Kimberly H. Vivas
ART DIRECTOR	David Geer
MANAGING EDITOR	Fran J. Donegan

Current Printing (last digit)
10 9 8 7 6 5 4 3 2 1

Ultimate Guide to Bathrooms, Fourth Edition
Library of Congress Control Number: 2006934266
ISBN-10: 1-58011-341-9
ISBN-13: 978-1-58011-341-0

CREATIVE HOMEOWNER®
A Division of Federal Marketing Corp.
24 Park Way
Upper Saddle River, NJ 07458
www.creativehomeowner.com

safety

Although the methods in this book have been reviewed for safety, it is not possible to overstate the importance of using the safest methods you can. What follows are reminders—some do's and don'ts of work safety—to use along with your common sense.

- Always use caution, care, and good judgment when following the procedures described in this book.
- Always be sure that the electrical setup is safe, that no circuit is overloaded, and that all power tools and outlets are properly grounded. Do not use power tools in wet locations.
- Always read container labels on paints, solvents, and other products; provide ventilation; and observe all other warnings.
- Always read the manufacturer's instructions for using a tool, especially the warnings.
- Use hold-downs and push sticks whenever possible when working on a table saw. Avoid working short pieces if you can.
- Always remove the key from any drill chuck (portable or press) before starting the drill.
- Always pay deliberate attention to how a tool works so that you can avoid being injured.
- Always know the limitations of your tools. Do not try to force them to do what they were not designed to do.
- Always make sure that any adjustment is locked before proceeding. For example, always check the rip fence on a table saw or the bevel adjustment on a portable saw before starting to work.
- Always clamp small pieces to a bench or other work surface when using a power tool.
- Always wear the appropriate rubber gloves or work gloves when handling chemicals, moving or stacking lumber, working with concrete, or doing heavy construction.
- Always wear a disposable face mask when you create dust by sawing or sanding. Use a special filtering respirator when working with toxic substances and solvents.
- Always wear eye protection, especially when using power tools or striking metal on metal or concrete; a chip can fly off, for example, when chiseling concrete.
- Never work while wearing loose clothing, open cuffs, or jewelry; tie back long hair.
- Always be aware that there is seldom enough time for your body's reflexes to save you from injury from a power tool in a dangerous situation; everything happens too fast. Be alert!
- Always keep your hands away from the business ends of blades, cutters, and bits.
- Always hold a circular saw firmly, usually with both hands.
- Always use a drill with an auxiliary handle to control the torque when using large-size bits.
- Always check your local building codes when planning new construction. The codes are intended to protect public safety and should be observed to the letter.
- Never work with power tools when you are tired or when under the influence of alcohol or drugs.
- Never cut tiny pieces of wood or pipe using a power saw. When you need a small piece, saw it from a securely clamped longer piece.
- Never change a saw blade or a drill or router bit unless the power cord is unplugged. Do not depend on the switch being off. You might accidentally hit it.
- Never work in insufficient lighting.
- Never work with dull tools. Have them sharpened, or learn how to sharpen them yourself.
- Never use a power tool on a workpiece—large or small—that is not firmly supported.
- Never saw a workpiece that spans a large distance between horses without close support on each side of the cut; the piece can bend, closing on and jamming the blade, causing saw kickback.
- When sawing, never support a workpiece from underneath with your leg or other part of your body.
- Never carry sharp or pointed tools, such as utility knives, awls, or chisels, in your pocket. If you want to carry any of these tools, use a special-purpose tool belt that has leather pockets and holders.

contents

INTRODUCTION
planning basics

Chances are good that if you own this book, you have already decided to remodel or add a new bathroom to your house. If your intention is to increase the value of the house, you've made a smart choice, especially if you decide to sell sooner rather than later. According to *Consumer Reports*, if you put your house on the market within a year after completing the project, you may recoup as much as 75 percent of what you spent. Even if you have no immediate plans to move, finally having that much-longed-for luxury master bath or convenient extra half bath may be all the payback you need. *Ultimate Guide to Bathrooms: Plan, Remodel, Build* can help you achieve your goals for a new bathroom.

The book provides lots of inspiration and information on today's most popular bath trends, including help in designing bathrooms of all sizes and uses, and picking the right fixtures and finishes. But the heart of *Ultimate Guide to Baths* is the 70 step-by-step projects that cover everything from removing old fixtures to installing a new spa tub. The collection of projects gives you a number of options. You can tackle all of the work yourselfer—to keep you from getting in over your head, there is a project rating system explained at right— or you can choose the projects with which you are most comfortable while a professional takes care of the rest. The system will help you get from point A (dreaming) to point B (doing) and, finally, point C (enjoying).

GUIDE TO SKILL LEVEL

Easy. Made for beginners.

Challenging. Can be done by beginners who have the patience and willingness to learn.

Difficult. Can be handled by most experienced do-it-yourselfers who have mastered basic construction skills. Consider consulting a specialist.

LEFT Begin your remodeling with a wish list of the elements and amenities you want your new bathroom to contain.

Once you decide what you don't like, make a list of what you do like. Gather pictures and product information from magazines, newspapers, and Internet sites. Keep all of these things together in a scrapbook or folder, along with business cards and ads for suppliers and professional services you might need.

What Are You Willing to Spend?

Maybe the real question is, How much can you spend? That depends on several factors: available cash; the amount of financing you can obtain; the amount of your monthly loan payments; and your overall goals. The total cost depends on the extent of the remodeling. Doing the work yourself can save money, but don't take on a job for which you have no skills or the time to complete. Remember that mistakes and delays are costly.

Architects. A licensed architect who regularly designs residential bathrooms is important if you plan to make significant structural changes.

Certified Bath Designers. Professional designers certified by the National Kitchen & Bath Association (NKBA), CBDs can help you with the layout of the room, and they know the latest trends and products.

Interior Designers. Interior designers are style and arrangement experts. You may want to consult an interior designer if you plan to make significant cosmetic changes rather than structural ones.

Design-Build Remodeling Firms. Many remodeling firms retain both remodelers and designers on staff.

Remodeling Contractors. A contractor is a good choice if you have already hired an architect to design the bath or if you are not making structural changes.

START WITH A PLAN

Your home is your personal space, so plan it carefully. Even if you ultimately hand the job over to a professional, do the homework.

Make a rough freehand sketch of the space; then take measurements. First record the length and width of the room, and then measure and note the doorways and window openings. Record each dimension in feet and inches

WHAT DO YOU WANT?

To answer the question of what you really want in a new bathroom, write down what you don't like about your current situation. Get the family involved. Here are some questions to help spark a discussion:

▌ Are there enough bathrooms in the house for the number of people who live there?

▌ Are the bathrooms conveniently located?

▌ Are there young children or elderly persons the family?

▌ Does anyone have a disability?

▌ Do the fixtures need updating, are there any leaks, or does the room simply need a cosmetic makeover?

▌ Is there adequate storage in the bathroom for everyone who uses the space?

▌ Is there good lighting? Ventilation? Do you see signs of mold or mildew?

▌ Are there enough electrical outlets? Are they protected with ground-fault circuit interrupters (GFCIs)?

▌ Do you prefer a bath or a shower?

▌ Do you regularly need to bathe and groom in the bathroom at the same time as other members of the household? How many?

▌ What kind of a budget do you have for the project?

▌ Is there another bathroom in the house that you can use until the project is complete?

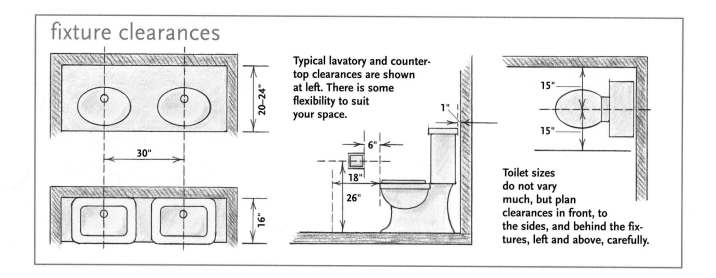

fixture clearances

Typical lavatory and counter-top clearances are shown at left. There is some flexibility to suit your space.

20–24"

30"

16"

6"

1"

18"

26"

15"

15"

Toilet sizes do not vary much, but plan clearances in front, to the sides, and behind the fixtures, left and above, carefully.

to the nearest ¼ inch. Then record the cabinetry and plumbing fixtures. Measure to the centerline of the sinks, toilets, and bidets, but also list their overall lengths and widths.

Next, transfer your measurements from rough form to graph paper to plan the new layout. Draw the room to scale, using ½ inch on your drawing to represent 1 foot. If you use graph paper with a ¼-inch grid, each square represents a 6-inch square.

Before you add the fixtures, make several copies of the plan so that you can explore different options. Or make scaled down paper templates of the fixtures and cabinets so that you can easily move them around on your layout. If you have collected pictures and spec sheets, use the dimensions given. You can find numerous sample layouts on pages 50–53 in Chapter 2, "Master Baths"; pages 70–73 in Chapter 3, "Family Baths"; and pages 83–85 in Chapter 4, "Half Baths."

Placing Fixtures

In a full bath, the most-used fixture is the sink, followed by the toilet, and then the tub or shower. The most efficient plan in this case puts the sink nearest the door, with the toilet next in line, and the tub at the far end. However, this is just a basic layout for a modest, typically 60- x 84-inch room. If you have more room, locate the toilet where it can't be seen from the door, even in a separate compartment if that's possible. If more than one person has to use the room at the same time to get ready for work or school, you can ease the traffic jam by making a place for the sink and vanity as far from the tub and shower as possible. And if more than one person uses the room at the

same time, be sure to plan for plenty of counter and mirror space.

When you have limited space, it's hard to maintain recommended minimum clearances around the bathroom fixtures, but try to adhere to them as closely as possible. (See the illustrations above.)

ADDING SPACE AND NATURAL LIGHT

Other than adding on to the house, there are a few things you can do to enlarge the bathroom. For example, consider expanding into an adjacent room or closet. Sometimes annexing a couple of feet from the room next to the bath can make a big difference in the layout of the bathroom without compromising the adjacent room's usefulness. A bump-out addition to an outside wall offers the chance to gain floor space as well, but the additional foundation work makes this solution expensive. It may be possible to extend the outer wall by as much as 3 feet without building a new foundation. This involves extending the floor structure with cantilevered joists over the foundation.

If the existing floor joists run perpendicular into the outer wall, add a "sister" to each joist, which means attaching a second joist to the one that is there, to cantilever out and overhang the foundation. But first get an architect or engineer to examine the structure to make sure it's sound. You will also have to make sure that this plan does not encroach into the setback required by the local zoning ordinance. (For more information on permits and zoning regulations, see page 12.)

Windows

Adding extra windows or a skylight can visually open up a small stuffy space. Operable units also provide natural ventilation. French doors and sliding doors provide access to a garden, the pool, or a deck, if you desire it.

Today's windows are made of wood, metal, or vinyl. Wood frames may be solid or made of pressed wood particles. The most common residential metal windows are made of extruded aluminum, but steel units are available, as are plastic (usually PVC) and fiberglass frames.

Wood windows are clad in aluminum or vinyl and need no upkeep, or they may come primed for painting or staining. Aluminum windows are surfaced with a permanent finish of baked enamel. Steel windows come primed for painting. The vinyl finish never needs painting.

Glazing. Fortunately, today's windows are better sealed against leakage and better insulated against heat loss through the glass. Select double-glazed windows (two separated panes) wherever you live. If you reside in a cold climate, you'll get even better energy efficiency with windows protected with a low-emissivity (low-E) film, either on the glass or as a separate film, and argon gas in the space between the two panes.

Window Types. Windows can be fixed (meaning you can't open them) or operable. Glass block is an example of a fixed window, but even clear-glass framed panels can be fixed. These windows let in light and views, but they don't admit air.

Examples of operable window types include double- and single-hung windows. The former has both an upper

ABOVE The layout of your bath will depend on available space and the type and size of the fixtures you choose.

and lower sash that ride up and down in their own channels. Single-hung windows are like double-hung units except that only their lower sash moves.

Casement windows are hinged vertically to swing in or out. You can operate them with a crank.

Sliding windows have top and bottom tracks on which the sash move sideways.

Awning windows are hinged horizontally to swing in or out. Refer to the illustration on this page to see examples of these five types of windows.

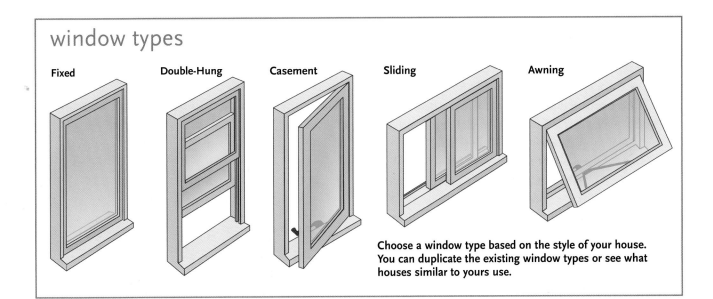

window types

Fixed **Double-Hung** **Casement** **Sliding** **Awning**

Choose a window type based on the style of your house. You can duplicate the existing window types or see what houses similar to yours use.

DO YOU NEED A PERMIT?

Before making any changes, find out whether you need a permit. Permits and inspections are a way of enforcing the building code. A permit is essentially a license to do the work, while an inspection ensures that you did the work in accordance with codes. Some municipal codes allow work by a homeowner on his or her house if a permit is obtained first. However, some municipalities won't let anyone but a licensed contractor work on wiring or plumbing.

To determine the regulations in your area, contact the local building department. Depending on the scope of the work, your permit application will probably include the following:

LEFT Skylights bring natural light into the center of the room. Choose units appropriate for your climate.

BELOW Large mirrors are useful for reflecting light and opening up the space.

Skylights and Roof Windows. An opening in the roof is an excellent way to flood a bathroom with light without taking up wall space. People often refer to any glazed opening in the roof as a skylight. That terms technically refers to the bubble-dome skylight of years ago. It's still available, but today there are flat-profile roof windows. However, bubble-dome skylights still make sense on a flat roof because they shed rain better. Fixed skylights are the most economical choice, followed by venting skylights, with operable roof windows at the top of the cost scale.

A tubular skylight is another option. It's smaller than a skylight, and it allows you to bring light into a dark bath even if the room isn't directly under the roof. There are various diameter sizes available. The distance between the roof opening and the bathroom ceiling below can range from the thickness of the rafters to many feet.

In conjunction with a roof window, the construction of a light shaft, which is usually larger than a tubular skylight, also brings light into the room. Splaying the shaft walls out from the roof opening to the ceiling distributes light to all corners of the bathroom. To promote light distribution, finish the shaft walls with drywall and paint them white.

- A legal description of the property from city or county records or from a deed.
- A site-plan drawing showing the position of the house on the lot and the approximate location of adjacent houses. It should also show the location of the well and septic system, if any exist.
- A drawing of the proposed changes and materials. Most building departments will accept plans drawn by a homeowner as long as they are clearly labeled.

Inspections

Whenever a permit is required, you'll probably have to schedule time for an inspector to examine the work. Actually, you may need to schedule a number of inspectors for different part s of the job. On a small project, an inspector might come out only for a final inspection. On a larger project, there may be several intermediate inspections before the final one. If you're working with a contractor, he or she will schedule the necessary inspections.

BELOW A well-planned project will provide you and your family with a bathroom that everyone can enjoy.

LEFT The small window and matching bench set the stage for the flanking vanities.

RIGHT Alcoves for toilets are becoming increasingly popular.

BELOW LEFT The arch of the tub alcove shown repeats the shape of the window.

BELOW RIGHT Half walls define activity areas without blocking light.

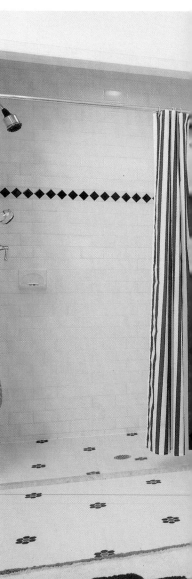

ABOVE A generously proportioned vanity fits into the nook shown here, setting it apart from the room.

BELOW Irregularly shaped rooms are often just right for creating separate activity areas, such as this dressing area.

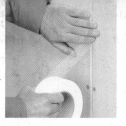

1 construction basics

This chapter could just as easily have been called "First Things First," because it is where you begin turning all of those ideas you have for a new bathroom into reality. But before you install the new double vanity or full-body jets for the custom shower, you will need to take care of the basics, such as removing the old bath fixtures, repairing damaged floors, and perhaps taking down a wall. Once the demolition is complete and if you have firm plans, you can form the bones of your new bathroom by getting the floors and walls in shape. If you are still in the planning stage, chapters 2, 3, and 4, beginning on page 38, cover the designs of different types of bathrooms.

Many techniques shown here, such as installing drywall, can be used in any room of the house. But most focus directly on the needs of the bathroom.

REMOVING AN OLD SINK AND VANITY

project

Begin the demolition process by removing the old sink and vanity. The first step is to shut off the water at the valves under the sink. Then remove the supply tubes that connect the shutoff valves to the bottom of the faucets. For hard-to-reach places, a basin wrench provides easy access to nuts. Before taking apart the trap assembly, slide a pail under the pipe to catch any waste water. Then loosen the trap nuts and remove the trap.

Remove the hardware that holds the sink in place, and cut any caulk around the lip of the sink. Pull the sink out of the top, and then detach the top from the cabinet underneath. Cut around the supply and waste lines to free the back of the vanity; then pull the base from the wall.

TOOLS & MATERIALS
- Open-end wrench
- Adjustable pliers
- Basin wrench
- Pipe wrenches
- Pail
- Flashlight
- Penetrating oil (if needed)
- Putty knife or utility knife
- Power drill with screwdriver bit
- Keyhole saw or utility saw
- Wood chisel

caution

USE ONLY A FLASHLIGHT OR A BATTERY-POWERED WORK LIGHT TO LIGHT THE AREA BELOW THE VANITY. IF WATER DRIPS DOWN ONTO A HARDWIRED ELECTRICAL LIGHT—ESPECIALLY A TROUBLE LIGHT WITH A BUILT-IN RECEPTACLE—AND CAUSES A SHORT, YOU COULD GET HURT.

1 Clear away everything from the bottom of the vanity, and turn off the water at the shutoff valves. If there are no shutoff valves, turn off the water at the main valve near your water meter or water well pressure tank.

5 Remove any retaining clips or other kinds of hardware that hold the sink to the countertop. Then separate the sink from the top by cutting the caulk seal around the sink using a putty knife or utility knife. Once the sink is loose, carefully lift it off the countertop.

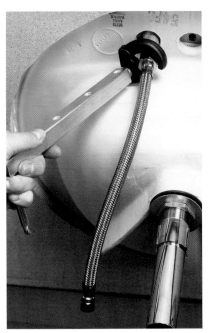

2 Single lever faucets come with copper tubes that extend down from the faucet valve. These tubes are joined to the shutoff valves by supply risers. Remove the nuts that hold the supply risers to the wall-mounted valves.

3 On bathroom sinks with dual faucets, each faucet is connected to its shut off valve with a separate supply riser. Free the sink by removing the hard-to-reach tubing nuts under the sink using a basin wrench.

4 To remove the sink connection to the waste line, first put a pail under the trap. Then loosen the nuts that hold the trap in place using adjustable pliers. Turn the nuts counterclockwise. If the nuts won't turn, cut out the trap using a hacksaw.

6 Loosen the vanity top by removing the hold-down screws at the corners of the cabinet; then lift it off and set it aside. To quickly free the vanity cabinet, cut around the shutoff valves and waste line using a keyhole saw or a reciprocating saw.

7 Remove the screws that hold the cabinet back to the wall. Then cut through any caulk or paint along the wall or floor that may hold the base in place. Pull the vanity away from the wall and discard it.

REMOVING OLD VINYL FLOORING

project

Installing new flooring is a great way to give any room a facelift. If the existing floor covering is in good shape, you can sometimes put new flooring directly over old. But in most cases, removing the old flooring first is the best idea. Start the job by prying off the baseboard and shoe molding. Then cut the flooring into strips, and pull up these strips with the help of a pry bar or a putty knife.

TOOLS & MATERIALS
▌Pry bar
▌Shims or scrap wood
▌Utility knife
▌Clothes iron, hair dryer, or heat gun
▌Paint scraper or wood chisel
▌Random-orbit sander

1 To remove vinyl flooring, first take off the baseboard and shoe molding trim. Use a pry bar and a piece of scrap wood to protect the trim and walls. Once the boards are off, use locking pliers to pull out the nails from the backside of the trim boards so that they can be reinstalled later.

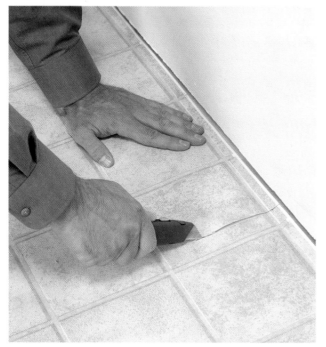

2 To make it easier to remove vinyl sheet flooring, cut it into strips that are 12 to 16 in. wide. Use a linoleum knife or a utility knife, and make sure to cut all the way through the flooring.

3 Use a flat pry bar or a wide putty knife to remove the flooring. Work one tip of the tool under a cut line and lift a corner. Then pull and pry at the same time. Once all the flooring is removed, scrape off the old adhesive using a putty knife, a paint scraper, or a sander.

taking up old flooring

Depending on the situation, your floor may require minimal or extensive remodeling. But before you start to tear apart your floor, let's look at the composition of a well-constructed bathroom floor.

Coverings. The surface that you look at and walk on is called the floor covering. Vinyl and ceramic tile rank as the most popular coverings, but other materials, such as wood and stone, are also used in bathrooms. Just below the floor covering is some sort of water-resistant underlayment, which provides a smooth, flat surface to support the floor covering. The underlayment may be made of a variety of materials, depending on the floor covering. (Never use particleboard, because in a bathroom environment it will absorb moisture and swell.)

Framing. Below the underlayment is the structural part of the floor. For wood floors, this consists of a subfloor—usually plywood or wood planks—supported by joists and beams below. Concrete slab floors are floor structure and subfloor rolled into one, though

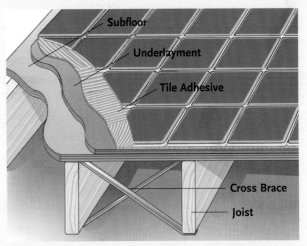

Below the floor covering in most modern homes is a layer of plywood or other panel material (the underlayment); below that, a plywood subfloor; and finally, the framing.

a plywood subfloor can be installed over a concrete floor that is continually damp, such as in a basement.

Insulation. You may need other materials to insulate the floor from heat loss and to keep water and moisture out of the structure. You can add thermal insulation between or below the floor joists or above a concrete slab. Plastic vapor barriers go between the thermal insulation and floor-covering material.

If you're planning to install new flooring, you may be able to apply it directly over the old covering, saving time and money. New resilient floor coverings (sheet vinyl and vinyl composition tiles) or ceramic tile can be installed over existing vinyl or linoleum if the old flooring (and the underlayment below it) is in good condition. But a curled or chipped edge, usually found around toilets and near tubs and showers, may indicate water damage below. If there is damage, you'll need to pry off the trim and pull up the old flooring. Peeling up a few tiles or a part of the sheet should reveal the condition of the underlayment and show you whether it also needs replacement. If the underlayment is severely damaged, peel it back to see whether you need to replace part of the subfloor.

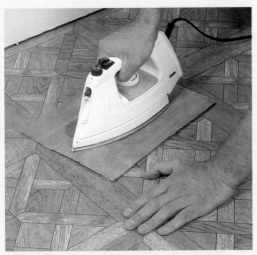

To remove resilient floor tiles, such as these parquet tiles, first heat them with a clothes iron to loosen the adhesive. A piece of thin fiberboard or plywood distributes the heat.

REPAIRING A DAMAGED SUBFLOOR

Bathroom floors are subjected to a lot of moisture. If this moisture penetrates the finished floor, it will saturate what's below. The first sign of trouble is a sponginess under foot. For less severe problems, you can usually replace just a small section of floor. But a serious problem can require replacing the whole floor.

Usually floor damage occurs around a toilet, so removing it is generally the first step in making repairs. Begin by emptying the water from the toilet tank and bowl. Then shut off the water supply valve; remove the supply tube; and unthread the nuts on the toilet hold-down bolts. Rock the bowl from side-to-side and lift it up.

To establish the depth of the underlayment that rests on top of the subfloor, drill a ¾ inch-diameter hole through the floor, and measure its depth. Set a circular saw blade to cut to this depth. If the damage clearly extends below the underlayment, set the blade depth to cut through the subfloor. If the entire floor is damaged, remove it down to the floor joists. In this case, you will need to replace the subfloor and the underlayment.

TOOLS & MATERIALS
- Plumbing tools (for toilets and sinks)
- Circular saw or saber saw
- Paint scraper or pry bar
- Rubber mallet
- Safety goggles and work gloves

EMPTYING A TOILET TANK CAN BE ANNOYING, BUT IT ONLY TAKES A FEW MINUTES. JUST USE A MEASURING CUP AND A BUCKET TO GET MOST OF THE WATER OUT. THEN SOAK UP THE LAST INCH OR TWO WITH A BIG SPONGE.

1 Turn off the water to the toilet at the shutoff valve; empty the water from the tank; and disconnect the supply tube. Remove the nuts that hold the toilet to the floor; then rock the bowl a few times from side to side. Carefully lift up and take it out of the room.

3 If the damage has gone through the underlayment and rotted the subfloor, set the saw to a depth that will cut through the subfloor. In these situations, make the cuts along the middle of the floor joists so that installing new subflooring will be easier.

2 Mark the extent of any water damage on the floor. Then set the blade depth on a circular saw to match the thickness of the flooring and the underlayment. Cut along the lines, and lift up the underlayment with a pry bar.

Joist

Closet Bend   Underlayment

4 If the whole bathroom floor has suffered water damage, it's a good idea to remove all the subflooring. Use a flat pry bar and a mallet to get under this plywood and pry it up. Be sure to wear gloves and eye protection, and put a rag in the toilet opening to keep scraps from clogging it.

KEEPING OUT MOISTURE

Most homeowners know that keeping surface water from penetrating floors and walls is essential if they want to prevent wood joists, studs, sheathing, and siding from deteriorating. But few realize that surface water is not the only menace. Airborne moisture can pose an even greater danger, and bathrooms are especially vulnerable to this type of moisture. The water vapor created by showering and bathing raises the indoor humidity to much higher levels than the outdoors. But once created, where does all this excess moisture go?

In winter, moisture migrates through walls, floors that are above crawl spaces, and roofs, con-

densing within the structural cavity. In time, it will cause insulation to lose its effectiveness, wood to rot, and paint to peel. An ideal time to address this type of problem is during a renovation, when structural framing is exposed.

Here are some tips:

▌ Install a continuous vapor retarder over wall studs and floor and ceiling joists on the warm side of the insulation. A continuous sheet of 6-mil polyethylene (usually called poly) stapled to stud and joist faces forms an effective vapor retarder. Tape the overlapping seams. Seal the sheet to any electrical or plumbing fixtures that exit the wall with tape or caulk.

▌ Install 1 or more inches of approved foam insulation over the studs and joists if you are rebuilding outside walls and ceilings. Tape all joints, and seal around outlets with caulk.

▌ Provide ventilating fans that exhaust to the outside, not into an attic or crawl space. Ventilating fans are a must in high-moisture areas such as bathrooms and kitchens.

▌ Cover the ground in an unheated crawlspace with 6-mil polyethylene.

REMOVING A BATHTUB

project

Most of the hard work in replacing a tub or shower is in removing the old one. The first step is to shut off the water; then remove all the standard hardware like the tub or shower spouts and the water faucets. Also, remove the tripwaste cover plate, the tripwaste itself, and the drain fitting. Then free the tub by removing the wall covering along the top of the tub and the flooring against the bottom edge. Remove the tub in one piece, or break it up and take it out in smaller sections.

TOOLS & MATERIALS
■ Screwdriver ■ Cold chisel
■ Sledgehammer or mason's hammer
■ Safety goggles ■ Putty knife ■ Pliers

1 Shut off the water supply to the tub, and open the faucet valve. Remove the overflow cover plate using a screwdriver. Also remove the showerhead, tub spout, and the faucet handle or handles. If you want to reuse these items, wrap them in duct tape or an old rag before grabbing them with a pipe wrench.

MOVING LARGE TUBS OR SHOWERS

When you are planning the space and selecting fixtures, you should also devise a plan for removing your old tub or shower and installing the new unit. When selecting a new fixture, make sure you can carry it through the house to the bathroom. But if you have your heart set on a unit that cannot be moved through existing hallways and doors, consider ways to move it through an outer wall. This process can be as easy as removing a first-floor window or as complex as removing a section of wall on the second or third floor.

5 The bottom edge of a tub is usually held captive by flooring material and sometimes underlayment. Use a cold chisel to remove ceramic tile, and make sure to wear safety glasses or goggles to protect your eyes. Use a flat pry bar to lift up vinyl flooring and plywood underlayment.

2 Once the cover plate screws are removed, carefully pull it away from the tub. The tripwaste mechanism is attached to the plate and will easily come out of the overflow tube.

3 The drain flange under the tub is attached to the tub with a threaded drain fitting. To remove it, slide the pliers' handles into the fitting and turn it counterclockwise.

4 Tubs usually have a lip around the top edge that is covered with the wall finish—in this case ceramic tile. Remove the tile with a wide cold chisel and mason's hammer.

6 The easiest way to remove a tub is in one piece. Once it's free from the wall and floor, tip it on its edge, and get some help to move it. Putting an old blanket or a canvas tarp under the tub will make it easier to slide across the floor. If you have to move it down a flight of stairs, get a couple of extra people.

7 If you can't move the tub in one piece, it needs to be broken into smaller sections. Cast iron tubs can be broken with a mason's hammer or a sledgehammer. Be sure to wear eye and ear protection. Steel and fiberglass tubs can be cut with a reciprocating saw.

WET-STRIPPING WALLCOVERING

project

Although some people paint and paper over old wallpaper, it's generally considered an inferior approach. The better idea is to remove the existing paper. To do this, first score the paper, then wet the surface with a steamer. Pull loosened paper off the wall with your hands or a paint scraper. Finish up by cleaning the walls with a sponge soaked in cleaning solution.

TOOLS & MATERIALS
- Scoring tool ▮ Rubber gloves
- Safety goggles ▮ Utility pail
- Steamer (may be rented or purchased)
- Wallpaper scraper (for plaster walls)
- Sponges or rags
- Phosphate-free trisodium
- Wallcovering remover

1 The first step in removing wallpaper is to score the surface with a scoring tool. This tool is usually shaped like a triangle with round disks at each corner. These disks have toothed wheels that perforate the wallcovering without damaging the drywall or plaster underneath.

3 Once the wallpaper starts to loosen, grab one corner and pull it down the wall at a shallow angle. Don't try to pull the paper off quickly because it will tear. A slow steady motion will yield better results.

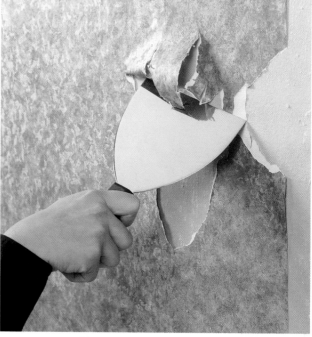

4 Some stubborn papers will not pull cleanly from the walls. Help to loosen these papers with a paint scraper. Hold the tool at a shallow angle, and don't be too aggressive or you risk damaging the wall. If the paper won't budge, wet or steam it again.

2 You can simply wet the perforated surface to loosen the wallpaper. But using a rented steamer makes the job go much faster. The steamer plate directs steam into the wallpaper and breaks the glue bond. Don't hold the plate in one area more than 15 minutes.

5 When all the wallpaper is off, clean the entire surface with a sponge soaked in phosphate-free trisodium and warm water. Be sure to wear rubber gloves, and rinse the sponge frequently. Let the walls dry for about a week before painting or installing new paper.

• OTHER STEAM REMOVAL METHODS

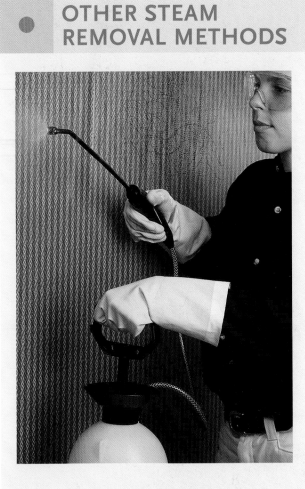

If you can't locate a steamer to rent, you can still wet-strip wallcovering by using a pail or garden sprayer. Here's how:

▌ **With a pail:** Fill the pail with a mixture of hot tap water and wallcovering remover. (Follow the manufacturer's recommended proportions.) Cover the floor with a waterproof tarp sealed at the edges with tape. Protect your hands with latex gloves; then dip a rag or sponge into the pail; and rub the wallcovering with it. Be sure to soak the material well before scraping it off—the wetter, the better.

▌ **With a garden sprayer:** First score the wallcovering as shown in Step 1. Then fill a sprayer (that has been thoroughly cleaned) with a mixture of hot tap water and wallcovering remover, following the manufacturer's instructions. Use the sprayer to saturate the wallcovering with the mixture. Then scrape off the wallcovering.

GUTTING A WALL

Think twice before you tear into a wall or ceiling. The job almost always adds up to more than you planned on. The dust and debris somehow find their way into all corners of the house—even if you take serious measures to contain the mess. But if you are committed to the idea, then protect yourself and the house on a couple of fronts. First, make sure to wear gloves, eye and hearing protection, and a heavy-duty dust mask. And keep the room closed off with polyethylene sheeting taped over the doorway. Also, try to locate a dumpster just below the bathroom window so that you don't have to haul debris through the house, which just spreads the mess to other rooms.

You also want to know just what is behind the wall before you cut into it, so be sure to check for wiring, ducts, and pipes.

Begin by shutting off the power and water to the room; then remove all the trim work. Knock a hole in the wall, or cut along the studs to start removing the drywall. The most efficient course of action is to pull off sections of wall with a flat pry bar. Remove the nails or screws from the edge of all the framing members.

TOOLS & MATERIALS
- Claw hammer ▮ Shims ▮ Pry bar
- Work gloves ▮ Reciprocating saw
- Cold chisel (for plaster)
- Goggles and dust mask
- Power drill-driver
  (to remove drywall screws)

caution

DON'T CUT INTO A WALL OR CEILING WITHOUT FIRST CHECKING FOR PIPES, WIRING, AND DUCTS. ALSO, COVER HEATING REGISTERS AND EXPOSED DRAINS TO KEEP THEM FREE OF DEBRIS DURING DEMOLITION.

1 Begin demolition by removing the wall and ceiling trim. If you don't plan to reuse these pieces, then just pull them off with a wrecking bar. But if you want to reuse them, carefully take them off with a flat pry bar. Once the molding is removed, pull out the nails from the backside using locking pliers.

2 The easiest way to start removing drywall is to drive a hammer into the wall. Once a hole is made, you can use a wrecking bar, a flat bar, or the claw on the hammerhead to pull off the drywall. Be sure to wear eye and breathing protection while you work.

● REMOVING CERAMIC TILE

You can remove small areas of ceramic tile with a cold chisel, prying tiles off one by one (left). But as the drywall underneath may have to be replaced anyway, it's far easier to cut away chunks with a reciprocating saw and remove the chunks whole (right). Always wear eye protection: flying pieces of tile can be dangerous.

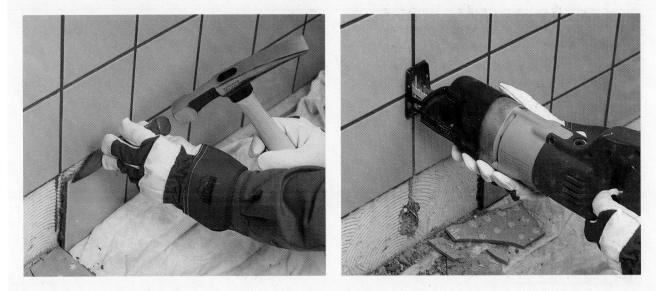

3 Removing drywall in large sections is easier by cutting out wall sections with a reciprocating saw. Use a short blade that cuts just through the drywall.

4 Use a pry bar to pull the drywall sections from the wall. If you cut along the sides of the studs, it should be easy to remove large sections at a time.

5 Once all of the drywall is removed, pull the nails along each stud using a pry bar or nail puller. If screws were used, remove these with a drill-driver.

INSTALLING DRYWALL

Drywall, also called wallboard, has a gypsum plaster core that is sandwiched between two layers of heavy paper. It usually comes in sheets that are 4-feet wide and from 8- to 16-feet long in 2-foot increments. Common thicknesses are $1/4$, $3/8$, $1/2$, and $5/8$ inches.

You can install these panels either horizontally or vertically. Horizontal installations are easier, particularly during the finishing stages. But vertical installations are easier if you are working alone. To prevent cracks, avoid making joints next to doors and windows.

Cutting and Hanging Drywall

Begin by cutting through the surface paper with a sharp utility knife and a straightedge guide. Break the panel against your knee or over a scrap board placed on the floor. Bend back the broken panel, and cut the back paper with a utility knife. Then cut any openings needed for electrical outlets or other obstructions. Nail or screw the panels in place, spaced every 6 inches around the edge and every 12 inches in the panel field. Lift panels with a site-made lever made of scrap lumber.

TOOLS & MATERIALS
▌ Basic carpentry tools
▌ Drywall saw
▌ 48-inch aluminum drywall T-square (or straightedge)
▌ Utility knife
▌ Power drill with drywall screw clutch
▌ Drywall hammer
▌ Drywall nails or galvanized drywall screws long enough to penetrate at least $3/4$ inch into the framing
▌ Panel lifter pail
▌ Drywall panels

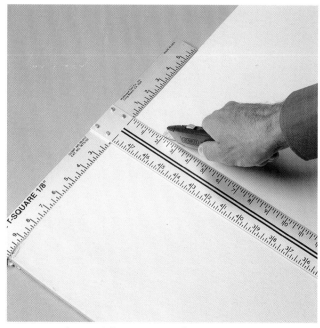

1 To make straight cuts on a drywall panel, first mark the sheet to proper size. Then score the surface paper using a utility knife and a metal straightedge. Always use a sharp blade in the knife, and cut only through the paper. Use a drywall saw to make jogged or curved cuts.

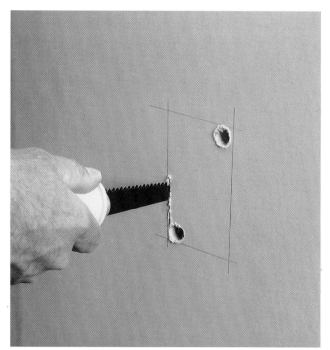

4 To make a cutout for a receptacle or switch box, lay out the box position on the panel. Then drill a hole at opposing corners, and cut along the layout lines with a drywall or keyhole saw.

3 After the panel is snapped, stand it on its edge and bend it slightly at the break. Then cut through the paper backing using a sharp utility knife. If the cut edge is too rough to fit, don't recut the panel. Just sand down the edge with coarse sandpaper.

2 Once the paper is scored, the panels are easy to break. Just put your knee behind the cut on the back of the panel, and pull both sides toward you. Or place a piece of scrap lumber under the cut, and push down on one side until the panel snaps.

5 When you need to lift a panel off the floor so that it fits tight to the one above, use a simple site-made lever. Put a wide board under the panel, then another smaller board under the wide board. Step on the end of the lever, and the panel will move up.

● NAILS OR SCREWS?

Drywall screws hold better than nails, but for small jobs and patches nails will suffice. Use 1⅝-inch ring-shank drywall nails for ½-inch drywall and 1⅞-inch nails for ⅝-inch drywall. Drywall screws should be at least ¾ inch longer than the thickness of the panel you are installing. To drive screws, use a drywall screw gun or a standard drill fitted with a drywall clutch. The clutch releases the screws before they sink too far into the drywall.

TAPING DRYWALL

project

If you plan to paint your finished walls, the quality of your drywall finishing job is crucial. The smallest dents and ridges will show through paint, especially high-gloss products. Wallpaper hides more, and ceramic tile or wood paneling require only one coat of compound and tape on the drywall.

For a top-notch job, begin by filling the screw and nail dimples with joint compound. Then start taping the joints between panels. There are two types of drywall tape: paper tape and self-sticking fiberglass mesh tape. Generally speaking, fiberglass tape works well on tapered joints (along the long edges of the panels) but doesn't work as well in corners and butt joints (across the ends of the panels). If you want to keep things simple, just use paper tape for everything.

First, apply a thin coat of compound across a joint; embed a piece of tape in this compound; smooth the tape in place; and cover it with another thin coat of compound. Use tape on inside corners and metal corner bead on outside corners. Once all the joints are dry, sand them smooth, and apply the last two coats of compound.

TOOLS & MATERIALS
▌ Utility knife
▌ 6-inch-wide drywall knife
▌ 12-inch-wide drywall knife
▌ Sanding block
▌ Aviation snips
  (if you need to cut metal corner bead)
▌ Pole sander with swivel head and
  120-grit sandpaper inserts or sanding
  screen (optional)
▌ Dust mask
▌ Ready-mix joint compound
▌ Perforated paper tape or fiberglass
  mesh tape
▌ Metal corner bead
  (only if outside corners are present)

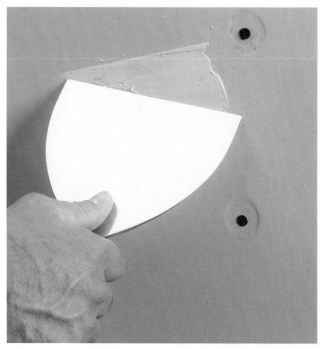

1 Begin the finishing process by filling the nail and screw dimples with joint compound. Use premixed compound instead of the type you mix yourself. Also, use a 6-in.-wide flexible taping knife. A flexible knife works better for pressing the compound into the depressions.

5 On outside corners, nail metal corner bead to the wall framing. Then apply joint compound to both sides of the bead, using the raised corner as a guide.

 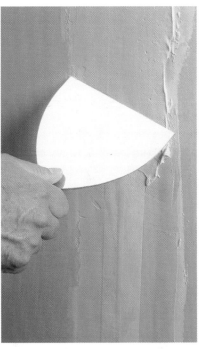 

2 All joints must be covered with compound and tape. First, spread a thin coat of compound across the joint. Then embed a piece of tape.

3 Once the tape is smooth, cover it with a thin coat of joint compound. Smooth the surface and remove extra compound using a 6-in. knife.

4 On inside corners, apply compound to both sides of the corner. Then place a folded piece of paper tape over the joint, and embed it in the compound.

6 Once the first coats of compound and tape are dry, sand all joints with a pole sander and 120-grit sandpaper. Smooth the rough spots and feather the edges. Make sure to wear eye protection and a heavy-duty dust mask.

7 Plan on applying at least two additional coats of compound, with each coat covering a wider area than the one before. Use a large (10- or 12-in.-wide) taping knife for the final coat. The smoother you apply the compound, the less sanding you'll need to do later.

INSTALLING BACKER BOARD

project

In wet areas, cement board is better backing for ceramic tile than regular or water-resistant drywall as it will not degrade if it should get wet. Although it's usually ½ inch thick and is installed much like drywall, it is heavier and harder to cut.

Begin by marking the cutline on the panel and cutting the panels to size using a utility knife. Then snap the panel, and cut through the fiberglass mesh on the back of the panel. Faucet holes are cut using a carbide-tipped hole saw in an electric drill. When making these cuts, it is best to take the holes slightly oversized to allow for minor adjustments when you place the panel on the wall.

Screw the panels to the studs using special cement-board screws. These should be driven ½ inch from the edges and spaced every 4 or 5 inches. In the field of the panels, 12-inch spacing is fine, but make sure you drive the screws into a stud. To finish the joints, all that's required is to apply self-sticking fiberglass tape that you press into place over the seams of the panels. No joint compound is needed because the entire surface will be covered with tile and grout.

TOOLS & MATERIALS
▪ Tape measure ▪ T-square ▪ Utility knife or cement-board cutter ▪ Masonry drill bit
▪ Saber saw (optional) ▪ Power drill with screwdriver bit and carbide-tipped hole saws
▪ Fiberglass mesh tape ▪ Thinset adhesive
▪ Cement-based backer board
▪ 1½-inch-galvanized cement-board screws

smart tip
FRAMING PREP

BECAUSE CEMENT BOARD IS MUCH LESS FLEXIBLE THAN DRYWALL, IT CAN CRACK WHEN SCREWED TO UNEVEN STUDS. SHIM ANY PROBLEM WALL STUDS.

1 Backer board is cut the same way as drywall. First mark the panel; then score this line using a sharp utility knife and a straightedge guide. Break the panel against your knee or over a piece of scrap wood placed on the floor.

2 Once the panel is broken, place it on its edge and cut through the fiberglass mesh on the back using a utility knife. This cut is generally rougher than drywall and can be smoothed to fit better with 80-grit sandpaper.

● ESTIMATING QUANTITIES FOR DRYWALL

Quality drywalling requires accurate estimates of material quantities. Nothing breaks your stride like having to run out to the store for materials once you've started a job. Here are some tips on how to estimate materials.

▮ **Joint Compound:** You'll need roughly a gallon for every 100 square feet of drywall.

▮ **Joint Tape:** To finish 500 square feet of drywall, figure on using 400 feet of tape.

▮ **Nails/Screws:** This figure can vary depending on stud spacing (walls framed 16 inches on center require more fasteners than those framed at 24 inches) and on your nail or screw schedule (panels attached with adhesive require fewer fasteners). Figure on one fastener for every square foot of drywall on your job. For example, an 18 x 18-foot ceiling (324 square feet) will require about 320 screws or nails. Because 1 pound of 1¼-inch drywall screws contains about 320 screws, you'll need a pound of screws for every 320 square feet of drywall.

▮ **Drywall Panels:** Estimating how much drywall you'll need to cover a room is a matter of square footage. Calculate the wall surface of the room, and divide that figure by the square footage of the panels you intend to use. For instance, a 4 x 8-foot panel measures 32 square feet. If you have a 1,000-square-foot room, you'll need just over 31 panels. Because they come in units of two, order 32 panels.

▮ **When estimating square footage,** don't subtract the door or window areas (except for bay windows or unusually large doors), because you'll need extra for mistakes.

3 Faucet holes can be cut in backer board with a power drill and a carbide-tipped hole saw. Mark the location with a center punch, and drill slowly.

4 Attach the panels to the wall framing with 1½-in. cement-board screws. Drive them every 5 in. around the perimeter and every 12 in. in the field.

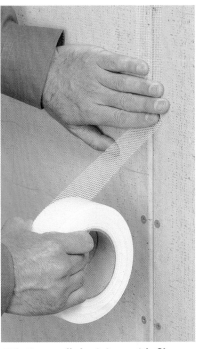

5 Cover all the joints with fiberglass drywall tape. No joint compound is needed underneath because the tape is self-sticking.

INSTALLING PLYWOOD UNDERLAYMENT

project

The correct underlayment will make your new flooring stay flat and resist water for many years. But it needs to be installed properly. First, prepare the existing floor so it provides a solid base; then cut the panels to size, and place them on the floor so the joints are staggered. Attach the panels using screws driven through the underlayment and subfloor below and into the floor joists.

TOOLS & MATERIALS
▌ Circular saw
▌ Power drill with screwdriver bit
▌ Measuring tape
▌ Chalk-line box
▌ Plywood
▌ Galvanized screws

1 To cut plywood underlayment, place the panel on scrap boards; mark the length on both edges of the panel; and snap a chalk line between the two marks. This is your cut line. Make the cut using a circular saw. Be sure to set the blade depth so the saw cuts through the panel but doesn't hit the floor.

2 Place the sheets along one wall. Start the second course of underlayment with a sheet that's shorter than the first, so the joints in the underlayment will be staggered. Maintain a uniform $1/8$-in. expansion joint between sheets and along the room walls.

3 Underlayment panels should be attached to the floor joists, not just the flooring. Find where the joists fall, and snap chalk lines above each. Drive screws that are long enough to reach through all the layers on the flooring and at least 1 in. into the joists.

36

SELECTING UNDERLAYMENT

Types of Underlayment

Always avoid particleboard, especially in the bathroom, because it will swell when wet, causing the floor covering to separate or bubble. Underlayment-grade plywood made from fir or pine is available in 4 x 8-foot sheets, in thicknesses of $\frac{1}{4}$, $\frac{3}{8}$, $\frac{1}{2}$, $\frac{5}{8}$ and $\frac{3}{4}$ inch. Lauan plywood, made from a species of mahogany, is often used under vinyl flooring. It's available in 4 x 8-foot sheets and usually in a single thickness, $\frac{1}{4}$ inch. If permitted by code, you can use oriented-strand board (OSB). Because both can expand when damp, plywood and OSB are not good choices for ceramic tile underlayment.

Cement-based backer board (also called tile backer board) is the better idea. It's made of sand and cement, reinforced with a sturdy fiberglass mesh. Commonly available in 36 x 60-inch sheets, the standard thickness is $\frac{1}{2}$ inch. This material is preferred for ceramic tile, terra-cotta and natural stone floors.

When to Install Underlayment

Resilient floor coverings (vinyl, rubber, and linoleum sheet flooring and tiles) and wood parquet can be laid over an existing layer of similar material if the original is in good condition. The existing covering must be tightly adhered, have no cupped edges, and be free of any water damage. If there is water damage, be sure to fix whatever is causing the water damage, such as a leaky pipe, before applying a new underlayment. If you don't, no matter what material you install, it will soon fail. If the existing flooring alone is not in good condition, remove it and smooth out the existing underlayment before installing new floor covering. If you can't remove the old floor covering, fill in any uneven spots and install a new underlayment over it.

Ceramic tile and stone can be set over existing ceramic tile if the original flooring is tightly adhered and in good condition. They can also be installed directly over a concrete slab floor. With the exception of shower stalls, tile and stone are usually set on an underlayment using a troweled-on adhesive called thinset. Showers require greater water resistance and sloped floors for drainage. The best way to achieve this is by setting the tiles on a mortar (thickset) base over a PVC or CPE membrane. (See "Installing a Sloping Mortar-Bed Floor," page 172.) The mortar base should be designed to provide a gentle slope to the drain in the shower. Over wood bathroom floors, the ideal underlayment for ceramic tile and stone is cement-based backer board that is attached to the floor joists. Underlayment-grade plywood is a second choice.

underlayment options

Floor Covering	Acceptable Underlayments
Resilient floor coverings	Old vinyl or linoleum flooring in sound condition Underlayment-grade plywood Lauan plywood
Wood parquet flooring	Old vinyl or linoleum flooring in sound condition Underlayment-grade plywood Lauan plywood Hardboard
Laminate flooring	Any sound surface
Solid wood flooring	Underlayment-grade plywood
Ceramic tile and stone	Old ceramic tiles in sound condition Concrete slab Cement-based backer board Underlayment-grade plywood

2 master baths

A master bath is a must-have on any homeowner's list of desired features. According to a recent survey conducted by the National Association of the Remodeling Industry (NARI), most people want the kind of convenience, comfort, and luxury that a new high-style master bath can provide. A bathroom equipped with personal spa amenities and outfitted in glamorous fixtures and materials offers the level of indulgence and pampering that people had to leave home to find until now. In fact, some new homes have two of them. One is located on the main level, and another one is upstairs. Homeowners know that while they may prefer the privacy of a master suite that is located away from the main living areas, there may come a time when the accessibility of a centrally located bedroom and bathroom is a necessity.

LUXURIOUS PERSONAL HAVEN

Master bathrooms in general have been getting grander in scale and in scope for more than a decade. For some people, a sumptuous bathroom may be a status symbol, but the reality is that contemporary life is hectic, people are working longer hours, leaving home earlier, and returning later than they used to a generation ago. "Me time" is getting harder to find. For this person, an at-home getaway is the answer.

OPPOSITE TOP This grand-scale master bath is actually a series of separate compartments for bathing, showering, toileting, and grooming. Special attention has been given to luxurious materials and decorating details.

OPPOSITE BOTTOM A large plan makes use of a center storage island with heated towel bars to divide the space into separate sink and grooming areas in a his-and-her design.

Top of the Line

At the highest end of the market, everything is designed for the convenience of two people. You don't have to wait your turn when there's both an oversized tub and a separate and spacious walk-in shower at your disposal. Cancel the day spa because both your bathtub and shower can be outfitted with strategically placed water or air jets designed to relax or invigorate you, head to toe, with a therapeutic message. (For more bathing options, see Chapter 9, "Tubs & Showers," beginning on page 148.)

Steam and More. Experts have been touting the health benefits of steam for years, and now many upscale homeowners request a steam-equipped shower or personal sauna to complete their at-home spa. Other luxurious master-bath amenities almost always include a separate toilet compartment (sometimes referred to as a "private toileting room"). Some homeowners also request a bidet.

In addition to two sinks and either a large double-sized vanity or two separate vanities, custom-designed dressing areas that are integrated into the suite (sometimes as the link from bedroom to bathroom) are expanding the concept of the walk-in closet. More than a place to store clothes, a dressing area is practically a room unto itself, except that it has no door. Dressing areas might feature custom cabinetry for clothes and linen storage, an exercise area, media equipment, or even laundry facilities.

ABOVE A deluxe shower system, above, comes as a prefabricated unit with an array of features: numerous pulsating jets, adjustable and hand-held showerheads, and even a TV.

Various types of fixtures and bulbs may be part of a high-end custom-designed lighting plan. In addition to general overall lighting and task lighting for applying makeup, shaving, and hairstyling, upscale bathrooms often feature decorative accent lighting underneath soffits, within coves, and even inside the tub. (See information on installing light fixtures on page 142.)

High-End Surfacing. Luxurious stone (mostly granite, slate, limestone, or marble in slab or tile form) is the preferred material, although ceramic tile is classic, especially custom or hand-painted versions. Exquisite glass tiles are also desirable because of their wonderful reflective quality. (See Chapter 6, "Stone, Tile & More," on page 102.) Stone and tile may be appealing to the eye, but they are also cold to the touch, so designers are specifying warming devices such as heat lamps over the tub and shower areas, radiant heating systems (under the floor), and toe-kick heaters (under the vanity) to keep bathers comfortable. Heated towel bars are also becoming a standard amenity in master bathrooms.

If people have fewer hours to relax, they want more from their relaxing experience. One way to do this is by incorporating elements of nature into the environment. Therefore, whenever it is possible, a deluxe master bath is also connected to an outdoor area. This may be a small private garden, a deck with an outdoor spa or hot tub, or

a pool area. Health-conscious homeowners may also want to make the master bath accessible to a swim spa that is used as part of a daily exercise routine. At the least, glass doors, large windows, skylights, or roof windows will enhance a bath's connection to the outdoors, especially if there's a beautiful view to enjoy. (See pages 10 and 11 of the introduction, "Adding Space & Natural Light," for more information about windows.)

smart tip

BALANCING PRIVACY AND LIGHT

To fill your master suite with natural light without sacrificing privacy, consider installing skylights, roof windows, and clerestory windows—small windows installed near the ceiling.

OPPOSITE Lots of cabinets add beauty and convenience to this master-bath design. A generous double vanity stores grooming items and toiletries, while the floor-to-ceiling bank of closets at the far end (leading to the dressing area) holds fresh linens and clothing.

BELOW Unpretentious bead board looks fresh in this master bathroom. A white marble countertop and a high-style faucet set add elegance to the simple design.

MARVELOUS AT MIDRANGE

Want a master bathroom that is as pleasing to your mind and body as it is to your pocketbook? Depending on the size of the room, you may be able fit a separate tub and shower into the layout. Locate a walk-in shower adjacent to the tub, for example. This conserves space and saves money because you don't have to pay to install long lines

LEFT Expanding into an adjacent room made way for a walk-in shower. Note the built-in seat in the corner.

ABOVE Reproduction fixtures, add a unique style and enhance the vintage look of this remodeled bathroom.

of plumbing. Using a glass enclosure around the shower compensates for the tight squeeze, keeping the room light and airy.

Another space- and money-saving option is a standard-size whirlpool. But if you prefer a shower and rarely if ever take a bath, eliminate the tub, especially if there is one in another bathroom in the house. Install a larger shower, one with a roomy seat for two, built-in storage nooks, and perhaps a spa feature, such as massage jets or a rainbar. However, don't overlook annexing a foot or two from an adjacent closet hallway or another room, or bumping out an outside wall a few feet over the foundation. Sometimes it's possible to position a fixture, such as

a sink, a shower, or even a toilet, at an angle, which conserves space and, if planned properly, doesn't require long plumbing lines.

Creating Privacy. If you can't accommodate a separate enclosure for the toilet, you may be able to install a partial partition with a half wall. Glass-block or sandblasted-glass walls offer some privacy without closing off the light, as well. If there is an existing linen closet and you can sacrifice the storage, it may be convertible, especially if it is adjacent to a plumbing line.

In a master bathroom with limited space, a double-bowl vanity is a more practical choice than a pair of pedestal sinks because you will need the storage the cabi-

net can provide. If you like the look of pedestal sinks so much that you're willing to sacrifice storage, try to space them far enough apart so that you can install a slim cabinet between the two. A shelf and a recessed medicine cabinet (deep enough to store an extra roll of toilet paper or a hair dryer) for each sink should compensate for some of the lost storage. When you select the pedestal sinks, look for a style that has a generous deck surrounding the bowl so that there is a landing spot for cosmetics, brushes, and the like when you're grooming. Make sure there's good task lighting in the area, even if you've provided adequate general lighting.

Light. If privacy demands that you keep windows to a minimum, consider supplementing a single or small window with a skylight or a roof window.

TOP RIGHT A partial wall creates privacy and adds storage space in a modest master bath.

RIGHT A decorative oval window adds light and elegance to this design.

BIG IDEAS, SMALL BUDGET

A handsome, practical master bath doesn't have to be the size of the Taj Mahal, nor does it require a marble countertop and tub surround. There are attractive and hard-working materials, such as standard ceramic tile and high-quality plastic-laminate products, that will serve you well. Stick to standard fixtures and fittings, avoiding special effects, fancy finishes, and special-order colors if you have limited funds. Another way to keep costs down: eliminate all spa amenities. However, the price range of whirlpool tubs is wide, and there are models available for the budget-minded, as well.

Again, depending upon your bathing habits, you could simply install a shower. A shower without a threshold that is separated from the rest of the room by a glass enclosure saves space and looks great. You would also be amazed by the flow options of many affordable adjustable showerheads today, so you do not have to resign yourself to one with just one standard flow setting. But it is interesting that consumer testing conducted recently by one major manufacturer revealed that most people use only one or two shower settings anyway.

Storage becomes a challenge in a small space, so a modest-size vanity with a single sink is a good idea. Storage nooks built between the wall studs can provide point-of-use storage for bottles and small toiletries in the bath or shower and near the sink. Shelving is another option, and makes a handy spot for holding extra towels and grooming supplies. As a bonus, good-looking bath linens can add a nice color accent to the room, especially if the permanent fixtures are a neutral color.

Sometimes thinking outside the box can expand the function of a small master bath in a unique way. If you want but can't fit two sinks, consider using a large trough-style or farmhouse-style sink and installing two separate taps or faucets.

TOP A slanted glass partition cleverly overcomes the challenge of a tight layout and allows for a uniquely designed roomy walk-in shower in this small bath.

RIGHT Colorful towels make a stylish display on an open shelf while providing point-of-use storage.

RIGHT A deep sink is a handy option in a bathroom. The corner spout keeps the basin area clear for wringing out hand washables or rinsing hair.

● BATHROOM LIGHTING

Good lighting puts illumination where you need it. A superb lighting scheme also enhances the mood of the room.

There are several types of artificial light and various sources. In all but the smallest bathrooms, ceiling-mounted lights are necessary for sufficient general illumination.

▌**Ambient lighting** is the general lighting that should illuminate the room. Recessed fixtures are a good choice. You can install them by the shower or tub, in the toilet compartment, and in the dressing room. The number of required recessed fixtures varies by the size of the room. (Don't try to get by with one large fixture in the center of the ceiling. It will cast shadows in the wrong places on any mirror.)

▌**Task lighting** is what you need for grooming. To look good in the mirror, task lighting should come at you from both sides, radiating from the middle of your face (about 60 to 66 inches from the floor for most adults). Avoid lighting the vanity area from above, which will cause shadows.

▌**Accent lighting** isn't necessary in a bathroom, but it can add a dramatic or decorative touch. Small strip lights mounted under a raised tub or lights recessed into a soffit above a vanity are good examples.

In general, when choosing bulbs, you may have to experiment. For your safety, you need to see where you're going and what you're doing. But bulbs generate heat, so choose ones that let you see the type of pill your taking but don't make you wilt.

LEFT A wall of glass block allows soft, diffused natural light to enter this bathroom, where hard, shiny surfaces can cause glare.

ABOVE A mirror reflects additional sunlight into a room that darkens when the door to the water closet is closed.

People often complain that their small bathroom is dark. If the only outside wall you have is in the shower, locate a row of small casement windows either close to the ceiling or just above your shoulders. That way you've got a view, but you're not on view. Skylights, roof windows, light shafts, and glass block (installed in any outside wall) are alternatives. Light, reflective colors on surfaces help, too.

And in any size bathroom, it's important to have good supplemental artificial lighting. Sometimes if the space is tiny, task lighting near the mirror or vanity can double as general illumination for the room. Sconces on either side of the mirror will provide the kind of glare-free lighting that will make you and the room look best. You'll have to check with your local building department about lighting codes in your area. In some places your bathroom lighting options are limited. For example, in California you will be required to install only fluorescent fixtures. Also, near the tub or shower you may be allowed to use only light fixtures that are specifically manufactured for installation in wet areas. (For more information on lighting, see "Bathroom Lighting," opposite.)

master bath plans

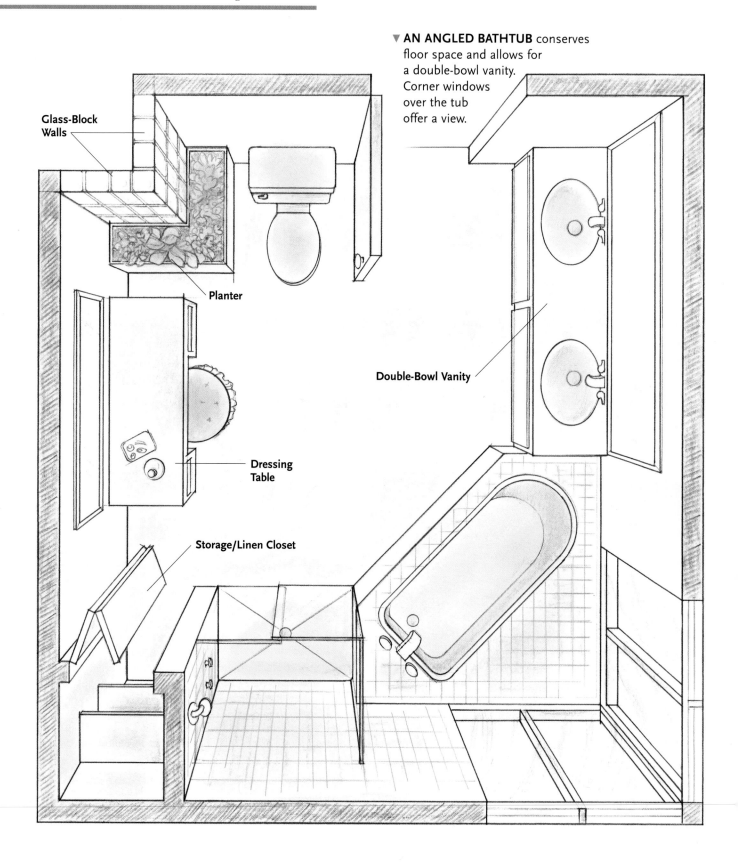

▼ **AN ANGLED BATHTUB** conserves floor space and allows for a double-bowl vanity. Corner windows over the tub offer a view.

Glass-Block Walls

Planter

Double-Bowl Vanity

Dressing Table

Storage/Linen Closet

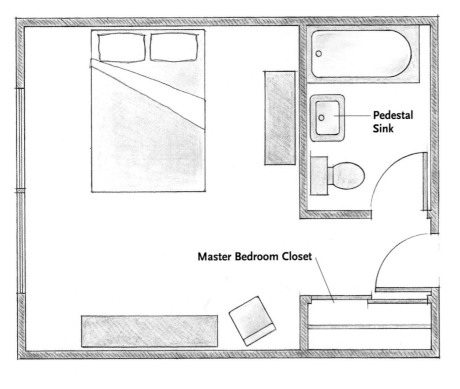

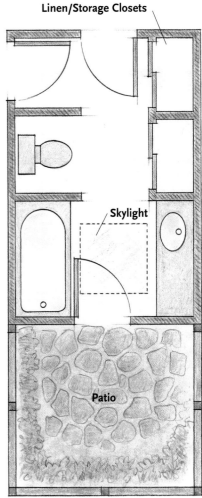

Pedestal Sink

◀ **A SMALL BATHROOM** tucked into the corner of a large bedroom adds convenience.

▼ **A SKYLIGHT** showers this room with lots of sunlight without compromising privacy.

Master Bedroom Closet

Linen/Storage Closets

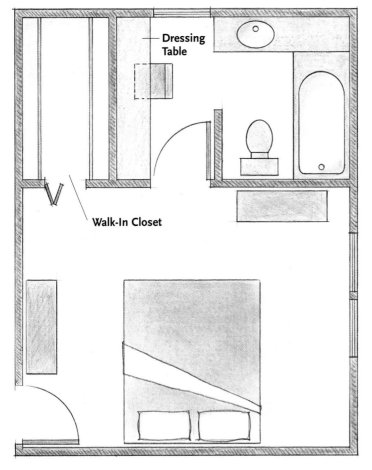

Dressing Table

Walk-In Closet

Skylight

Patio

◀ **LOCATING THE TOILET** opposite the vanity improves sightlines from the bedroom.

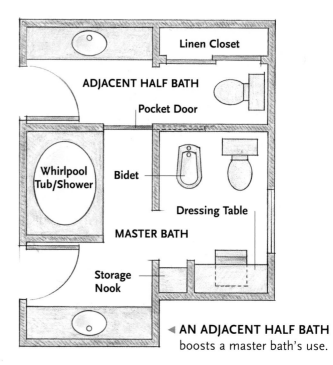

▲ **AN ADJACENT HALF BATH**
boosts a master bath's use.

Linen Closet

ADJACENT HALF BATH

Pocket Door

Whirlpool Tub/Shower

Bidet

Dressing Table

MASTER BATH

Storage Nook

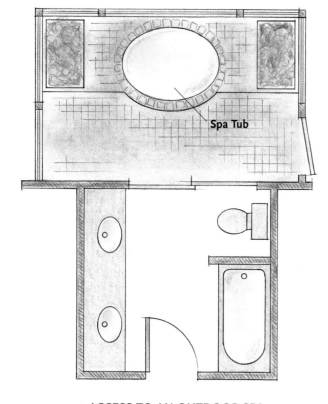

Spa Tub

▲ **ACCESS TO AN OUTDOOR SPA**
makes this master bathroom
an ideal at-home getaway.

▼ **A SEPARATE GROOMING AREA** creates a
more efficient use of space for two people.

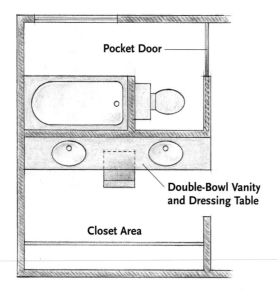

Pocket Door

Double-Bowl Vanity
and Dressing Table

Closet Area

▼ **A POCKET DOOR** conceals a water closet in
this design of compartmentalized space.

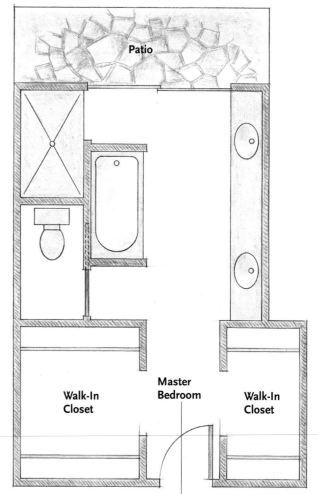

Patio

Walk-In
Closet

Master
Bedroom

Walk-In
Closet

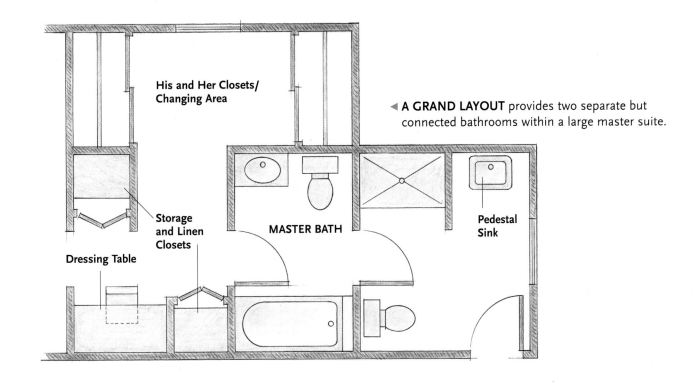

His and Her Closets/ Changing Area

◀ **A GRAND LAYOUT** provides two separate but connected bathrooms within a large master suite.

Storage and Linen Closets

MASTER BATH

Pedestal Sink

Dressing Table

◀ **AN L-SHAPED COUNTERTOP** makes way for a pair of sinks as well as a dressing table.

Double-Bowl Vanity and Dressing Table

Pocket Door

Whirlpool Tub

Bidet

▲ **POCKET DOORS** offer access from the his and her zones of this room into the space for a shared oversize tub.

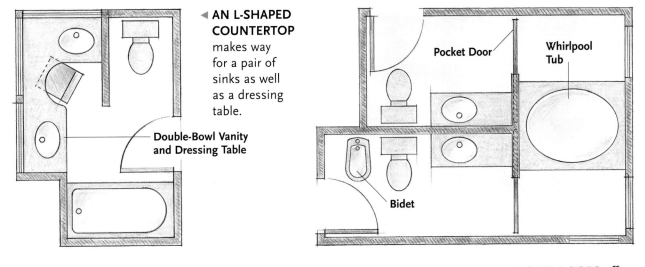

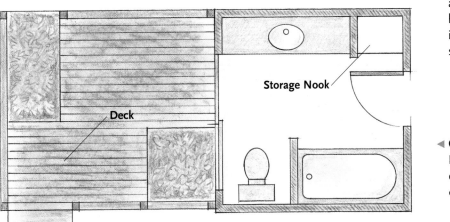

Deck

Storage Nook

◀ **OPENING THE ROOM** to the deck enlarges the feeling of a midsize plan.

3 family baths

Addressing functional issues for a family bath is complex because individuals each have preferences and needs. If yours is a household of kids, adults, and the elderly, you may want to pay particular attention to the specifics recommended in the section "Individual Needs." Here are some things to think about when you're creating a bathroom for the entire family.

Begin by looking at the physical space. Compartmentalizing is the best way to make the room multifunctional. Designate separate zones for bathing, showering, grooming, and using the toilet. But remember, if you separate the bathroom into smaller areas, you run the risk of making the room dark or cramped. Anything that divides with privacy while also allowing light to enter will ease the closed-in feeling, such as glass block or frosted-glass partitions.

ROOM FOR EVERYONE

If the space is large, investigate the possibility of constructing smaller back-to-back bathrooms in lieu of one large shared room. The plumbing lines for both rooms will be right there, which will save you money. Another option for making a bathroom more functional is to locate the tub and shower in the center of the room and install the other fixtures—toilet, bidet, and sinks—on either side in their own separate areas. To make this arrangement work, you need a large space and a floor plan that keeps each side of the room accessible to the door. This allows more than one person to use the room at the same time. If space is tight, consider what some people are doing: install a deep soaking tub in the master bedroom if the rooms are adjacent to one another. This is a way to create a luxurious master retreat and gain space in the family bathroom to accommodate an extra vanity, a large closet, or a large walk-in shower.

BELOW Placing the tub in the center of the room serves as a divider for fixtures placed along the walls.

TOP RIGHT Uncluttered space is easy to keep clean and is more functional when several people share the bathroom.

RIGHT Good natural and artificial light is important for safety and because it keeps this room cheerful.

Storage. Although storage is a big deal in any bathroom, sufficient storage in a family bath is critical. This busy room can get cluttered, especially if everyone leaves their stuff all over the countertop or on other surfaces. Besides cosmetics, grooming products and appliances, and medications, there may be toys as well as linens and cleaning supplies to keep organized yet handy. Whenever it's possible, give each person a suitable amount of personal storage space, even if that means designating a shelf in the linen closet or medicine cabinet for each family member who uses the room. Stackable bins, extra racks, and hanging baskets can boost your bathroom's storage capacity, too. Supplement this with wall shelving or compact freestanding units that go under the sink or above the toilet tank. One or two built-in nooks inside the shower or tub wall can keep shampoo and soap off the ledge of the tub, keeping the area clutter free. Don't leave these or other items on the floor where you or someone else can trip on them—especially in a small space. Make

ABOVE Two vanity cabinets, each one paired with three-way mirrors, make perfect sense in a family bath.

LEFT A customized vanity provides a distinctive look and space for a slide-out-of-the-way seat.

BELOW A combination of drawers and cabinets is a practical solution for containing a range of bath items.

LEFT A pegged rack that's reserved for the kids will encourage them to hang up their towels.

BELOW Large open tub surrounds are perfect for storing bathing items.

use of the back of the bathroom door, where you can install shallow wire racks that can store extra bottles of shampoo and other hair-care products, bath soaps and oils, and so forth. Carve out vertical niches between the studs, installing them from floor to ceiling if necessary. If you're using dividing walls to separate zones, create small storage nooks or compartments in these walls, too. Good-looking hooks can take care of additional towels and robes.

TOP OF THE LINE

Including spa amenities in a family bath makes sense whether or not it is the only full bathroom in the house. A whirlpool tub with an in-line heater is something that everyone can enjoy. See Chapter 9 on page 148, "Tubs & Showers," to find out more about deluxe features that can enhance your whirlpool experience.

If you're not going to install a whirlpool tub, consider an enamel-coated cast-iron model. It's expensive, but it will last a lifetime. Other options might be an extra-deep soaking tub or an oversize tub that accommodates two bathers. A custom-built separate shower with built-in seating, massaging jets, and multiple showerheads may be overkill if you already have these luxuries in a master bath. And you might pass on a steam-equipped unit if young children live in the house, as it can be dangerous for them.

Delicate hand-painted or glass sinks may be impractical in high-traffic bathrooms, but other designer features can substitute, such as a pair of porcelain bowls that are mounted on top of the counter. Today, stone surfaces—

TOP Luxury items and spa amenities, such as this whirlpool tub, are often included in today's family bathrooms.

BOTTOM A reproduction telephone-style faucet set lends an upscale note to a refurbished antique clawfoot tub.

smart tip

BUILT-IN STORAGE

BUILT-INS GREATLY INCREASE YOUR STORAGE OPTIONS. REMOVE THE DRY-WALL, AND ADD SHELVES BETWEEN WALL STUDS FOR SMALL ITEMS. TRIM THE OPENING WITH DECORATIVE MOLDING.

LEFT Using different-color knobs on drawer fronts is one way to assign storage space in a shared bath.

BELOW Custom cabinetry can add to the cost of a bath remodel, but it can be tailored to an entire family's needs.

RIGHT Graceful arches and partitions divide the space without creating a boxy look.

floor, walls, and tub and shower surrounds—are the height of fashion and luxury, especially when they are made of granite, marble, or limestone. Stone usually requires more maintenance, too, although some fabrications can now be permanently sealed with a special coating that makes the material impervious to water damage. Solid-surface laminate material, which can be as expensive as some stone, is not porous and offers more design versatility in the sense that it comes in a variety of colors and can imitate the look of different materials and textures. It's also not as hard and cold as stone. Solid-surfacing material can be used to fabricate sinks, countertops, tub and shower surrounds, and floors.

Customization. Custom cabinetry in a family bath

really makes sense because it can be tailored to accommodate a variety of personal storage needs. It can be part of a dividing wall or a large built-in vanity and hutch, complete with sinks, mirror, and lighting. It can incorporate special touches, such as a pullout step that's built into the toekick area to give youngsters a lift at the sink. Base cabinets can be built to accommodate a higher- or lower-than-standard countertop that's tailored to individuals' heights.

In a zoned space, it's important to include lighting in each area—at the tub and shower, at the vanity, and in the toilet area—in addition to general lighting. For more lighting information, see the sidebar "Bathroom Lighting," on page 48.

MIDRANGE DESIGNS

In general, you can have some of the basic fixtures already mentioned—a whirlpool tub and a double vanity, for example—without spending top dollar. It's the materials and custom work that can drive up the cost of the bathroom, so stick to less-pricey plastic laminate, standard ceramic tile, or stone tile (as opposed to slab stone). If you want a separate shower, a prefabricated unit will be more affordable than a custom design.

Another factor that inflates a budget, and perhaps the costliest one, is an addition. Look for other ways to gain space, such as stealing a few feet from an adjacent room or annexing space from a hallway or closet. Replace a small window with a bay (as long as it doesn't compromise privacy), or install one or two roof windows to add light and a sense of spaciousness.

Tub Choices. The larger the tub, the higher the price, so buy a 60-inch model to fit your budget. Besides, the larger the tub, the more water you'll need to fill it. The most popular tubs today are made of acrylic, which is less expensive than cast iron. Lightweight acrylic usually does not require additional framing support, as a cast-iron tub might.

RIGHT Children share this bathroom and, save for a few replaceable accent tiles, the design can grow with them.

OPPOSITE TOP A stepstool caters to younger members of the family who have difficulty reaching the sink.

OPPOSITE BOTTOM Lever-style faucet and door handles are easier for young and old hands to operate.

STYLE ON A BUDGET

Many Americans live in houses with one bathroom that is old and not much bigger than a closet, but they can't spend a lot of money to change things. If that sounds like your situation, don't give up. You can make affordable improvements that will update the face and the functional aspects of the room.

If you're on a tight budget, don't make any structural changes and don't move plumbing lines. Another costly change is replacing an old bathtub. As long as the plumbing behind the wall is in good shape, why bother? If it's an old cast-iron tub, don't remove it; refinish it. You can do this in one of two ways: have it reglazed or relined. The first option restores an old tub by having it recoated professionally with enamel. The second option, which is also a professional job, involves installing an acrylic form or liner over the tub. The form is molded to conform to the exact shape of the old tub; then it is glued securely onto the old tub. Either way, you'll pay about the same price as you would for a good quality new tub, but you'll save lots more because you won't have to rip out and replace the plumbing. With gentle, nonabrasive care, re-enameled or relined tubs will look good for 5 to 10 years.

RIGHT Adding a bright color scheme provides an affordable cosmetic makeover.

BELOW Replacing the sink and toilet with a coordinated set can be done quickly and on a budget.

BELOW LEFT Reglazing an old tub costs less than replacing it. New fittings add flair and improved function.

Fittings. It pays to splurge a little on the quality of the fittings. Cheap faucets simply don't last, so you'll end up spending more in the long run. You'll also want to invest in a quality toilet. Today's low-flush models are often so-so flush, so ask around for reviews and recommendations. If you know other people who have recently replaced a toilet, find out whether they are pleased with its efficiency. Remember that the priciest toilet may perform as poorly as the cheapest one. However, you can save money if you buy a two-piece model. One-piece toilets are slick, but you are paying more for style than engineering.

bathroom planning guidelines

The National Kitchen & Bath Association (NKBA) has developed a list of bathroom planning guidelines that help both bath design professionals and homeowners who are designing a bath remodel on their own—whether or not expansion is an option. Here are some of those guidelines. Follow them as best as you can in your situation.

1a. Doorways at least 32 inches wide and not more than 24 inches deep in the direction of travel.

1b. The clear space at a doorway must be measured at the narrowest point.

1c. Walkways should be a minimum of 36 inches wide.

2. Clear floor space at least the width of the door on the push side and a larger clear floor space on the pull side for maneuvering to open, close, and pass through the doorway.

3. A minimum clear floor space of 30 x 48 inches either parallel or perpendicular should be provided at the lavatory.

4a. A minimum clear floor space of 48 x 48 inches provided in front of the toilet with 16 inches of clear floor space extending to each side of the fixture's centerline.

4b. Up to 12 inches of the 48 x 48 inches of clear floor space can extend under the lavatory when total access to a knee space is provided.

5. A minimum clear floor space of 48 x 48 inches from the front of the bidet should be provided.

6a. A minimum clear floor space of 60 x 30 inches at the bathtub for a parallel approach.

6b. A minimum clear floor space of 60 x 48 inches at the bathtub for a perpendicular approach.

7. A minimum clear floor space at a shower less than 60 inches wide should be 36 inches deep x shower width + 12 inches. A shower 60 inches wide or greater requires a space of 36 inches deep x shower width.

8. The clear floor spaces required at each fixture may overlap.

9. Turning space of 180 degrees planned for in the bathroom. Minimum diameter of 60 inches for 360-degree turns and/or T-turn with a space of 36 x 36 x 60 inches.

10. A minimum clear floor space of 30 x 48 inches is required beyond the door swing in the bathroom.

11. For more than one vanity, one may be 30–34 inches and another 34–42 inches high.

12. Kneespace provided at the lavatory, 27 inches above the floor at the front edge and 30 inches wide.

13. The bottom edge of the mirror over the lavatory should be a maximum of 40 inches above the floor or a maximum of 48 inches above the floor if it is tilted.

14. The minimum clear floor space from the centerline of the lavatory to any side wall is 15 inches.

15. The minimum clearance between two bowls in the lavatory center is 30 inches, centerline to centerline.

16. In an enclosed shower, the minimum usable interior dimensions are 34 x 34 inches measured wall to wall.

17. Showers should include a bench or seat that is 17–19 inches above the floor and a minimum of 15 inches deep.

18. A 60-inch shower requires a 32-inch entrance. If the shower is 42 inches deep, 36 inches is required.

19. Shower doors must open into the bathroom.

20. No steps at the tub or shower area. Safety rails should be installed to facilitate transfer.

21. All showerheads equipped with a pressure-balance/temperance regulator or temperature-limiting device.

22a. Shower controls accessible from inside and outside the fixture and located between 38–48 inches above the floor and offset toward the room.

22b. Tub controls accessible from inside and outside the fixture and located between the tub rim and 33 inches above the floor, below the grab bar, and offset toward room.

23a. A minimum 16-inch clearance from the centerline of the toilet or bidet to any obstruction on either side.

23b. For adjacent toilet and bidet installation, the 16-inch minimum clearance to all obstructions should be maintained.

24. The toilet-paper holder installed within reach of person seated on the toilet, slightly in front of the edge of the toilet and centered 26 inches above the floor.

25. Compartmentalized toilet areas should be a minimum of 36 x 66 inches with a swing-out door or pocket door.

26. Walls reinforced to receive grab bars in the tub, shower, and toilet areas.

27. Storage for toiletries, linens, grooming, and general bathroom supplies provided 15–48 inches above the floor.

28. Storage for soap, towels, and personal items should be installed within reach of person seated on bidet or toilet or within 15–48 inches above the floor.

INDIVIDUAL NEEDS

The first step in making special accommodations is to assess the specific physical limitations of the person who will be using the bathroom. This will help you tailor the layout and fixtures to meet his or her needs.

Limited Mobility

Some decrease in the ability to reach and bend is experienced by most people as they age, although young people can certainly have these limitations, too. Adaptations that can make bathrooms easier to use include raised toilet seats, tub seats, and grab bars around the tub, shower, and toilet.

If your family member has trouble reaching high objects, provide storage for personal hygiene and medicines at a level between 36 and 60 inches from the floor. A hand-held shower is useful for people who must sit while showering.

To make life easier for someone who has difficulty turning faucets on and off, replace a faucet that has knob handles with one that has levers. Replace the light's toggle switch with a large rocker plate. Instead of small glass knobs on the vanity drawers, use easy-to-grip C-shaped handles. Provide shallow, open shelves and racks wherever possible, rather than deep storage behind doors.

Reduced Sight

Any changes you may make to improve bathroom access for someone with poor eyesight will make the room easier for all to use. Start at the floor, and eliminate sudden changes in elevation. Be sure to use an extra-long nonslip mat on the tub or shower floor.

You can also mount the light switch on the outside of the entrance door, and use the type that glows. Provide brighter levels of lighting in the bathroom than you might otherwise install. And make sure that there are no unlit corners, such as in the tub/shower area.

RIGHT This accessible bathroom design has provided plenty of space for a wheelchair to maneuver, carefully placed grab bars, and an extra-wide wall-mounted sink accessible to a seated person.

Wheelchair Accessibility

Accommodating wheelchairs in a bathroom can be difficult. In addition to including specially designed plumbing fixtures, the layout must include space for the wheelchair user to get in and out of the room and, once inside, to turn around.

Any doors in the pathway to the bathroom should have at least 32 inches clear width—that is, between the stops. Provide at least 60 inches in front of an in-swinging bathroom door. Better still, avoid swinging doors altogether, if possible. They always pose an obstacle to wheelchair users. Consider substituting a pocket door. In some cases, such as a private bath off of a bedroom, you might even consider skipping the door altogether.

The floor inside of the bathroom should have a clear 360-degree area measuring 60 inches across to allow the wheelchair user to turn around.

Bathing and showering also require special planning. Remember that the shower and adjacent area for maneuvering can consume a lot of floor space.

ABOVE This well-designed shower stall allows someone in a wheelchair to enter and exit easily. The convenient fold-down table holds bath items.

RIGHT All of the fixtures in this bathroom have been designed for easy use by a person with limited mobility. Note the grab bars behind the toilet and all around the shower area.

Permanent versus Temporary Changes

It doesn't make sense to construct permanent physical changes to accommodate a family member whose limitations are temporary. After determining what the person can and can't do, look for practical and inexpensive ways to make temporary adaptations to the bathroom.

For example, add grab bars that clamp onto the side of the tub or surround the toilet. Don't use towel bars for this purpose as these are not designed to support the weight of a person. Extensions are available to raise the height of a standard toilet seat. Visit a medical products supplier to see what's on the market. You may even be able to rent some of these products.

If a household member is permanently disabled, lasting changes may be warranted. You need to determine whether it is possible to adapt an existing bathroom or whether a new bathroom must be added. If a larger room is needed for wheelchair use, consider adapting an unused or underused bedroom or bumping the bathroom into an existing closet. (See the minimum clearances for wheelchair use in the illustrations below.) If the family member's limitations make for longer bathroom time, you may want to try to add a second full or three-quarter bath to ease the morning rush and make it possible for all of you to be on time for work or school.

Barrier-Free Fixtures

You can adapt existing fixtures by either adding grab bars and various devices that adjust heights or replacing them with fixtures specifically designed for people who use wheelchairs or who have limited mobility. Here are some of the options.

Sinks. Sinks for wheelchair access must allow for knee space below and project out far enough to allow the user to reach the faucets. Insulate exposed hot-water pipes beneath the sink to prevent users from burning their legs, and adapt fittings to the user's needs.

Wheelchair-accessible sinks measure about 20 inches wide and project out from the wall 18 to 27 inches. Mount the sinks 34 inches from the floor to the underside of the front edge. One model can be mounted on an adjustable wall bracket, allowing users to choose the most convenient height. For wheelchair access to a sink, allow 36 inches of clear width at the floor level.

Showers. There are two types of showers for people who use wheelchairs. One contains a seat: the person wheels up to the shower and uses grab bars to hoist himself or herself onto the seat. Constructed out of fiberglass or acrylic, these units measure 36, 42½, or 56 inches wide by 37 inches deep by 84 inches high. They come equipped with handholds, soap ledges, and adjustable

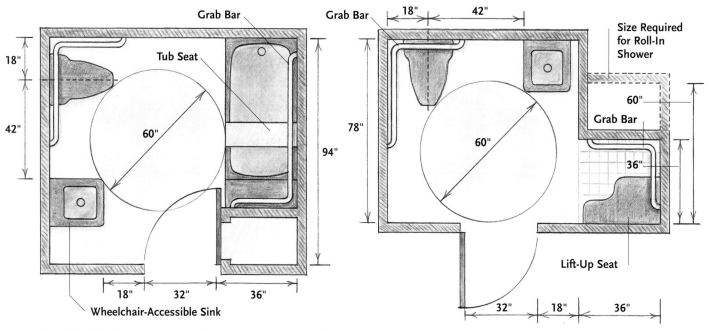

ABOVE LEFT These are the minimum clearances and accessories required for wheelchair access in a bathroom with a tub. The 60-in. clear circle allows a person in a wheelchair to turn inside of the room.

ABOVE RIGHT Two types of showers are geared for wheelchair use. People who can leave the wheelchair can move onto the seat of a small shower. If the person must remain in the wheelchair, install a roll-in shower.

handheld showers. In the second type, the user can wheel into the compartment and shower while remaining in the wheelchair.

Toilets. Toilets for wheelchair users are basically the same as standard toilets, but the seat is 17 to 19 inches above the floor instead of the more usual height of around 14 inches. Grab bars, preferably at the back and at least on one side, are essential for maneuvering between the wheelchair and toilet. Allow at least 36 inches of clear width for access around the fixture.

You can adapt a standard toilet by placing a portable extension seat over the existing toilet. This approach is useful if the fixture must also be used by small children, who may have trouble reaching a higher seat. Some extension seats come with grab bars attached to the sides. Look for these items in medical product supply stores.

smart tip
GRAB BARS

Grab bars are fast becoming standard accessories in bathrooms. Even if you don't need them now, you may in the near future—even if it's while recovering from an injury or in the last few months of pregnancy. The shower shown here has been modified with the addition of a grab bar and a large lever-type faucet control. Many manufacturers offer grab bars in a variety of styles and finishes to suit any bathroom decor or design. (For proper installation, see "Installing a Grab Bar," page 240.)

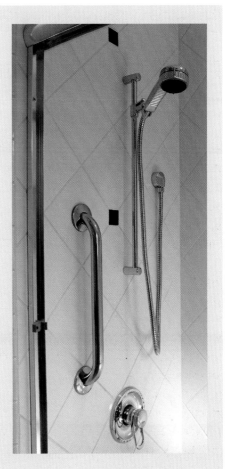

● ACCESSIBLE FIXTURE PLACEMENT

The table at right shows the minimum floor clearances, in inches, recommended by the National Kitchen and Bath Association (NKBA) for placing fixtures in a bathroom that meets accessible design criteria. If you don't have enough floor space to meet them, at least use these minimum clearances as guidelines, but tailor them to your personal situation and available space as necessary.

Fixture	NKBA Minimum
Lavatory	30 x 48*
Toilet	48 x 48**
Bidet	48 x 48***
Bathtub	60 x 30****

In the case of a shower that is less than 60 inches wide, the minimum clearance should be 36 inches deep by the width of the shower plus 12 inches. A shower that is more than 60 inches wide requires 36 inches of clear floor space by the width of the shower.

* Up to 19 inches can extend under the lavatory.

** At least 16 inches must extend to each centerline of the toilet.

*** You may reduce it to 30 x 48 if space is tight, but that may compromise full use.

**** For a parallel approach. For a perpendicular approach, clearance should be 60 x 48.

family-bath plans

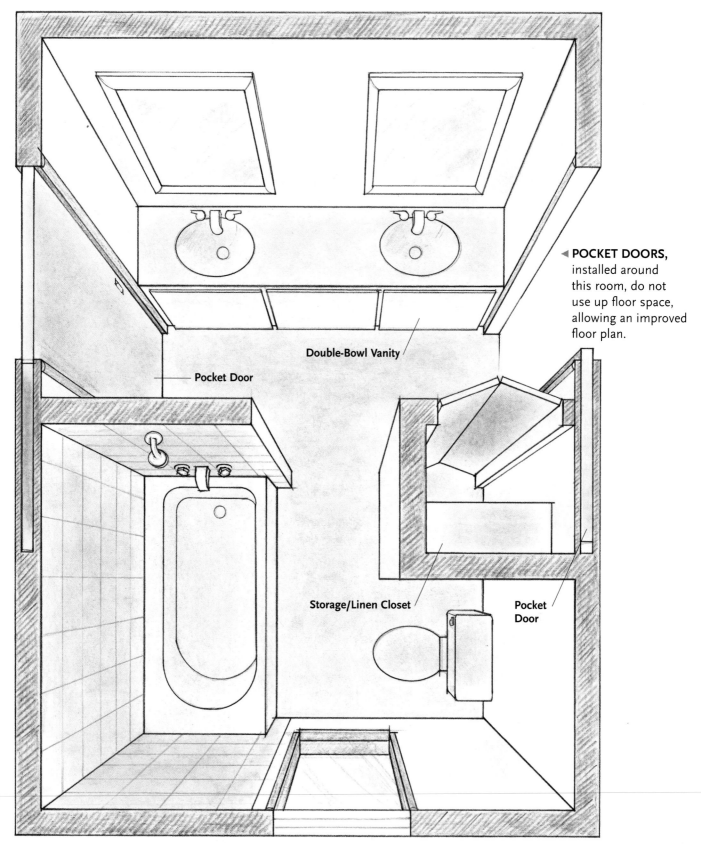

▲ **POCKET DOORS,** installed around this room, do not use up floor space, allowing an improved floor plan.

Double-Bowl Vanity

Pocket Door

Storage/Linen Closet

Pocket Door

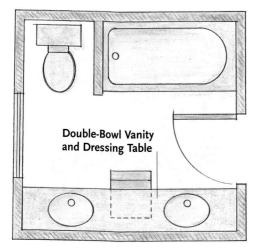

◀ **A PARTITION** next to the toilet expands the use of this shared bathroom without adding on to it.

Double-Bowl Vanity and Dressing Table

▶ **IN A MODEST ROOM,** installing standard-size fixtures may yield space for a linen closet.

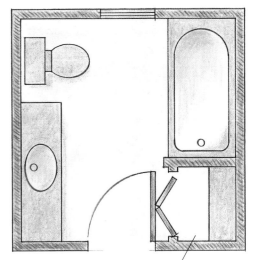

Linen/Storage Closet

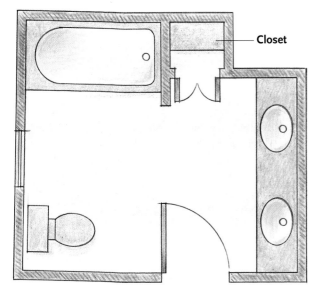

Closet

▲ **A DOOR** that opens into the dressing area of the room provides a better sight line.

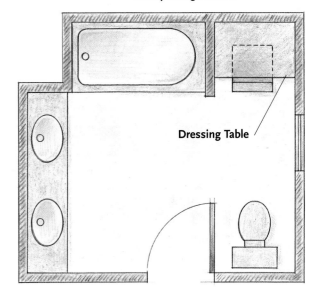

Dressing Table

▲ **IN A SIMILAR LAYOUT,** the toilet is obscured from sight by the door swing.

▼ **ACCESS TO THE BATHROOM** is provided by two separate entrances at either end.

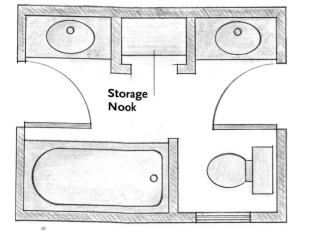

Storage Nook

▼ **PEDESTAL SINKS** and a large storage area are separated from the bathing zone in this layout.

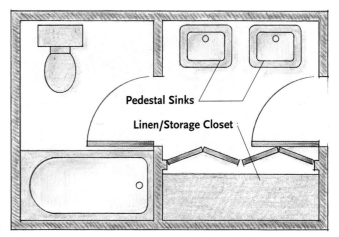

Pedestal Sinks

Linen/Storage Closet

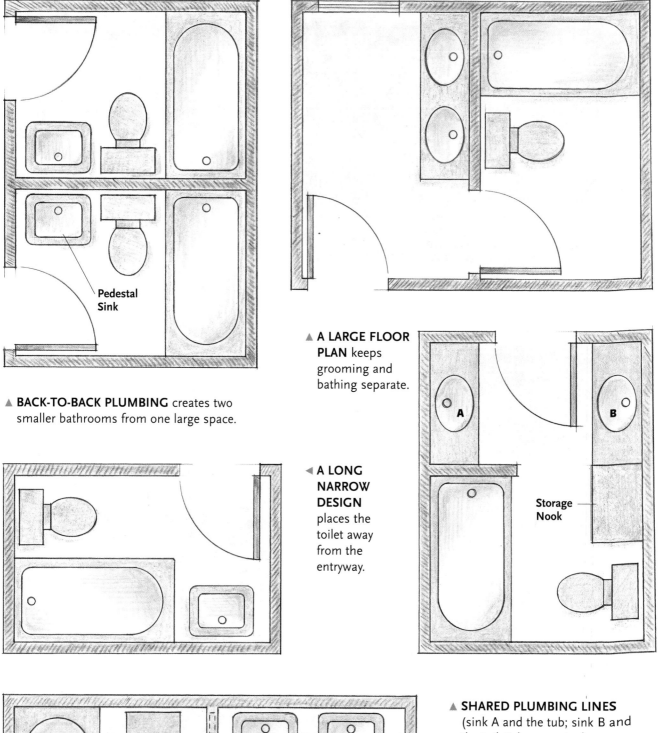

▲ BACK-TO-BACK PLUMBING creates two smaller bathrooms from one large space.

Pedestal Sink

▲ A LARGE FLOOR PLAN keeps grooming and bathing separate.

◄ A LONG NARROW DESIGN places the toilet away from the entryway.

Storage Nook

▲ SHARED PLUMBING LINES (sink A and the tub; sink B and the toilet) keep costs down.

◄ LOCATING THE SINKS, which are the most-used fixtures, nearest the door is logical.

Pocket Door

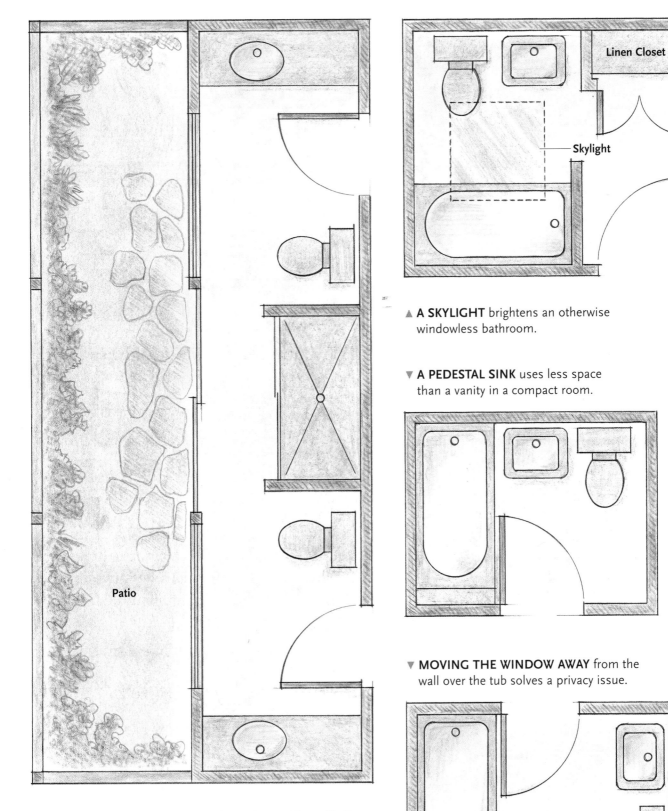

▲ **A SKYLIGHT** brightens an otherwise windowless bathroom.

▼ **A PEDESTAL SINK** uses less space than a vanity in a compact room.

▼ **MOVING THE WINDOW AWAY** from the wall over the tub solves a privacy issue.

▲ **A LARGE FAMILY BATH** that is located just off of the patio contains an oversized shower and views to the outdoors.

4 half baths

A half bath is often the smallest room in the house, but it may also be one of the most important and efficient ones, providing exactly what you need often in tight quarters or awkward spaces. A half bath is also referred to as a "powder room." This appellation can be traced to Colonial America when men and women wore powdered wigs. The wealthiest people built special rooms onto their houses where—away from clothes, furniture, and drapery—servants powdered the wigs. Today, a half bath normally includes a toilet and a sink. However, a shower might also fit into the room. This arrangement is called a three-quarter bath—and it's a practical idea if there is only one other bathroom in the house. Some homes also combine a half bath with a laundry room. You'll find of all of these arrangements in the Half-Bath Plans section.

THIS SMALL SPACE

If you're thinking of adding a powder room, you might consider locating it near a laundry area or in a convenient spot that is away from the most public areas of the house—a pantry or a back hall closet are excellent spaces to reinvent this way. Ideally, you don't want to sit in the living room in full view of or within earshot of the toilet if you can help it. But if the only place you can fit the room is in the front-hall closet, pay careful attention to sight

OPPOSITE A unique marble and stainless-steel vanity adds distinction to a small powder room.

ABOVE Gold-plated fittings and the gilded mirror add sparkle to a closet-size powder room.

RIGHT Light colors, white fixtures, and understated prints open up this small half-bath.

lines—and position the toilet accordingly.

If your powder room is miniscule, you can find small-scale fixtures specifically designed for tight spaces, from the tiniest sinks to the narrowest toilets. (See Chapter 10, "Toilets & Bidets," on page 180, and Chapter 12, "Sinks & Faucets," on page 216.) Another space-saving option is a toilet or sink designed to fit into a corner. One way to conserve floor space is to hang the door so that it opens out instead of into the room. A better idea is to install a pocket

door, which runs on a track and slides out of the way and back inside the wall when someone opens the door.

You might think that because this is just the powder room, it makes sense to skimp on fixtures or even on the decor of the room. But it's likely that this bathroom may see more traffic than any other one in the house. It's a better idea to invest a few more dollars in a toilet that flushes efficiently on the first try and on a sink and faucet set that will work properly and retain their luster over time.

TOP OF THE LINE

This is a room where you can show off, especially because it's used by guests. So decorate the powder room with a flourish. Even if it's boxy, pick out a dramatic color or an over-the-top wallcovering pattern. This is the perfect place for a delicate hand-painted sink or a glass above-counter basin. Likewise, if you don't have to worry about mold and mildew, consider a beautiful painted finish for the wall and vanity.

A powder room is also a great place to splurge on an elegant marble countertop or a one-of-a-kind custom vanity fabricated from an antique piece of furniture. Or instead of going to the trouble and expense of retrofitting an antique into your plans, check out some of the furniture-like manufactured vanities on today's market. Because the damaging effects of moisture are less of a concern, layer on the fabrics to dress up this room. Formal curtains, a skirted lavatory, or even an upholstered chair or vanity stool can add beautiful decorator touches that can make this room special.

Personal Touches. Include a piece of art in the room or an antique mirror. Draw attention to a framed painting or print with a picture light or a small recessed eyeball fixture that you can focus on the art.

An elegant powder room should also have nice linens and special soaps and lotions kept handy for the use of your guests. Although this may not be the place where you normally groom your hair or apply makeup, a suitable mirror and sufficient lighting are always essential elements in good bath design.

LEFT Visible from the entry hall, an above-counter lav atop a restored dresser looks elegant paired with formal lamps and a mirror.

ABOVE A black marble countertop adds glamour to an antique dressing table that has been converted for the powder room.

BELOW A large mirror over the sink helps this small room seem bigger than it really is.

LEFT A beveled mirror that spans the length of the wall above the toilet and the sink, visually enlarges the space.

RIGHT Even a small mirror can work magic. Here it washes a space with reflected sunlight from a roof window.

BELOW All glass walls make this powder room shimmer. Chrome fittings and the right lighting heighten the drama.

MIDRANGE AND PRACTICAL

Of course, you don't have to install gold-plated taps to create an upscale look. Reliable quality fixtures that don't need pampering may be more practical in a room that gets a lot of traffic. Surfaces that clean easily and don't require much maintenance, such as ceramic tile, plastic laminate, or solid-surfacing material, make more sense than stone or glass, especially if the kids will use this room as much as anyone else.

A modest powder room is a good place for a pedestal sink because you don't really need a lot of surface space for cosmetics and the like. A small shelf above the sink is all that's necessary. You may want to keep a small cabinet or basket nearby for extra rolls of toilet tissue, towels, and soaps, too. Baskets are also useful for attractively storing cleaning supplies in a handy location. There is a wide array of stylish faucets that come with sealed finishes, so they repel water spots and hold up to wear better than ever. Add washable wallcoverings or paint to the list of sensible options as well.

LEFT Fluted trim and crown molding dress up a plain medicine cabinet in this modest but attractive half bath.

BELOW A small corner sink that can be mounted to the wall saves the most amount of space in tight places.

BOTTOM LEFT Adjacent laundry and powder rooms have the advantage of shared plumbing lines.

JUST FUNCTIONAL

Sometimes having an extra toilet in the house is all you really need. In that case, a half bath needn't be fancy. All you have to concern yourself with is finding a place for a modest toilet and a small sink. That may be a closet, an area at one end of the laundry, or a corner of the basement. But make sure that you are not violating any building codes with your installation. First obtain the necessary permits for the work. Just because you think a little nook under the attic eave is a perfect spot for a half bath doesn't mean that the local building department is going to agree with you. Find out first. (See "Do You Need A Permit?" on page 12.)

Codes allowing, you can even make the tightest location pleasant. Add a skylight or small window; it's not that expensive, and it can make a big difference. Use light colors and mirrors; eliminate clutter; and by all means, keep the room well lit and adequately ventilated.

BELOW Bold color is an inexpensive way to add style. Here, bright-green walls look fresh and up to date.

LEFT An outrageous sink and artful handpainted tile strike a one-of-a-kind note in this powder room.

half-bath plans

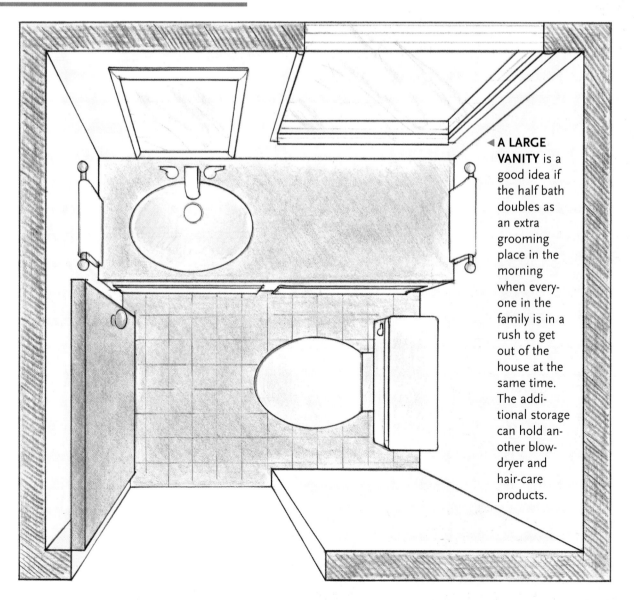

◀ **A LARGE VANITY** is a good idea if the half bath doubles as an extra grooming place in the morning when everyone in the family is in a rush to get out of the house at the same time. The additional storage can hold another blow-dryer and hair-care products.

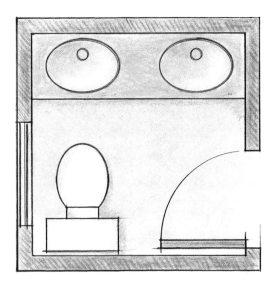

▲ **A DOUBLE-BOWL VANITY** may be smart if there's only one other bathroom in the house.

▼ **TURN A LAUNDRY-ROOM CLOSET** into a toileting room.

Pocket Door

Stacked Washer/Dryer

Oversize Sink

▶ **INSTALLING A SHOWER** turns a half bath into a three-quarter bath.

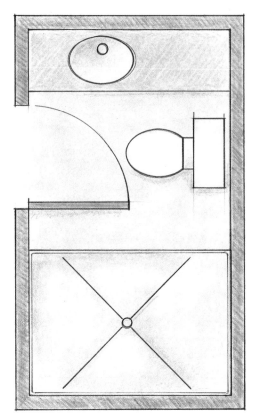

▶ **LOCATE THE SINK** and the toilet on the same wall to conserve floor space in a small room.

Pedestal Sink

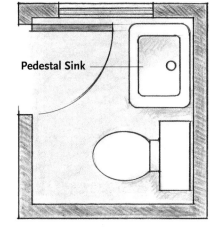

▼ **IN A LONG NARROW ROOM,** place the toilet and the sink on opposite walls.

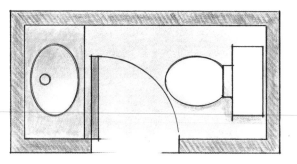

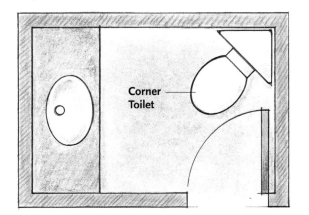

▲ **PUT THE TOILET** in the corner to improve the clearance for the door swing.

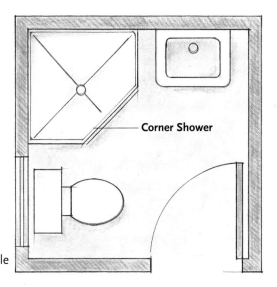

▶ **A CORNER SHOWER UNIT** makes it possible to convert a half bath into a three-quarter bath.

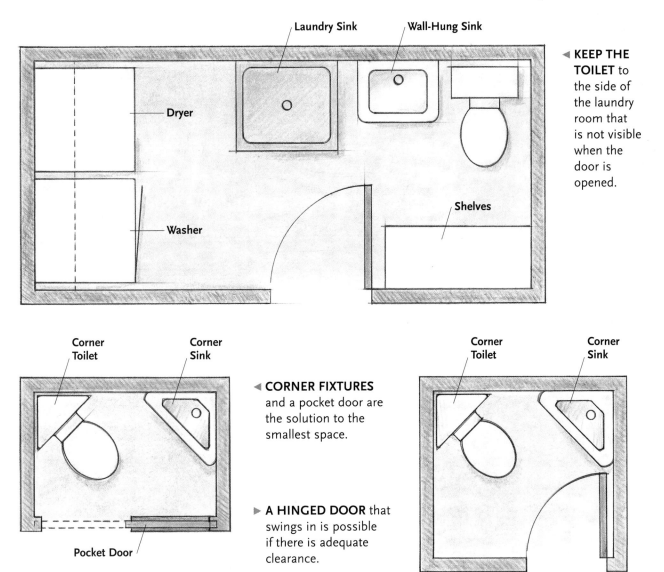

◀ **KEEP THE TOILET** to the side of the laundry room that is not visible when the door is opened.

◀ **CORNER FIXTURES** and a pocket door are the solution to the smallest space.

▶ **A HINGED DOOR** that swings in is possible if there is adequate clearance.

5 windows

Remodeling a bathroom often includes removing the small original windows and opening up the space with larger windows. Or you can add a skylight to flood the area with natural light without worrying about privacy issues or using up valuable wall space.

In either case, there are a variety of window and skylight styles from which to choose. You will want to get one that looks best with the rest of the room, of course, but don't forget to consider the energy qualities of the units. Today's windows and skylights are much more energy efficient than those produced in the past. Construction is much tighter, so there is reduced air infiltration around the frames. And improved coatings for the glazing can stop heat loss from the house or block unwanted heat gain from outside.

INSTALLING NEW SASH IN AN EXISTING FRAME

project

You can replace worn sash without replacing the entire window. The first steps are to measure the window openings carefully and order your new sash. Then remove the old ones, and fill the window-weight cavities with insulation. Cut the liners to size and install them. Then slide the sash into the liners. Finish up by installing window stops to hold the sash in place.

TOOLS & MATERIALS
- Wood chisel or pry bar ▮ Utility knife
- Hacksaw ▮ Sash-replacement kit
- 8d (2½-inch) finishing nails
- Loose-fill (vermiculite) and spray foam insulation
- Cup and cardboard guide for insulation

1 Using a sharp utility knife, cut the paint seal that runs along the sash stop boards and the window jambs. Then carefully push a flat pry bar under the stops and pry them off. Pull the nails from the backside of these trim boards.

4 Carefully measure the jamb opening, and cut the new jamb liners to fit, using a hacksaw or a power miter box. Then attach them to the old jambs following the directions that came with the kit. In many cases, you simply screw the liners to the jambs.

5 Install the top sash first by angling one corner of it into the outermost track on one of the liners. Make sure the pin on the corner of the sash (inset) engages in the track channel.

2 Pull the bottom sash away from the window opening, and remove the cords or chains that are connected to the sash weights. Set the bottom sash aside, and pry away the parting strips that separate the top and bottom sash from the grooves in the side jambs.

3 Remove the sash weights, cords, and pulleys from the side jambs; then enlarge the pulley opening using a drill and spade bit. Using a piece of cardboard and a cup, pour loose-fill insulation into the weight cavities; fill the upper cavity with spray foam insulation.

6 Slide the other sash corner into its channel, and push the sash down to the sill. Then lift the sash, and push the bottom into place.

7 Install the bottom sash in the inside liner tracks. Push the bottom against the sill, and then force the top into place.

8 Finish up the job by installing window stop trim boards. If you removed the old ones carefully, you can reuse them.

REMOVING OLD WINDOWS

To remove the old window unit entirely, take off the inside and outside trim. If you work carefully, you may be able to use them for the new window. Once the trim is removed, cut or pull the nails that hold the jambs in place. At this point, loose-fitting units will slide out easily. Tighter units may have to be pried out. If the rough opening is too big for the new window, add boards to the jambs to close it in.

TOOLS & MATERIALS
- Pry bar ▌Pliers ▌Wood chisel
- Hammer ▌Wood shims (as needed)
- Reciprocating saw
  with metal-cutting blade
- Lumber (for packing out the rough
  opening, as needed)
- Work gloves and safety goggles

1 To replace an entire window, start by ordering new units that are the same size as old windows. Then remove the window by prying off the exterior trim using a flat pry bar. Be careful with the trim. You may be able to use it on the new window.

3 Once the trim is off, check to see how the window is attached to the wall. Older windows are nailed through the jambs, so cut these nails using a reciprocating saw. New windows have a nailing flange, so just pull the nails from this flange.

4 After the installation nails are gone, some loose-fitting windows can just be pushed out of the opening. Tighter fits will need to be pried out. Removing the unit from the outside reduces the mess on the inside of the house.

2 Move inside and pry off the interior trim. Again, if you work carefully, you may be able to reuse these boards. Once they are free, pull the nails from the backside of the board using locking pliers.

5 The new window will specify what the rough opening should be. If yours is too wide, fill in the opening by nailing lumber to the jambs. Add the same amount to both sides so the new window will stay centered in the opening.

MAKING A NEW HEADER

If you're putting in a larger window, you'll need to install a new header—the built-up framing member that spans the top of the rough opening. The header would be strong enough if you made it simply by doubling two pieces of two-by lumber of the appropriate width. However, because two-by lumber is actually 1½ inches thick, a doubled two-by would be only 3 inches thick. Because 2x4 studs are actually 3½ inches wide, you need another half-inch of thickness so that the header will be flush with the inside and outside of the stud wall.

The answer is a piece of ½-inch plywood cut to the width and height of the header and sandwiched between the two-bys, as shown in the photo. Assemble the header with 12d nails.

½" Plywood Spacer

Two-by Lumber (Width per Local Code)

12d Nail

CUTTING AN OPENING IN THE OUTSIDE WALL

FIRST MARK THE DIMENSIONS ON THE SIDING. THEN CUT THROUGH THE SIDING AND THE SHEATHING USING A CIRCULAR SAW. TACK ON A GUIDE BOARD TO KEEP THE SAW STRAIGHT.

Guide Board

enlarging a window opening

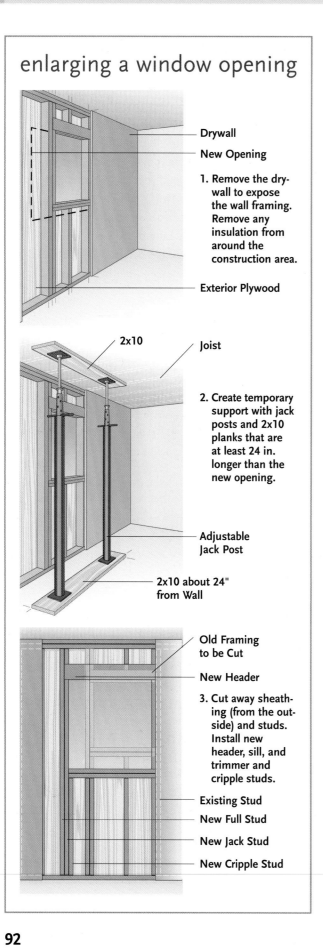

— Drywall

— New Opening

1. Remove the drywall to expose the wall framing. Remove any insulation from around the construction area.

— Exterior Plywood

2x10

— Joist

2. Create temporary support with jack posts and 2x10 planks that are at least 24 in. longer than the new opening.

— Adjustable Jack Post

2x10 about 24" from Wall

— Old Framing to be Cut

— New Header

3. Cut away sheathing (from the outside) and studs. Install new header, sill, and trimmer and cripple studs.

— Existing Stud

— New Full Stud

— New Jack Stud

— New Cripple Stud

INSTALLING NEW WINDOWS

project

A major bathroom remodel is a good time to increase the size of typically small bathroom windows. But you must take care to support the ceiling above when enlarging any window opening. The drawings at left show how to do this.

Once the opening is ready to go, slide the new window into the opening from the outside of the house. Have an inside helper guide the window into position. Center the window in the opening, and make it level and plumb using shims driven between the window unit and the surrounding framing. When you're satisfied with the window position, nail the flange to the sheathing. Then nail the exterior casing boards over the nailing flange. Finish up the outside chores by caulking around the perimeter of the window and the trim with exterior-grade caulk. Clean up any excess caulk, and touch up the paint as required.

Move inside, and fill the gap between the window unit and the rough opening with fiberglass or low-expanding foam insulation. Don't overfill the gap, or you risk distorting the side jambs and making the sash difficult to operate.

TOOLS & MATERIALS
- Window unit
- Pry bar
- Shims
- Level
- Hammer
- Roofing nails
- Exterior casing
- Casing nails
- Caulk
- Fiberglass insulation or low-expanding foam insulation
- Work gloves
- Interior casing

1 Once the opening is prepared, slide the new window in place from outside. Have an inside helper center the unit from side to side; then check for level and plumb. Wedge cedar shims between the window and the framing to keep the window properly aligned.

2 Most new windows have a flange that's nailed to the wall with galvanized roofing nails. Drive these nails every 4 or 5 in. on the sides and top. The bottom of the window usually has flexible flashing instead of a nailing flange.

3 Cut trim boards to fit the space between the window frame and the siding on all four sides. Nail them using galvanized casing nails.

4 Once the casing boards are installed, caulk the perimeter of the window frame and the casing boards with exterior caulk.

5 Move to the inside and fill the space between the window and the framing with fiberglass or low-expanding foam insulation.

window options

CLOCKWISE FROM LEFT The right window treatment, such as the one shown here, provides both privacy and a sense of style to the room. A solar tunnel, such as the one shown in the ceiling below, lets you enjoy the benefits of a skylight without installing a skylight shaft. Adding a large window along the tub wall, below left, usually injects a sense of drama into the room.

CLOCKWISE FROM ABOVE

Large windows and skylights help incorporate the outside view into the design of the room. A round window, right, brings a unique design touch to the bathroom. When selecting windows, be sure to match the scale of the window, left, to the room.

INSTALLING ROOF WINDOWS AND SKYLIGHTS

Installing a roof window or skylight is possible for some do-it-yourselfers, but before deciding to go ahead, be sure you are up to the task.

You'll need to do some of the work inside a cramped attic and part of it crawling around on the roof. If you build a light shaft between the roof and ceiling, you're in for measuring and cutting framing and finishing materials that have tricky angles.

When you have selected your skylight or roof window, read and follow the manufacturer's instructions. Your first job will be to locate the window location on the ceiling.

Planning the Location

First, use a keyhole saw or a saber saw to cut out a piece of the ceiling drywall about 2 feet square, somewhere near the center of where you want the shaft opening to be. Standing on a stepladder and armed with a flashlight, look through the test hole, and inspect the roof and ceiling framing to determine the final location for the opening. Although where you want the sunlight to fall is an important factor, you should also locate the ceiling opening to minimize reworking the framing.

Most skylights and roof windows are designed to fit between two rafters (or three rafters with the middle one cut out). You will need to orient the ceiling opening the same as the roof opening, ideally with joists for its sides. You can make the ceiling opening somewhat larger than the roof opening by adding a light shaft with angled walls. The end of the skylight opening nearest the eaves is usually directly underneath the skylight, and the end nearest the roof's ridge flares out to allow in more light. (See "Framing the Opening," on page 99.)

Cutting the Ceiling Opening

When you have decided where the skylight will go, remove the insulation at that spot in the attic, and mark the final opening of the bottom of your light shaft on the ceiling drywall. Cut along the outline using a keyhole saw or reciprocating saw, and remove the ceiling drywall or plaster. If there is a joist in the middle of the opening, don't cut it until you're ready to frame the new opening. When you are ready, you will need to add headers to carry the weight of the missing joists.

INSTALLING A SKYLIGHT

project

Begin by marking the location of the light shaft opening on the ceiling and driving a nail through the ceiling at each corner. Then go up into the attic; remove the insulation from above this area; and transfer the location of the four nails to the rafters above using a plumb line.

Reinforce the rafters by nailing 2x4 braces across them, above and below the opening. Then, layout the position of the headers at the bottom and top of the opening using a sliding T-bevel. Cut the hole in the roof as shown on page 99, and install the window. Remember, all roof openings need to be flashed. Some skylights have integral flashing. But for many skylights and roof windows this usually means weaving aluminum step flashing between each course of roofing shingles.

Lay out the position of the ceiling headers using a 2x4; then cut out any ceiling joists that are in the way and install the headers. Cut out the ceiling drywall; and then frame the light shaft opening. Begin with the 2x4s that form the ceiling; then fill in the sidewall studs. Cover this framing with drywall, and add insulation between all the framing members.

TOOLS & MATERIALS
- Basic carpentry tools
- Electric drill ▌ Goggles
- Roofing compound
- Chalk-line box ▌ Sliding T-bevel
- Framing lumber (as needed)
- Framing anchors
- 12d (3¼-inch) and 16d (3½-inch) common nails
- Roofing cement ▌ Trowel
- Circular saw with carbide-tipped blade
- Keyhole saw (or reciprocating saw)
- Skylight
- Aluminum step flashing (usually comes in bundles of 100)

1 Lay out the light-shaft hole on the ceiling, and drive a nail through the drywall at each corner. Then transfer the location of these nails to the roof rafters using a plumb line. Connect these marks with heavy lines drawn on the sheathing.

2 Reinforce the rafters by nailing 2x4s across the rafters above and below the marked opening. Then establish the four corners of the opening by driving nails up from each corner so that they poke through the top surface of the roof.

3 Cut away the roof shingles and sheathing, as shown on page 99. Then mark the location of the support headers at the bottom and top of the opening.

4 Cut out any rafters that fall within the opening, and install headers above and below to carry the load of the missing rafters.

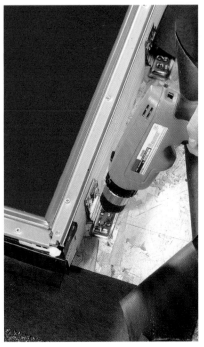

5 Install the window unit according to the manufacturer's instructions. Make sure that any mounting hardware is securely screwed to the roof.

continued on next page

continued from page 97

6 The window has to be properly flashed to prevent leaks. Different manufacturers have different approaches. But usually step flashing (above) is installed between every layer of shingles.

7 Use 2x4s to frame the light shaft. Hold a straight one between the two openings to mark the location of both headers that support any ceiling joists that were removed.

8 Cut and nail headers to both ends of the ceiling opening to carry the weight of the missing joists. Once the headers are installed, cut out the ceiling drywall and screw the drywall to the perimeter of the opening with drywall screws.

9 Build a frame around the opening using 2x4s. Install the angled members first, then the short studs. Once the framing is done, install drywall on the inside surface. Add insulation between the framing members on the attic side of the light shaft.

CUTTING A ROOF OPENING

If you've left the nails that you drove in at the corners of the roof opening, that makes it easier to snap a chalk line on the shingles to mark the opening. Cut asphalt shingles along this line using a utility knife and straightedge to bare the roof sheathing below. Drill a test hole to gauge the depth of your roof sheathing; you want to set your circular saw blade at that depth so that you don't damage the rafters underneath.

Use the circular saw to cut the opening through the roof sheathing. If you need to cut through wood shingles, place a board below the saw. By doing this, you can ease the saw forward without bumping into the bottoms of the shingles. When cutting through the roof sheathing, keep in mind that you will probably hit nails, so use a carbide-tipped blade.

smart tip

CONTROLLING ENERGY COSTS

THE BIGGEST FACTOR IN THE ENERGY PERFORMANCE OF A SKYLIGHT OR A ROOF WINDOW IS ITS ORIENTATION TO THE SUN. UNITS PLACED ON A SOUTHERN ROOF WILL GAIN MORE HEAT THAN THOSE INSTALLED ON A NORTH-FACING ROOF. IN COLD CLIMATES, PURCHASE WINDOWS WITH A LOW-E GLAZING. AND UNITS WITH U-VALUES BELOW 0.35 ARE CONSIDERED EXTREMELY ENERGY EFFICIENT. TO COMBAT OVERHEATING, MAKE USE OF OPERABLE SHADES OR BLINDS.

framing the opening

A skylight requires that you build two new rough openings—one in the roof rafters and one in the ceiling joists—as well as a light shaft, which will run through the attic.

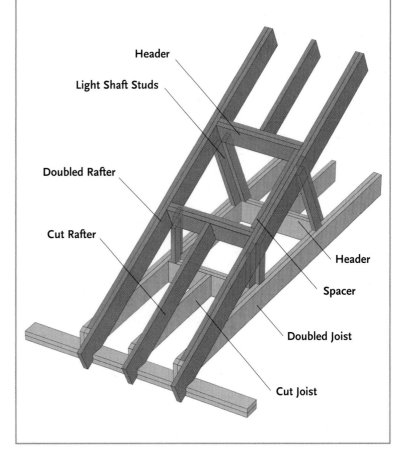

Header

Light Shaft Studs

Doubled Rafter

Cut Rafter

Header

Spacer

Doubled Joist

Cut Joist

BUILDING A GLASS-BLOCK WALL

project

Design your installation so it makes use of only full blocks, which makes the job much easier. Begin by mixing some mortar and adding an expansion strip and joint anchors to the wall and a bed of mortar to the floor. Lay each block in this bed; then start the next course. Finish up by smoothing the joints with a jointing tool.

TOOLS & MATERIALS

- Lumber for curb forms, blocking and extra joists
- 10d nails (3 in.)
- Concrete mix for curb (optional)
- Glass block
- Glass-block mortar mix
- Masonry trowel
- Plastic tub
- Foam expansion strips
- Metal wall anchors
- ¼-in. plastic joint spacers
- Wire joint reinforcement
- Jointing tool
- Silicone caulk and caulking gun
- Rubber gloves

1 When you are ready to start laying up the blocks, mix the white-colored glass block mortar in a plastic tub or a wheelbarrow. Use as little water as possible to make a stiff mix. You have the consistency right if you can form a "baseball" out of the mortar.

BELOW Glass-block walls and windows not only add a distinctive design element to the bath but also allow filtered light into the room without sacrificing privacy. These blocks aren't difficult to install, but the framing in the room may need to be beefed up to support the additional weight. Check with an engineer or architect for what's required.

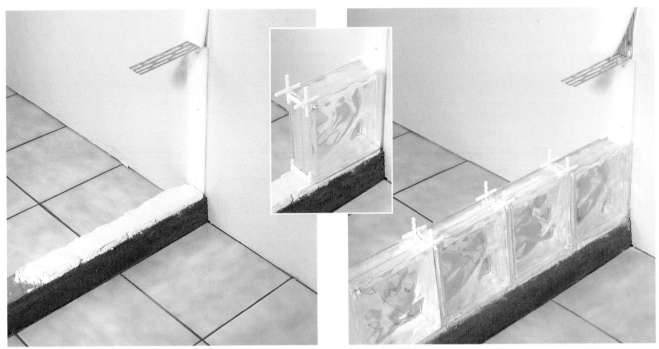

2 Staple an expansion strip and a joint anchor to the wall above the curb (optional) or the floor. Then spread ½-in. bed of mortar on top of the curb or the floor. Set the first block in place, and add plastic mortar spacers to the outside corners (inset).

3 Complete the first coarse of blocks by adding mortar to both sides of each block and spacers to one side. Tap them in place carefully with a rubber mallet. If you push too hard, you may force too much mortar from the bed. Check each block for level.

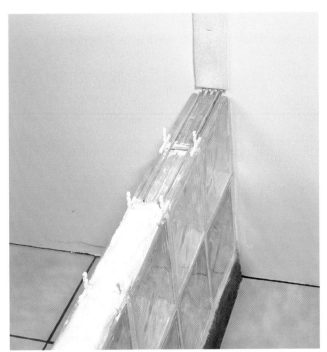

4 Once a course of block is complete, cover the top of the blocks with a new bed of mortar. Embed any wall anchors in this mortar. Then add lengths of wire joint reinforcement on top of the mortar and carefully push them into place.

5 When the wall reaches the ceiling, carefully slide the blocks on the last course in place so that the mortar joints on the sides and bottom are not distorted. Twist off the end of the spacers; then smooth the joints with a jointing tool (inset).

6 stone, tile, and more

Moisture and steam can take their toll even in well-ventilated bathrooms. So it's important to select materials for walls, floors, and countertops that can hold up to water and look stylish as well. Ceramic tile, of course, is always classic, as is solid-surfacing material and plastic laminate. Natural stone, particularly granite, continues to be today's most-popular material. However, concrete and engineered stone—a material made of high concentrations of natural quartz, color pigments, and polymers—are winning over bathroom designers and homeowners in increasing numbers.

Here's a rundown on all of these materials, including their uses and their pros and cons, plus a look at what other homeowners are doing with them.

STONE, NATURALLY

There is no doubt that the natural look is in and that stone is a beautiful and hardworking natural material. Granite, marble, and slate are probably the most expensive materials you can choose for a floor, countertop, and tub or shower surround. Two other stone materials, limestone followed by concrete, are finding their way into the creative hands of designers today, and depending on the application, may be moderately to greatly more affordable to install. When you're considering any of these materials,

remember that they are cold underfoot and hard. A glass bottle that is dropped on a stone or concrete countertop or floor will shatter. Also, stone may pose a safety hazard on the floor because it gets slick when it's wet. Older persons and children are at particular risk. If you choose a stone floor, use a slip-resistant carpet over it.

Granite and marble come in ¾- or 1¼-inch-thick slabs or as ¼- or ⅜-inch tiles. Slabs are the more expensive of the two because you can't just buy a piece of one. If you see a slab of stone that you like, you must purchase the entire thing. Then you must pay to have it cut and installed by a professional to very exact specifications. If you're only interested in a modest-size vanity countertop, you could try to find a remnant. Talk to a fabricator who might be able to help you with this. Otherwise, think of

how you could use the rest of the slab somewhere else in the house—on a small kitchen island, as a fireplace surround, or as a tabletop.

Stone tiles, on the other hand, can be a do-it-yourself project. Just remember to buy extra tiles in case you make a mistake cutting and to have on hand should you need to replace a few tiles in the future. Color lots vary between one another, and if you buy tiles from a different lot later, they may not match. In fact, before you pay for a box of tiles, open it and examine each tile individually and against one another.

OPPOSITE Gorgeous granite is still the favorite for everything from countertops to floors to walk-in showers.

BELOW Marble epitomizes design elegance. However, it is a high-maintenance material that can be damaged easily.

Granite

Granite is considered the ultimate in luxury today. In fact, according to a survey conducted by the Remodelers Council of the National Association of Home Builders (NAHB), most bathroom remodelers choose granite over all other countertop materials. Why do so many bath designers and homeowners like granite so much? Among other things, granite is handsome. An igneous rock, granite has a visible crystalline coarse-grain texture. Its speckles and fine grains have been formed from quartz, feldspar, mica, and bits of other materials that are present in the stone.

Also, granite comes in a variety of colors: shades of green, brown, gold, blue, violet, and mauve, as well as almost pure black and almost pure white. Another reason for its popularity is that it is practically—but not completely—nonporous, which means water won't damage it. Dark colors will show fingerprints and water marks on a highly polished granite countertop, but you can seal the surface periodically (about every six months) to keep it looking new. You can buy the sealant, which may also be

ABOVE Marble tiles with a black granite inset, closely match the marble slab that was used to fabricate the vanity countertop and the shower.

LEFT A slab of green granite was used to fabricate the deck of the tub surround and the countertop of a double-bowl vanity in a master bathroom.

called a cleaner, at a home-improvement store. But make sure the label states that it is for granite. Sealing granite is as easy as polishing furniture.

Engineered Stone. Fabricated "stone" has existed in Europe for years. Now the North American market is quickly catching on to it because engineered stone looks and feels almost exactly like granite. But engineered stone is not porous, so it doesn't need sealing and is therefore easier to maintain. You can effortlessly clean engineered stone using normal bathroom cleansers. Engineered stone is available in a wider and more consistent color range than granite, and unlike natural stone, it comes with a 10-year warranty.

ABOVE Terrazzo tile is a cementious material containing bits and pieces of granite and marble, which is honed to a smooth finish. Terrazzo tile comes in a wide color range.

RIGHT A concrete countertop complements an above-counter lav. Concrete can crack, however, so you may want to limit it to a bathroom that does not get a lot of use.

Marble and Limestone

Marble, including travertine, serpentine, and onyx, has a timeless beauty that traditionalists always admire. Technically, marble is crystallized limestone plus other materials that create the stone's dramatic veining and rich colors, which range from white and light ecru to deep brown, black, gray, green, red, and pink. But marble is also a soft, porous stone that can be gouged and stained easily. Like granite, marble is popular for floors, walls, and surrounds. It must be treated gently and sealed regularly, but even attentive care may not protect it against damage. Yet marble remains synonymous with luxury.

Limestone. This absorbent sedimentary stone was formed by the skeletons and shells of sea creatures. Although it can be polished (and must be sealed), it appears more textured and rustic than granite or marble. You can easily find limestone in tile or slab form in shades of buff or gray. Yellow and pink limestone are available, but not as readily. Imported limestone may be dark brown, red, or black.

Concrete

Poured concrete is inexpensive and offers much opportunity for creating unique countertops, floors, and surrounds. Fabrication and installation are difficult, however, and usually require professional expertise. You can mold, carve, or rout it. Add color to concrete, and inlay pieces of tile, stone, or glass into it to form random or planned designs. Concrete is versatile and can be used for countertops or floors. It is porous, so it must be sealed, and it can crack easily. Still, concrete is affordable and stylish, especially within the context of a contemporary or naturalistic design.

WOOD WALLS

Wood adds warmth to bathroom walls but may absorb moisture, depending on the finish. Aim for smooth-textured surfaces with as few joints as possible, and avoid wood altogether in continuously damp areas such as behind toilets. You can get wood veneer paneling in 48 x 96-inch sheets, prefinished or unfinished. Imitation wood veneer, consisting of a particleboard core printed with a wood pattern, is also available. It's cheaper than wood, but it doesn't have the same look of the real thing.

TILE

You can't go wrong with ceramic tile, a staple in bathroom design for decades. Impervious to water, durable, and easy to maintain, ceramic tile is a perfect material for any surface in the bathroom. Ceramic tile lets you add color, pattern, and texture to a wall, floor, or countertop. Use it to enclose a tub or shower or to create art. Tile is versatile. It comes in a variety of shapes, sizes, and finishes. Use hand-painted or raised-relief designs to create a mural or a mosaic. If hand-painted tile is too costly, more affordable silk-screened designs are so good today that you probably won't see the difference. For the budget-minded, there are mass-produced standard tiles. Visit a tile showroom or a home center, and you will be impressed with the selection. You'll also see examples of how you can mix and match embossed tiles, accent and trim strips, edges, and contrasting colored grout (the compound that fills the joint). For long-lasting wear, always apply a grout sealer.

Tile comes in two finishes: glazed and unglazed.

Unglazed Tile. To make unglazed tiles impervious to water, you will have to apply a sealant. Unglazed tiles always come in a matte finish. It's best to reserve unglazed tiles for installation in areas or on surfaces that will not be overly exposed to water.

Glazed Tiles. Already coated with a sealant during the manufacturing process, glazed tiles can stand up to water. You can use them on all bathroom surfaces. You'll notice that the glaze can be matte finished or highly polished. Floor tiles should be soft-glazed. Anything else will be slippery and hazardous underfoot. Ask the tile retailer about the slip-resistance rating for any tile you may be considering for the bathroom floor.

ABOVE Even standard tile can be highly decorative. Here, a designer stuck to basics and created a simple but lively pattern.

smart tip

GROUT MAGIC

YOU ARE NOT LIMITED TO PLAIN OFF-WHITE GROUT FOR YOUR TILE INSTALLATIONS. GROUT COMES IN A RANGE OF COLORS; CHOOSE ONE THAT ENHANCES YOUR INSTALLATION.

SYNTHETIC MARVELS

New advances in technology have made synthetic materials better than ever. Many of them are economical, and all of them are smart. Perhaps with the exception of the cheapest grades, products such as solid-surfacing material, laminates, and vinyl promise long-term wear and require little maintenance.

Solid-Surfacing Material

If you're looking for something that is handsome, extremely durable, and easily maintained, solid-surfacing material is it. A synthetic made of polyester or acrylic, solid-surfacing comes in a wide array of colors and faux finishes that may mimic everything from stone to leather. Solid-surfacing material is impervious to water, and any dents or abrasions that may occur over time are easily repaired with a light sanding. You can use solid-surfacing material to fabricate countertops, sinks, and shower enclosures. It's not cheap, costing as much per linear foot as granite or marble. Professional installation, which is strongly recommended, and finishing techniques, which include routing or carving, drive up the price tag. Solid-surfacing material comes in ½- and ¾-inch thicknesses, widths of 30 and 36 inches, and lengths up to 12 feet.

BELOW A countertop that is made from solid-surfacing material is good-looking and will stay that way for years.

LAMINATE

Plastic laminate is hard to beat for a bathroom counter-top. It's economical and requires almost no care. Plus, it resists moisture superbly. You can find it in hundreds of colors, patterns, and textures. Plastic laminate comes in 48- x 96-inch sheets of varying grades or thicknesses. To get your money's worth, buy the best quality, which won't chip easily. At the top of the line is "color-through" laminate. Unlike laminate with color on the surface only, this type will not show seam lines at the edges because the color is solid all the way through.

Laminate Flooring. Manufacturers of laminate flooring offer dozens of designs that look almost exactly like real wood or stone. However, unlike natural materials, these products are economical and can boast easy mainte-nance, as well as moisture and stain resistance. You can purchase laminate flooring in either tongue-and-groove planks or as tiles for a relatively easy do-it-yourself proj-ect. In most cases, laminate material installs right over the old floor.

Resilient Flooring

Thin floor coverings composed of resilient materials such as vinyl, rubber, cork, or linoleum are attractive and durable. While softer than tile, resilient flooring feels hard compared with carpeting. Its surface resists water, but it can be slippery when wet. Offset this hazard with throw rugs placed strategically next to tubs and showers.

Resilient flooring comes in a wide range of colors and patterns in both tiles and sheets. Tiles come in $3/32$- and $1/8$-inch thicknesses and are usually 12 inches square; sheet flooring comes in rolls 6 or 12 feet wide. Easier, by far, to in-stall than sheet flooring, tiles are never as resistant to water

● GLASS—ALL THAT GLIMMERS

Glass block is the perfect solution to the often vexing problem of how to enclose a space for privacy without obscuring the light. In addition to using it on an out-side wall, it can be used as a partition, next to a toilet for example, or as an enclosure for a walk-in shower.

Glass block is non-load-bearing, however, so a wall made of this material will need structural support. Talk to a professional if you plan to install it yourself. Basically, it comes in 3- and 4-inch thicknesses. Vari-ous applications (a curved shower stall versus a non-curved wall, for example) have different thickness requirements.

Another option is architectural glass. Beautiful de-signs can be etched or sandblasted into the glass, making them works of art. This is a custom job that must be left in the hands of an artisan.

Luminous glass tiles are highly decorative. Design-ers like to use them in showers and on backsplashes or as accents to ceramic or stone tiles. They are imper-vious to water and hard, yet they can be scratched eas-ily. Only embossed or textured glass tiles are advisable for floors. Glass-tile sizes range anywhere from $1/2$-inch squares to 8-inch-square versions. These tiles are glamorous and expensive, and require skill to install.

Glass countertops have a slick look that coordinates well with contemporary wood cabinets. Like glass walls, they can be customized with special effects, such as a crackle finish, and cut into any size or shape.

because of the number of joints that can open if the substrate expands. For the best water resistance, set resilient tiles in a troweled-on adhesive. Self-adhesive tiles, while easy to install, can pull up at the corners over time. Resilient tiles are easily cut by scoring them with a scribing tool or utility knife and snapping them in two. Sheet flooring can be cut with a high-quality utility knife.

All resilient flooring is easy to maintain, needing only occasional waxing. The shiny surface layer of so-called no-wax floor covering eventually wears down. In time, you'll need to wax to restore the original luster. While resilient floor covering is ideally installed over a substrate of underlayment-grade plywood, you can also apply it over resilient flooring, but only if the existing floor is tightly adhered and smooth.

BELOW Resilient flooring is a popular floor covering choice because it is inexpensive and easy to maintain.

PAINT AND WALLCOVERING

Paint is the easiest and cheapest way to finish a wall. Today, acrylic and latex paints, which have been greatly improved to hold up against moisture, are preferred over the old alkyd-based paints, which are harmful to your health and the environment.

When selecting paint for the bathroom, you could use one with an acrylic gloss enamel finish, which withstands moisture best. But a bathroom has lots of glossy surfaces, and the reflective value of a high-gloss paint may be too intense. Instead, choose a semigloss or low-luster finish. If you're concerned about moisture, buy paint that contains a mildewcide that has been applied to the product during the manufacturing process.

Wallcovering is another attractive option for walls, and there are many colors and motifs from which to choose. Wallcovering can be style- or period-specific, so you can use it to establish a theme in a room: formal or casual, juvenile or sophisticated. You can pair it with a border or simply combine a border treatment with paint. In a bathroom, the only practical option is a vinyl product, unless it's a half bathroom where there is no threat of moisture damage. Fabric-backed vinyl is basically washable, strippable, and mostly indestructible. Paper-backed vinyl is a lighter alternative that is typically prepasted, peelable, and washable. Heavy screen-printed vinyl requires vinyl adhesive with a fungicidal agent instead of standard paste.

7 plumbing

Most bathroom improvements include some change to the plumbing system. The modifications can be as simple as installing a new faucet or as complicated as rerouting pipes and installing a luxurious whirlpool tub and spa. Whatever is in your plans, this chapter will help you learn the basics of working with pipe and give you direction on installing bath fixtures.

Complex projects will require consultation with the building inspector to learn how local codes will affect your plans. Plumbing codes tend to be stringent with little room for modification, so be sure to follow them to the letter. Tackle only those projects that you are sure you can handle. The cost of repairing botched work often exceeds the cost of the original project.

PLUMBING BASICS

Bathroom plumbing has to do three things:
▌ Deliver hot and cold water to the fixtures
▌ Remove waste to the sewer or septic system
▌ Vent the waste pipes to the outside
Here's what's required to achieve these goals.

Getting Water to the Fixtures

Every fixture except the toilet requires separate hot- and cold-water supply pipes. Locate a shutoff valve in a convenient place below the fixture. This way, you can make repairs without shutting down the water to the entire house. By shutting off the main valve, not only will every fixture be out of commission for hours, or even days, but you'll have to run back and forth between the master shutoff valve and the bathroom.

Hot- and cold-water pipes were previously made of galvanized steel joined with threaded connectors. Cutting and threading pipes was difficult and required specialized tools. Today, do-it-yourselfers can install their own hot- and cold-water pipes, thanks to rigid and flexible copper pipe alternatives, which are far simpler to work with and more economical to install and rework when mistakes are made. Chlorinated polyvinyl chloride (CPVC) plastic is also used for supply pipes. The material is popular because it is easy to work with, but some municipalities may not sanction its use.

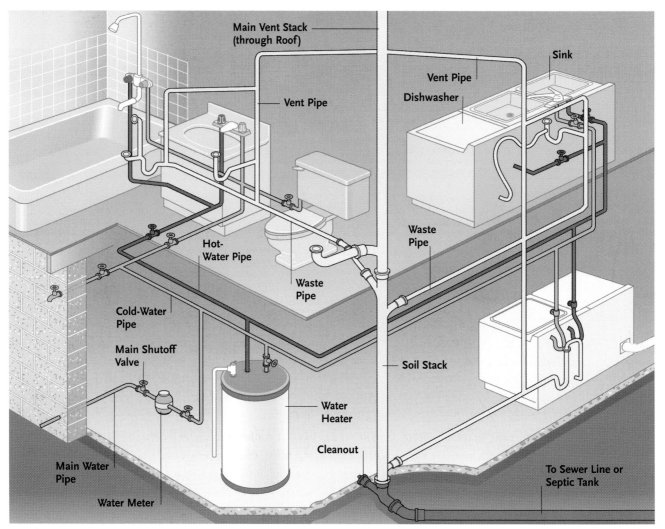

ABOVE Here is a typical household plumbing system. Water arrives from the municipal system or a private well. The cold-water supply lines branch from this main line; hot-water lines are first routed through the water heater. All fixtures receiving water are also connected to drainpipes and vent pipes. All drain and vent lines converge on the soil stack, which extends through the roof.

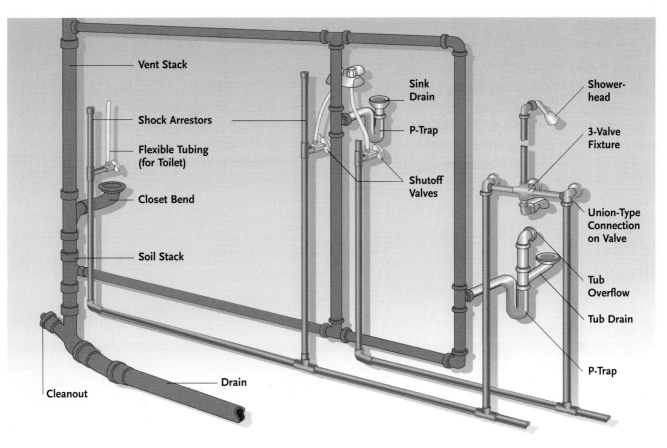

ABOVE This is a plumbing rough-in for a typical bathroom, with the toilet, sink, and bathtub along one wall. The sink faucets and showerhead are shown for clarity; they are not included in the rough-in work.

Waste and Vent Pipes

The pipes that remove waste to the sewer and vent fixtures to the outside work together as a drain-waste-vent (DWV) system. Waste pipes carry off water, while vent pipes allow outside air into the system. The soil stack is a single large-diameter pipe that carries waste down to the sewer and vents air through the roof. Getting water to the fixtures requires pipe that is $\frac{1}{2}$ or $\frac{3}{4}$ inch in diameter; home waste lines are 3 or 4 inches in diameter, depending on the number of fixtures served.

As with water-supply pipe, installing a DWV system was pretty much a plumber's realm in the past. Cutting heavy cast-iron sections and then uniting them by pouring melted lead into bell and spigot joints was beyond the capabilities of most homeowners. By contrast, plastic pipe can be installed by anyone with moderate skills and ability. What could be simpler than cutting pipes with a handsaw and joining them with solvent cement?

Waste Pipes. The waste lines in the DWV system consist of pipes that are sloped to drain to the sewer. Like branches of a tree, small-diameter pipes from sinks,

showers, and tubs feed into the soil stack, which usually sits in the wall just behind the toilet. Each of the fixtures requires a trap, a curved part near the fixture drain to trap water, preventing sewer gas from entering the room. Toilets contain built-in traps. To allow the trapped water to refill instead of being sucked into the sewer, a vent is located between the trap and the sewer line.

Venting. In a simple arrangement with a sink, toilet, and tub on the same wall, the soil stack is simply extended through the roof to provide a vent. When plumbing fixtures are on more than one wall, set apart from each other, or more than a few feet away from the main vent, it is often more practical, and more in-line with the plumbing code, to provide additional vents. Check with your building inspector for specific requirements that pertain to your system.

When planning to relocate fixtures or add new ones, try to use as much of the existing waste and vent pipes as possible. Snaking small-diameter water pipes through existing floors and walls is much easier than dealing with large DWV pipes.

plumbing

PLUMBING TOOLS

Most of the projects in this chapter will require basic plumbing tools, pictured opposite. Tools used to cut and join copper, ABS, and CPVC plastic pipe are listed, but specialized tools that are used for cast-iron waste lines and galvanized steel pipes are not. Pictured below are more specialized tools that may come in handy for certain projects.

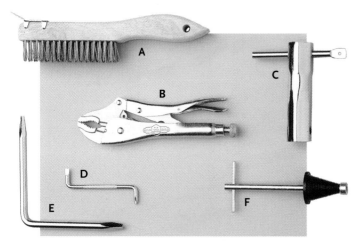

ABOVE Helpful plumbing tools include: (A) wire brush, (B) locking pliers, (C) deep faucet stem wrench, (D) off-set screwdriver, (E) valve-seat wrench, (F) valve-seat reamer.

The Basic Kit

Every household should have these basic tools on hand: a toilet plunger for freeing clogs in toilets and sinks; a closet auger for clearing out more serious blocks in drains, waste pipes, and soil pipes; and a variety of wrenches for making simple repairs to fittings. More complex repair work and installation requires different, specialized tools—not just specific wrenches but valve-seat reamers, pipe cutters, and tube benders.

You should also include a round file and sandpaper in your basic tool kit. In place of a relatively expensive pipe reamer, you can use a file to remove burrs from the inner edge of freshly cut copper pipe. Use medium-grit sandpaper or emery cloth to clean the exterior surface of the end of copper pipes, which is important when soldering pipes together. You'll also need the propane torch, flux, and solder for that job. A Phillips and a flat-blade screwdriver for #8 and #6 screws are also important basic tools because machine screws in faucets and cutoff valves often need tightening or loosening during repairs.

USING A PROPANE TORCH

If you're going to be working with metal pipe—whether copper, steel, or cast iron—you'll need to become familiar with the propane torch. Although it has the potential to be a dangerous tool, a few precautions and the proper safety gear will keep you safe from harm. Use a sparking tool to safely ignite the gas. Turn on a gentle supply of gas, and squeeze the sparker handle. Once you ignite the gas, increase the flow to enlarge the flame. It's wise to wear gloves and eye protection when you handle heated pipes.

Before you try to heat up a pipe with a torch—to thaw a frozen section or to resolder a joint—first drain the line. You can't get copper hot enough to make solder flow when it is filled with water. Also, open a faucet just beyond the repair so that any steam that develops can escape. Be careful when using propane torches in tight spots where the flame may lick past the pipe and heat up building materials nearby. Use extra care working in framing cavities, particularly in older homes where the wood is very dry.

BASIC PLUMBING TOOLS

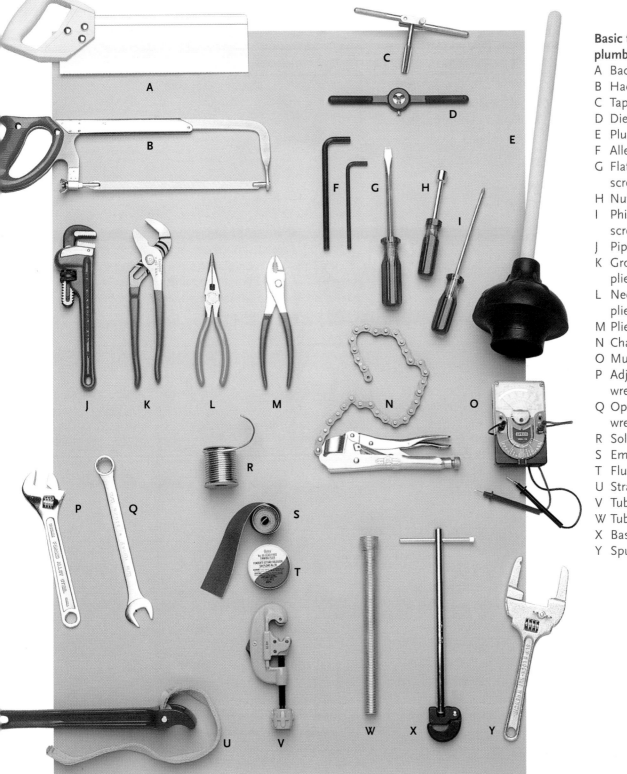

Basic tools for plumbing include:
A Backsaw
B Hacksaw
C Tap
D Diestock
E Plunger
F Allen wrenches
G Flat-blade screwdriver
H Nut driver
I Phillips screwdriver
J Pipe wrench
K Groove-joint pliers
L Needle-nose pliers
M Pliers
N Chain wrench
O Multitester
P Adjustable wrench
Q Open-end wrench
R Solder
S Emery cloth
T Flux
U Strap wrench
V Tubing cutter
W Tubing bender
X Basin wrench
Y Spud wrench

CUTTING AND JOINING PLASTIC PIPE

Plastic pipe is easy to install. Just measure the length you need and cut the pipe in a miter box. Then test fit the pipe and fitting to see if it works where it's supposed to work. Join the pieces with primer/cleaner, followed by solvent cement. Working quickly, push the pieces together; give them a slight turn; hold for 10 seconds—and you're done.

TOOLS & MATERIALS
▌Plastic pipe ▌Backsaw or hacksaw
▌Miter box ▌Work gloves and goggles
▌Pipe primer ▌Pipe ▌Solvent cement
▌Compression clamp fittings
  (when working with cast iron)
▌Utility knife ▌Emery cloth

1 A simple wooden miter box is a great tool for making square cuts on plastic pipe. Just place the pipe in the box, and hold it tightly against the side. Then make the cut with a backsaw, and remove the burrs from the cut end using emery cloth.

3 The first step in joining pipe is to clean the end of the pipe and the inside of the fitting with pipe primer. For PVC pipe, this cleaner is usually colored purple.

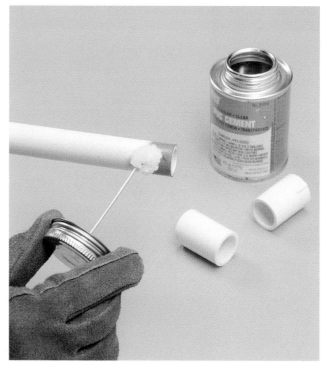

4 Once the primer is dry, apply a liberal coat of solvent cement to the end of the pipe and the inside of the fitting. Open the windows and use an exhaust fan to remove the cement fumes from the room.

2 Once the pipe is cut, install the appropriate fitting and check if the assembly fits where it needs to go. If things look good, join the two.

BASIC PLASTIC DRAINAGE PIPING

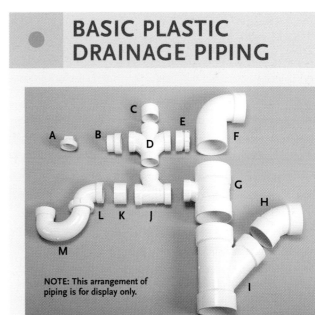

NOTE: This arrangement of piping is for display only.

Plastic drainage piping includes the following: (A) clean-out plug, (B) threaded adapter, (C) coupling, (D) cross, (E) ground-joint adapter, (F) street 90-deg. elbow, (G) 3 x 1½-in. T-fitting, (H) 45-deg. elbow, (I) 3 x 2-in. Y-fitting, (J) sanitary T-fitting, (K) coupling, (L) trap arm, (M) trap.

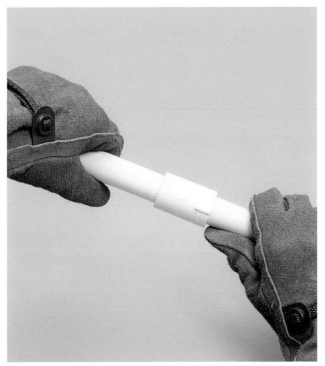

5 Immediately after applying the cement, push the two parts together; turn them about ¼ turn; and hold them for 10 seconds. This fuses the assembly so the pieces can't be taken apart.

WHICH PIPE?

Which type of pipe you can use for projects in this book depends on your local code. However, some typical uses are

- **Copper (rigid and flexible):** Hot- and cold-water supply pipes
- **Galvanized steel:** hot- and cold-water supply pipes; drainpipes
- **Cast iron:** Main supply and DWV pipes
- **PB (polybutylene):** Hot- and cold-water supply pipes
- **ABS (acrylonitrile butadiene styrene):** drain and vent pipes, drain traps
- **CPVC (chlorinated polyvinyl chloride):** Hot- and cold-water supply pipes
- **PVC (polyvinyl chloride):** drain and vent pipes, drain traps

Rigid Copper

Galvanized Steel

Cast Iron

PVC

COPPER FITTINGS

You can join both rigid and flexible copper tubing with soldered joints and fittings, including couplings, which join pipes in a straight line; reducers; 45- and 90-degree elbows to make bends; and reducer fittings, which join pipes of different diameters.

Compression fittings are often found on water-supply tubes and shutoff valves for fixtures. This is because, unlike soldered joints, compression fittings can be taken apart easily. They can also be used in spots where it's impractical or dangerous to solder, such as in an unventilated crawl space. These couplings become watertight when you tighten the threaded nut, drawing a flange against the end of the pipe. Couplings are available with threaded nuts on both ends or with one end threaded and the other straight, for soldering.

Flared fittings are usually only permitted for flexible copper pipe (Type L) used on gas lines, but some local codes may permit them in areas where soldering is not safe, as long as the pipes are not behind finished walls. Two tools are required for flared fittings: the flaring tools and the flaring set. The base part of the flaring tool clamps around the end of one of the pipes being joined, and the top of the flaring set forces the lip of the pipe against the clamp. This creates a bell-shaped flare. A flaring nut placed on one side of the joint threads into a flaring union on the other.

Coupling

Female Adapter

Male Adapter

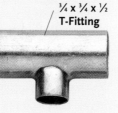
¾ x ½ x ½ T-Fitting

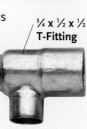
¾ x ¾ x ½ T-Fitting

Compression Ring / Coupling Nut

CUTTING COPPER PIPE

project

Usually copper pipe comes in 20-foot lengths, which means that you'll have to do some cutting no matter what job you are doing. To make these cuts, use a tubing cutter or a hacksaw, and remove the resulting burr from the inside of the pipe. Then clean the outside of the pipe and the inside of the fitting, and get the torch ready for soldering.

TOOLS & MATERIALS
▌ Copper tubing
▌ Tubing cutter or hacksaw & miter box
▌ Multipurpose plumber's tool or wire brush

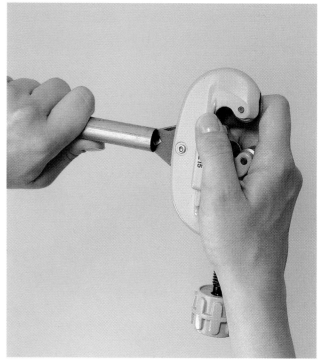

3 Once the cut is made, remove the interior burr with the burr remover that's part of the tubing cutter. You can also remove the burr with a round file.

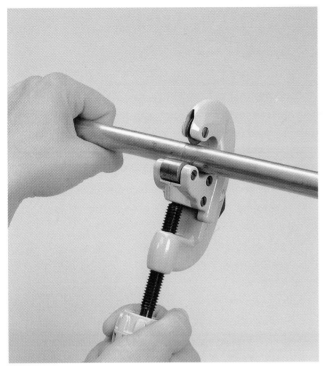

1 A tubing cutter is the preferred tool for cutting copper pipe. Mark the pipe to length; then tighten the cutting wheel against the pipe. Slowly turn the tool around the pipe, tightening the wheel as it cuts.

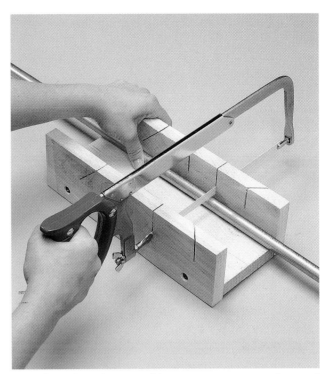

2 If you don't have a tubing cutter, you can make good cuts with a hacksaw. Just be sure to use a miter box for this chore. You can build one by screwing together three scrap boards.

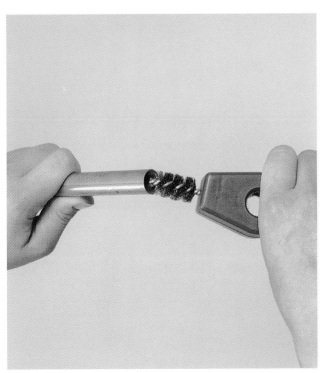

4 A plumber's multipurpose tool can do several pipe prep chores, like deburring pipes (above) and cleaning the inside of copper fittings prior to soldering.

5 Use emery cloth or a multipurpose tool to clean the end of copper pipe before soldering. If dirt or other impurities are left on the pipe, the solder may not bond properly and the joint will leak.

SOLDERING COPPER PIPE

Before soldering copper pipe, make sure to don leather gloves and safety goggles to protect yourself against molten solder burns. Start by applying flux to the parts and pushing them together. Heat the joint, and press the solder onto the pipe. Protect combustible items with a piece of flashing, and wipe the joints clean when they are done.

TOOLS & MATERIALS
- Copper pipe ▮ Emery cloth
- Bristle brush
- Flux (soldering paste)
- Solder ▮ Propane torch ▮ Sparker
- Sheet metal ▮ Work gloves
- Clean rag ▮ Pipe fittings

INSULATING PIPES

For pipes that will carry hot water, it's smart to save a little on your energy costs with pipe insulation. Fit preformed polystyrene insulation tubes around hot-water pipes, and tape them in place. You can also wrap the pipes in strips cut from fiberglass batts. Either system will not only reduce heat loss but also prevent pipe sweating in the summertime. If you have pipes running through an unheated crawl space, insulate (or protect with a heating cable) both hot- and cold-water pipes to keep them from freezing.

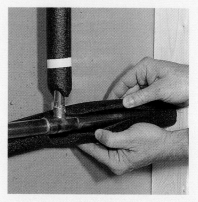

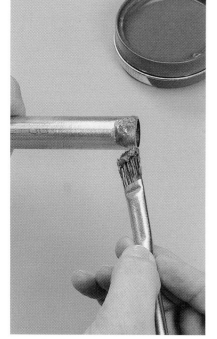

1 The first step in soldering copper pipe is to coat the pipe end and fitting with flux. Use a small brush, and make sure everything is coated liberally.

2 Slide the fitting over the end of the pipe and twist it so that the flux is spread around the entire joint.

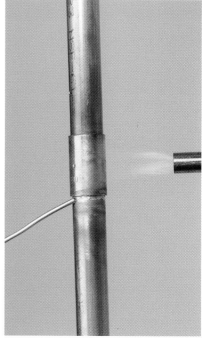

3 Push the other pipe into the coupling, and heat the fitting with a torch. Press the solder against the joint until the joint is filled.

IT'S EASY TO BURN YOURSELF WHEN SOLDERING PIPE. ALWAYS MAKE SURE THAT YOU TURN OFF YOUR TORCH WHEN IT'S NOT IN USE. REMEMBER ALSO THAT SOLDERED JOINTS ARE VERY HOT; ALWAYS LET THEM COOL BEFORE TOUCHING THE PIPES.

SHUTTING OFF THE WATER

Before you begin work on a section of pipe, you'll need to shut off the water supply to that part of your plumbing system. The main shutoff valve for your house's system, shown top right, will be near the spot where the municipal pipe enters your home or, if you have well water, near the storage tank. Other cutoff valves farther along allow you to turn off just part of the water system, such as to one bathroom, while still allowing you to have water in the rest of the house. Most fixtures, such as sinks and toilets, should have their own shutoff valves, shown bottom right, usually located right where the supply lines come through the wall or floor.

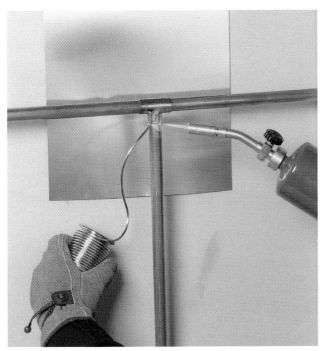

4 When soldering joints close to combustible materials, use a piece of flashing to protect these areas. Usually you can just tape the flashing in place with a piece of duct tape.

5 Once both sides of a joint are filled with solder, remove the torch and wipe the joint clean with a rag. Wear sturdy leather gloves to protect your hands from burns. Test your work by turning the water back on. If the joint leaks, heat the joint to melt the solder and start again.

8 wiring

Before installing that new whirlpool tub or lighting scheme, you will need to bring the bathroom's electrical system up to current standards. Protect outlets with ground-fault circuit interrupters (GFCI), which will reduce the hazards of shock. A ventilating fan expels unwanted moisture that can lead to mold and structural damage. For convenience as well as safety, you may need to add additional electrical circuits for special equipment.

Rewiring can be done without tearing up walls and ceilings, but it's easiest when the framing is exposed. Working with wiring isn't difficult if you take the time and effort to understand what's required—but it is extremely unforgiving. A bad connection means a circuit won't work. But more importantly, a bad connection creates a dangerous situation that can lead to serious injury.

WIRING BASICS

If your house is more than 50 years old, its electrical system is very likely outdated. Chances are that successive owners added bits and pieces over the years in no coherent fashion. Knowing this, you can choose to rewire the whole house at once or update it as you remodel the rooms. If you go room by room, at least be sure that the main electrical service is up-to-date and capable of carrying the additional loads required by many modern fixtures and appliances.

Getting a Power Source

Electricity enters your home through overhead or underground wires, where it passes through a meter before entering the main service panel (also called a fuse box or circuit-breaker panel). The meter measures the amount of electricity you use. At the main service panel, the electricity is divided into branch circuits, each of which is protected by a fuse or circuit breaker. Power travels in a closed loop through the circuit's hot wires to outlets or fixtures and returns to the service panel via neutral wires, unless it is interrupted by an open switch or short circuit. The fuses or breakers protect these circuits from overloading—that is, from drawing more power than the wires can handle.

Your bathroom lights and power outlets may be wired to a single circuit protected by a 15- or 20-amp breaker in the panel. If you rewire or change a few light fixtures or outlets, you won't need to change the power source. If you add new devices, you may overload the circuit, so get the advice of an electrician before proceeding.

Assuming the wiring is sound and you want to leave the wall finishes intact, you can replace a light fixture, switch, or outlet by removing the existing device and installing the new one. If you want to add an outlet or light, you can tap into the box of a fixture or come off of a box containing an outlet. If you tap off an outlet box, replace the box with a larger one to contain the additional wiring.

Grounding

Electricity always seeks to return to a point of zero voltage (the ground) along the easiest path open to it. If you touch an electric fence, electricity will flow from the fence through your body to the ground—the electrical path is then "grounded" through you. A short circuit in wiring is a similar situation. Electrical current exits the closed loop of the circuit—a hot wire is off its terminal and touches the metal box of a light fixture, for example—and returns to the source by some other means. If the system is properly grounded, this short would be a fault to ground and pose no hazard. If it's improperly grounded and you touch the wiring path—and it could be something as innocuous as the metal pull cord on that light fixture—the electricity will ground itself through your body.

To guard against this, your house's electrical system has grounding wires, which give the electricity a permanent alternative path for its return to the source. Each outlet and fixture has its own grounding wires that return electricity to the main panel—the third, grounding plug of most appliances extends this protection to them. The entire system is also grounded to your cold-water pipes or, if you have plastic plumbing, to a grounding rod buried underground next to your foundation—or to both.

Codes and Permits

All electrical procedures and materials are governed by local building or electrical codes. These codes are for your protection. You may need to obtain a permit before beginning some projects. Always consult with a municipal building inspector.

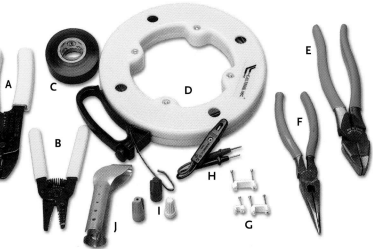

ABOVE Basic tools for wiring include (A) multipurpose tool, (B) wire stripper, (C) electrical tape, (D) fish tape, (E) lineman's pliers, (F) needle-nose pliers, (G) cable staples, (H) circuit tester, (I) wire connectors, and (J) cable ripper.

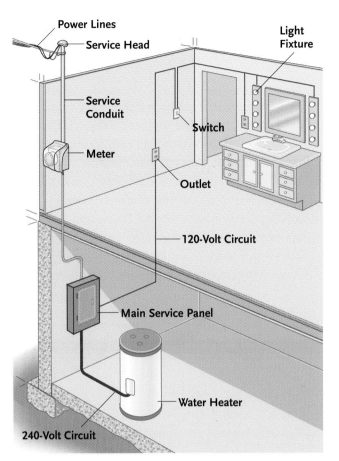

ABOVE Electrical circuits are run from the main panel; they may contain outlets, fixtures, and switches. Large fixtures, like water heaters, require dedicated circuits of higher voltage.

Power Lines
Service Head
Service Conduit
Meter
Light Fixture
Switch
Outlet
120-Volt Circuit
Main Service Panel
Water Heater
240-Volt Circuit

caution

ELECTRICITY CAN BE DANGEROUS, BUT IF YOU USE COMMON SENSE, YOU CAN WORK WITH IT QUITE SAFELY. IT'S MOST IMPORTANT TO REMEMBER ALWAYS, WITHOUT FAIL, TO TURN OFF THE POWER AT THE MAIN SERVICE PANEL BEFORE WORKING ON A CIRCUIT. USE ONE HAND TO DISCONNECT OR REACTIVATE A FUSE OR CIRCUIT BREAKER, AND KEEP THE OTHER HAND IN YOUR POCKET OR BEHIND YOUR BACK. BEFORE STARTING WORK, CHECK THE CIRCUIT WITH A NEON CIRCUIT TESTER TO BE SURE THAT IT IS SHUT OFF. IF YOU ALWAYS FOLLOW THIS RULE, YOU WILL NEVER SUFFER AN ELECTRICAL SHOCK.

● BASIC ELECTRICAL TERMS

▌ **Amperes,** or amps, measure current flow. An amp rating is marked on many appliances. Electrical suppliers have charts showing the amp rating for various American wire gauge (AWG) sizes. The rating for your house's circuits is marked on the circuit breaker or fuse—generally 15 or 20 amps for most room circuits and 30 or 50 amps for heavy-duty circuits, such as those serving a kitchen range, a clothes dryer, or a water heater.

▌ **Volts** measure the force of electrical pressure that keeps the current flowing through the wires. Products are marked with a voltage capacity, usually 120 or 240 volts. You can't hook up a product designed to operate at 120 volts to a 240-volt electrical outlet—it will burn out. The shape of the receptacle will prevent you from inserting the wrong type of plug.

▌ **Watts = volts x amps.** The wattage rating of a circuit is the amount of power the circuit can deliver safely, determined by the current-carrying capacity of the wires. Wattage also indicates the amount of power that a fixture or appliance needs to work properly. Appliances with large motors, such as air conditioners, should not exceed 50 percent of a circuit's capacity because of start-up overcurrent—motors need more current to start than they do to run. Large appliances often need dedicated, or separate, circuits.

WIRING AND CONDUIT

Single wires are insulated to carry electricity or are bare (sometimes insulated green) for grounding. Most household wiring is contained in cable, inside flexible metal (as in AC or BX) or plastic insulation (as in NM). Wires have size numbers that express wire diameter as a whole number. For example, 14-gauge wire is 0.064 inch in diameter; 12-gauge is 0.081 inch. Smaller numbers indicate larger diameters that carry more power. The National Electrical Code requires a minimum of 14-gauge wire for most house wiring.

Wires have color-coded plastic insulation to indicate their function. Hot wires carrying current at full voltage are usually black, red, or white with black marks (made with a marking pen or bands of electrical tape), but can be other colors. Neutral wires carrying zero voltage are white or gray. Grounding wires are bare copper or clad in green plastic insulation. A small piece of wire, called a pigtail, connects two or more wires to the same terminal.

Bare Wire

Insulated Solid Wire

Insulated Stranded Wire

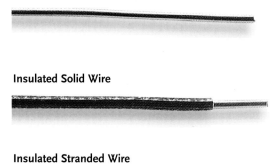

Nonmetallic Cable (NM)

Armored Cable (AC)

When you run cable and hook up outlets, fixtures, and switches, the individual wires inside each cable may need to be spliced together with the wires from other lengths of cable using wire connectors. To join wires, strip ½ inch of insulation, hold the wires parallel, and twist them together clockwise using a screw-on plastic wire connector. The twisted part should be long enough to engage the wire connector without exposing any bare wire when you attach it. Tighten the connector by hand; don't use pliers.

Conduit

Insulated wires are sometimes run through metal or plastic pipe called conduit. Metal conduit comes in three types: rigid (preferred for outdoor applications), intermediate, and EMT (electrical metal tubing). Standard conduit diameters are ½, ¾, 1, and 1¼ inches. There are fittings to join conduit for straight runs and at 45-degree angles, and a special tool, called a hickey, for making more gradual bends in metal tubing. You may be required by codes to use conduit for wires run underground or in open, unfinished walls, such as in a garage or basement. You can cut both metal and plastic conduit with either a pipe cutter or a hacksaw. A pipe cutter is the best tool—

the shoulders of the cutter keep the pipe square in the device and ensure an even cut. When cutting with a hacksaw, wrap the cutline with masking tape first to reduce burring, which can damage wires' insulation when it is pulled through. For more information, see "Plastic Pipe," pages 118 to 119, and "Copper Pipe," pages 120 to 123.

Boxes

Each switch, outlet, and light fixture must be installed into a metal or plastic electrical box that is attached to the framing of the structure. Boxes come in a variety of different sizes and shapes. Ask your building inspector which types of boxes are acceptable for your intended use. Round or octagonal boxes are generally used for ceiling fixtures or junction boxes (boxes used to contain only wiring). Rectangular boxes usually contain switches or outlets. You can choose among boxes that come with various types of fasteners, screws, nails, brackets, and clips suited for new construction or for retrofitting into walls.

ABOVE The main types of electrical boxes include (A) standard plastic receptacle and switch box, (B) metal octagonal box, (C) plastic ceiling fixture box, (D) standard metal receptacle and switch box, (E) MP bracket switch box, and (F) metal "pancake" fixture box.

wiring boxes

The National Electrical Code limits the number of wires you can install in any one box. Wire connections outside a box are not permitted at all. A single switch or duplex (two-plug) outlet and all the necessary wiring will fit into a 2½-inch-wide plastic or metal box. More than one device in a box—or more wiring than needed just to serve the device—calls for a wider or deeper box. Use the table at right to determine the required box size.

maximum number of wires permitted per box

Type of Box (Size in Inches)	Wire Gauge		
	14	12	10
Round or Octagonal			
4 x 1½	7	6	6
4 x 2⅛	10	9	8
Square			
4 x 1½	10	9	8
4 x 2⅛	15	13	12
Rectangular Boxes			
3 x 2 x 2¼	5	4	4
3 x 2 x 2½	6	5	5
3 x 2 x 2¾	7	6	5
3 x 2 x 3½	9	8	7

WIRING GUTTED ROOMS

Gutting floors, walls, or ceilings down to the framing gives you the opportunity to replace outdated wiring and locate electrical fixtures just where you want them. The easiest kind of wiring to install directly onto exposed framing is plastic-sheathed, nonmetallic cable, called NM cable or sometimes by the brand name Romex. NM cable contains a black-sheathed hot wire, a white neutral wire, and a bare grounding wire.

Always check with the electrical inspector to see which type and gauge of cable is acceptable for your project and by your local code. As a rule of thumb, you will probably get by with 12-gauge cable for bathroom lights and outlets. Special equipment such as whirlpools, heaters, and appliances will require 12-gauge wire or larger. (Use the product literature as a guide.) Appliances such as these usually require their own dedicated circuits.

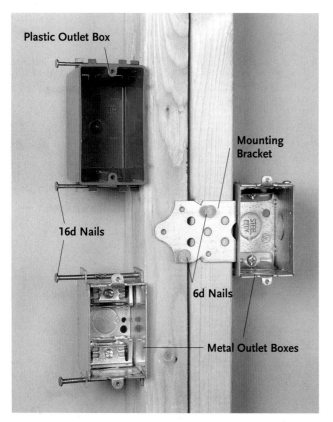

Plastic Outlet Box

Mounting Bracket

16d Nails

6d Nails

Metal Outlet Boxes

ABOVE Boxes for switches and outlets are made of plastic or galvanized steel. Many boxes are fastened to the studs with two roofing nails through slots in the top and bottom (left). Some are nailed through a tab to the face of the stud (right).

RUNNING CABLE IN OPEN WALLS

project

Before reworking any branch circuit, shut off the power to the circuit at the main service panel. Then determine where you want the boxes, and nail them in place.

Next, drill cable holes through the framing using a 3/4-inch-diameter drill bit. Keep these holes at least 1 1/4 inches back from the front edge of the studs. As you thread cables into the holes, remember to attach them with staples for single cables and plastic cable stackers for multiple cables.

Attach each box so that its front edge is flush with the surrounding finished wall surface. And once the cables are inside the box, staple the cables to the framing members within 8 inches of the box. In places where you notched the studs or joists, cover the cable with protective steel plates.

TOOLS & MATERIALS
- Power drill-driver with 3/4-inch bit
- Cable
- Cable staples or cable stackers
- Junction boxes
- Switch boxes
- Outlet boxes
- Metal stud plates or wire shields
- Saw (if cutting notches)
- 1 1/2-inch roofing nails
- Insulated hammer
- Cable clamps

smart tip

WHEN YOU ARE INSTALLING NEW CABLE, THERE ARE USUALLY A LOT OF HOLES TO DRILL. RECEPTACLES ARE CENTERED 12 IN. ABOVE THE FLOOR OR 10 IN. ABOVE COUNTERTOPS. SWITCHES ARE INSTALLED 48 IN. ABOVE THE FLOOR. MAKE A STICK WITH THESE HEIGHTS MARKED ON IT TO QUICKLY LAY OUT THE BOX LOCATIONS.

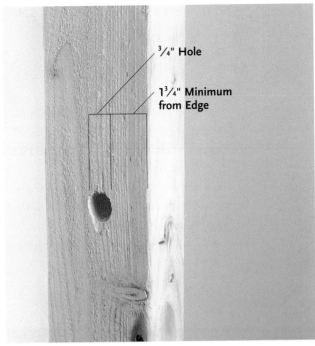

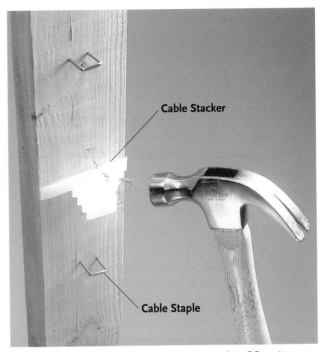

1 Cable holes should be drilled in the middle of the framing members. In the case of a 2x4 (above), this means 1¼ in. in from the edge of the board. Standard cable holes are ¾-in. diameter.

¾" Hole

1¾" Minimum from Edge

2 Cables should be attached to the side of framing members to keep them out of harm's way. Hold a single cable with a cable staple. But if you have to attach multiple cables to the side of one stud, use plastic cable stackers.

Cable Stacker

Cable Staple

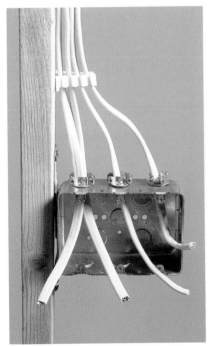

3 Install all boxes so the front edge of the box is in line with the finished surface of the wall. Usually this means the box protrudes ½ in. beyond the face of the stud.

4 Once the cables are inside the box, staple the cables every 48 in. and within 8 in. of the box.

5 In places where the cable is installed in notches, instead of holes, shield the cable from punctures from nails or screws with protective steel plates.

WIRING FINISHED ROOMS

Snaking new wiring through finished floors, walls, and ceilings can be difficult, but it's far from impossible. The trick is to remove small sections of drywall (or plaster) in key areas that give you the access you need.

You start by cutting a box hole in the drywall where you want you new outlet to be. Then you cut access holes as shown in the drawings on this page and the facing page. Sometimes, power will be available from another receptacle in the room. At other times, you'll have to fish it up from the basement or down from the attic.

Drill any appropriate holes through the framing members and then start pulling cable. Use a fish tape for this job, and tape the end of the tape to the end of your cable. This is a job that almost always calls for two people: one to pull the cable and the other to feed the cable.

In some ways, the most difficult part of the job is to patch the access holes you've made. Fill these with drywall, and finish them with one coat of joint compound and tape, followed by two coats of joint compound. Sand all the joints smooth; then prime and paint.

RUNNING CABLE BETWEEN FLOORS

project

Snaking new wire between floors can be a difficult job. But careful work and using a fish tape can make the job much easier. Start by cutting a box opening in the wall and marking its location by driving a nail into the floor. Then go into the basement and drill a hole up through the subfloor. Push a fish tape into the basement, and hook the cable to the tape. Pull both up through the box opening.

TOOLS & MATERIALS
- Power drill-driver with ¾-inch bit
- Fish tape
- Basic electrical tools
- Keyhole saw
- Electrical boxes
- Electrical tape ▌ Electrical cable

● RUNNING CABLE VERTICALLY

To pull the cable from somewhere inside the wall up to the ceiling, first remove part of the corner at the wall-ceiling joint above the wall hole. Cut a notch in the top plates to make a space for the cable run. Thread fish tape from the ceiling opening to the wall/ceiling joint opening and then down the wall. Attach the cable to the tape, and pull it back up through the structure and out the ceiling opening. Nail a metal protective plate over the cable in the corner notch before patching the opening. The procedure is similar if you are running cable to a second-floor receptacle. Use the notch to get into the second-floor wall; then use the tape to snag the cable through the receptacle hole upstairs. Leave at least 8 inches of cable protruding out of the box to allow for your connections.

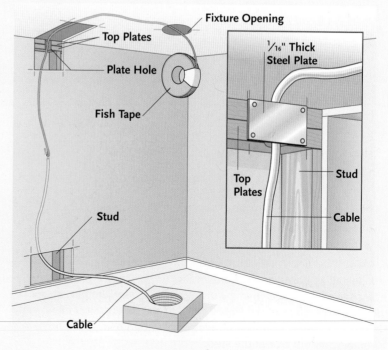

Fixture Opening
Top Plates
Plate Hole
Fish Tape
Stud
Cable

1/16" Thick Steel Plate
Top Plates
Stud
Cable

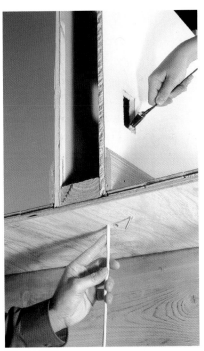

1 Cut a box opening in the wall; then drive a nail through the floor to mark the box location. From the basement, drill a hole up through the floor.

2 Feed a fish tape through the box hole into the basement. Hook the end of the cable onto the end of the fish tape; secure using electrical tape.

3 Slowly pull the cable up through the box hole. Have a helper in the basement guide the cable so it does not get caught on anything.

RUNNING CABLE HORIZONTALLY

If you want to run cable to another point on the wall—say you're adding a few outlets to an existing circuit—try to make the horizontal run in the open basement ceiling. If you can't run cable horizontally below the bathroom floor (such as when you're wiring a second-story bathroom), you can run it through the bathroom's walls.

First, cut out temporary access holes into the drywall along the run, one for each stud. Using a right-angle drill, cut a hole into each stud at the level of the box. If you don't have a right-angle drill, cut notches with a saw. For short runs, just pull the cable from one hole to the next by hand. For longer runs, use fish tape.

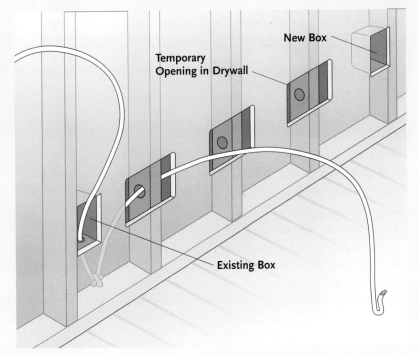

New Box

Temporary Opening in Drywall

Existing Box

ADDING A NEW CIRCUIT

Bath remodeling plans almost always call for adding new electrical circuits to meet the increased demands. To start this job, turn off the main panel switch, and remove the cover. Check for the best location for the new circuit, and install the circuit cable. Strip the sheathing and insulation, and install the cable wires and the circuit breaker. Finish up by installing the panel cover and turning on the power.

TOOLS & MATERIALS

- Basic electrical tools ▪ Flashlight
- Cable (the type required by code)
- Circuit breakers of the required amperage and of the same make as your panel
- Cable clamps

1 To add a new electrical circuit to your service panel, start by opening the door and turning off the main circuit breaker. Then take off the panel cover by removing the four screws located near the corners of the box.

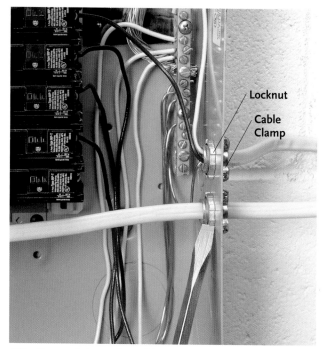

Locknut

Cable Clamp

5 Finger-tighten the cable connector against the side of the panel. Then drive the locknut in a clockwise direction using a flat-bladed screwdriver and a hammer. The locknut will dig into the panel and hold the connector securely in place.

Hot Bus

Neutral Bus

Grounding Bus

6 Strip the sheathing from the end of the cable; then remove about $1/2$ in. of insulation from the individual wires. Install the white wire in the neutral buss bar along with the other white wires. Install the ground wire in the grounding bus bar.

2 Pull back any insulation to find the reference wire. Then establish the fan location. It should be installed against a framing member to provide adequate support. Drill small holes through the ceiling at the corners of the fan.

3 Press the fan housing against the ceiling so its corners fall within the four holes you drilled from above. Trace around the housing to mark the ceiling, and cut the drywall using a keyhole or saber saw (inset).

5 Extend the vent duct up to the point where it goes through the roof. Then attach an aluminum vent collar to the end of the duct using duct tape.

6 Cut a vent hole through the roof using a saber saw. If you don't have one, use a reciprocating saw or a keyhole saw.

7 Once the hole is cut, pull up the vent duct and attach it to the vent hood. Seal the adjacent shingles with roof cement.

WIRING A VENTILATING FAN

There are a couple of code-approved ways to provide power to a fan housing. Usually the easiest approach is to bring a power cable to the fan and then run a switch leg cable down to the wall switch. In this configuration the wire connections are made as follows: the white wires from the fan and the power source are joined; the black wire from the power source and the switch cable are joined; and the black wire from the power source is joined to the white wire (wrapped with black tape) on the switch cable. All these connections are made with wire connectors.

At the switch box, there is just a single cable. Code the white wire with black tape; then connect the black wire to one switch terminal and the white-with-black tape wire to the other.

Another approach is to run power to the switch box and then run a switch leg up to the fan. In this option, the white wires from the fan and the power cable are joined, and the black wires from the fan and the power source are joined.

Once all the wiring connections are done, install the fan motor in the housing and plug it in to the power receptacle that is provided. Finish up by attaching the grille to the bottom of the fan housing.

TOOLS & MATERIALS
▌ Cable ripper
▌ Multipurpose tool
▌ Insulated screwdriver
▌ 14/2 NM cable with ground
▌ Switch
▌ Pigtails
▌ Switch box
▌ Wire connectors

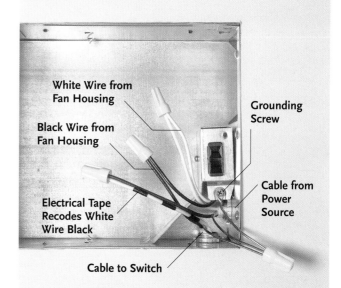

White Wire from Fan Housing

Black Wire from Fan Housing

Grounding Screw

Electrical Tape Recodes White Wire Black

Cable from Power Source

Cable to Switch

1 Every electrical outlet has to be supplied with power either directly from a branch circuit or from a controlling switch. In the photo above, the power comes directly from a circuit and then is directed down to a controlling switch.

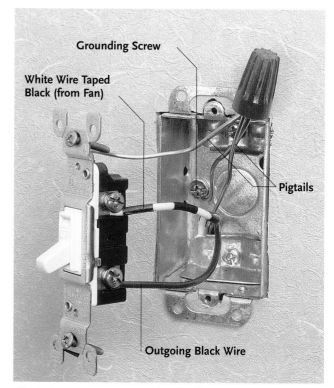

Grounding Screw

White Wire Taped Black (from Fan)

Pigtails

Outgoing Black Wire

2 When power goes to the fan first and only a single cable goes to the switch below, the wiring connections are simple. The black wire goes to one terminal. The white wire (which should be wrapped in black tape) goes to the other terminal.

caution

BECAUSE VENTING AN EX-HAUST FAN CAN BE DIFFI-CULT, IT'S TEMPTING TO OMIT THE DUCT ALTOGETHER AND JUST VENT THE EXHAUST FAN INTO THE ATTIC SPACE. NO BUILDING CODES PERMIT THIS AND THEIR MOTIVATION ISN'T BASED ON AN EXCESS OF CAUTION. BY DUMPING LARGE AMOUNTS OF WATER VAPOR INTO THE ATTIC, YOU VIRTUALLY ENSURE THAT WATER WILL CONDENSE OUT OF THE VAPOR AND COAT THE FRAMING MEMBERS. THIS GREATLY INCREASES THE LIKELIHOOD OF SERIOUS DAMAGE CAUSE BY ROT.

duct locations

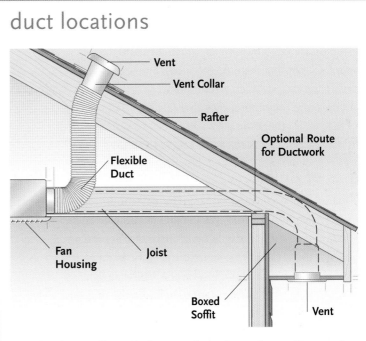

Running the vent from a bathroom exhaust fan to the outside can take some creativity. The most direct route is usually straight up through the roof. But the one that is most protected from the weather is running the duct between ceiling joists and out through the soffit.

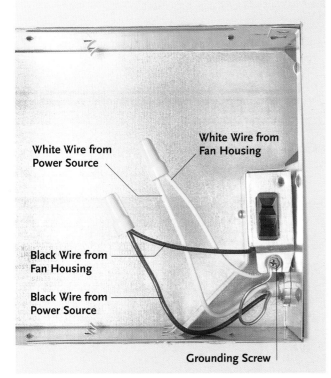

3 When the power goes to the switch first and only a single cable goes to the fan, connect the fan by joining like-colored wires with wire connectors.

4 After installing the fan housing, put the fan into the housing and plug its pigtail extension cord into the receptacle provided in the housing. Cover the whole assembly with the fan grille.

LIGHTBULBS

Lightbulbs are rated by lumens, which measure the amount of light that the bulb produces, and watts, which measure the rate at which electrical energy is used. Watts don't measure brightness; though a 100-watt incandescent bulb is brighter than a 40-watt one, a 13-watt fluorescent may be brighter than the 40-watt incandescent.

Types of Bulbs

Compared with an energy-guzzling 100-watt incandescent, compact fluorescents use 75 percent less electricity and last longer. But the harsh, bluish light of a fluorescent is also not necessarily what you want over the bathroom mirror. If you are stuck with fluorescent fixtures, a lighting expert can help by choosing warmer bulbs or cooler tubes to suit the situation. Halogen bulbs have a kind of clear-white quality, and are about 25 percent brighter than standard incandescent bulbs of the same wattage, but they require special fixtures. They are also extremely hot and should be treated with caution. High-intensity-discharge (HID) bulbs, such as halide and high-pressure sodium, are also bright and efficacious but require special fixtures.

INSTALLING A CEILING FIXTURE

project

The hardest part of this job is getting the box and cable installed. (For help on this job see "Running Cable Vertically," on page 132.) Once both are in place, strip the sheathing and wire insulation from the cable and screw a hanging strap to the box. Join the wires from fixture and the box; then tighten the fixture in place. Install the proper lightbulb (or bulbs), and screw on the fixture globe.

TOOLS & MATERIALS
▌Insulated screwdriver ▌Electrical box
▌Knockout punch ▌Cable ripper
▌Needle-nose pliers ▌Wire stripper
▌Cable clamps ▌Wire connectors
▌Light fixture ▌Threaded nipple
▌Mounting strap

● LIGHTING CAPACITY

Before deciding on a fixture, be sure to have enough lighting capacity. Determine how much you need by matching the power consumption in watts to the floor area to be lighted: for fluorescent lighting, 1.2 to 1.6 watts per square foot; for incandescent lighting, 3.5 to 4 watts per square foot.

Unfortunately, there is no simple rule of thumb for task lighting. Because task lighting must focus on a specific target to be effective, the location of the lamp is as important as the amount of light it yields.

To light a mirror with incandescent lamps, figure on at least three bulbs of 15- to 25-watt capacity at each side or a series of strip lights (pictured at right) around the sides and top of the mirror. Strip-lighting fixtures are generally available in 18- 24-, 36-, and 48-inch lengths.

An enclosed tub or shower also requires lighting. Choose a recessed vapor-proof fixture with a 60- or 75-watt bulb. For safety, position the switch so that it is out of reach from inside the compartment.

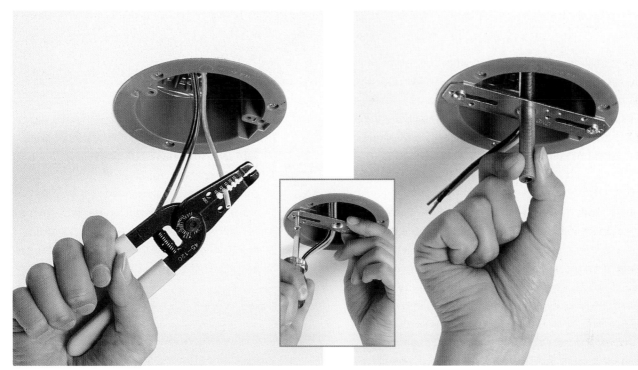

1 Begin by cutting a box hole in the ceiling and installing a retrofit ceiling box and cable in this hole. Remove the cable sheathing, and strip the ends of the wires with wire strippers.

2 Screw a metal hanging strap to the bottom of the ceiling box (inset). Then turn a threaded nipple into the strap collar. This nipple will hold the light fixture in place.

3 Join the fixture wires to the box wires by combining like-colored wires with wire connectors. Add a short pigtail wire to the ground wires, and tighten it under the grounding screw.

4 Slide the fixture over the box, and turn the retaining nut onto the threaded nipple. Tighten the nut until the fixture is against the ceiling. Add the recommended bulbs, and install the globe that came with the fixture.

143

RECESSED LIGHTS

Recessed lighting fixtures for damp areas such as bathrooms must be clearly marked "Suitable for Wet Locations" or at least "Suitable for Damp Locations." These fixtures must be installed so that water cannot enter the wiring compartments. Recessed lights that are designed for wet locations can even be used inside a shower or over a tub or whirlpool. Make sure you use shatter-resistant white acrylic lenses that eliminate the danger of glass breakage are best. Always put the switch out of reach of those in the tub or shower to reduce the risk of electrocution.

Some recessed systems must be installed before the ceiling is closed. If that is not possible, be sure to buy a system that you can install from below in a finished ceiling. Also check to make sure that the housing you are considering is compatible with the clearances you have for both depth and proximity to insulation. Low-profile downlights and rectangular fluorescent fixtures called "troffers" can be used in spaces as shallow as 4 inches.

Unless the fixture is rated safe for insulation contact, insulation batts should be cut back so that they are at least 3 inches away from the fixture's housing. If the ceiling has loose-fill insulation, you'll need to install baffles to keep the insulation away from the fixture.

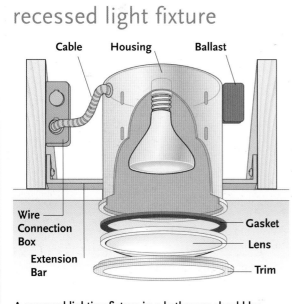

recessed light fixture

Cable Housing Ballast

Wire Connection Box
Extension Bar
Gasket
Lens
Trim

A recessed lighting fixture in a bathroom should be clearly marked as suitable for wet or damp locations. It must have a watertight cover with a gasket.

INSTALLING A RECESSED LIGHT FIXTURE

project

Recessed lights come in different configurations. But generally, the unit features a light housing mounted on sliding brackets with a separate electrical box for making the wiring connections. Start the job by installing the unit between ceiling joists. Then open up the electrical box; install the switch cable; and replace the box cover. Install a bulb, lens, gasket, and trim ring.

TOOLS & MATERIALS
- Insulated screwdrivers
- Nails or screws
- Hammer (if necessary)
- Power drill-driver Cable ripper
- Needle-nose pliers Cable clamps
- Multipurpose tool Wire connectors
- Recessed lamp housing

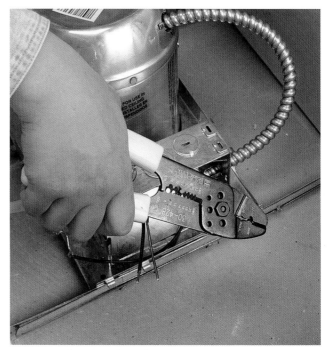

3 Strip the sheathing from the switch cable, and then remove approximately $1/2$ in. of insulation from the end of each wire.

1 Begin by establishing the location of the light unit, and cut a hole in the ceiling drywall. Then take the fixture into the attic; pull back the insulation; and adjust the extension bars until the fixture is centered over the hole. Screw the brackets to the sides of the joists.

2 Take off the side cover to the box, and using a flat-bladed screwdriver, remove one of the box knock-outs. Install a cable connector in this hole; then slide the switch cable through the connector, and tighten it in place.

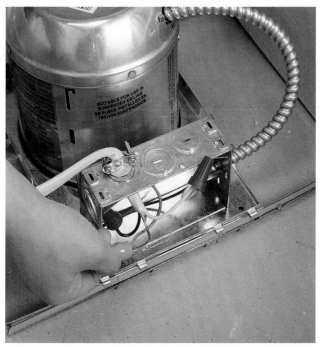

4 Join the like-colored wires from the switch cable and the fixture cable with wire connectors. Hand-tighten each connector. Make sure to install the proper size connector. In this case, the connector must be rated for at least two 14-gauge wires.

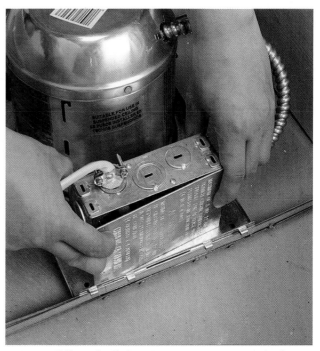

5 Carefully tuck all the wire connections into the box, and replace the side cover. Then go back to the bathroom, and install the gasket, lens, and trim ring.

INSTALLING VANITY LIGHTING

A common bathroom wiring scheme for over a vanity calls for a light fixture above the sink, a receptacle on both sides, and a switch closer to the door to provide easy access when entering the room. Rough in the wiring; then install and finish the drywall. Wire the first receptacle, then the light fixture, followed by the second receptacle, and then the switch that operates the light.

TOOLS & MATERIALS
- 20-amp GFCI receptacle
- 15-amp standard receptacle
- Single-pole switch ▌ Lighting fixture(s)
- 12/2ɢ NM cable ▌ 12/3ɢ NM cable
- Insulated screwdrivers ▌ Long-nose pliers
- Light-fixture box ▌ Switch box
- Outlet boxes

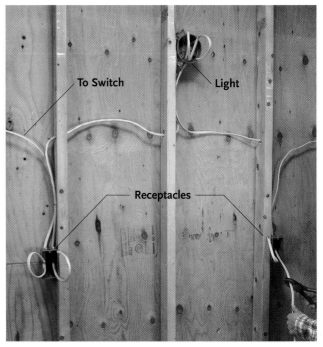

1 Install a two-wire power cable (yellow-colored above) to the receptacle on the right and then to the light fixture. Use three-wire cable to connect the light fixture to the receptacle on the left.

4 Attach the light fixture mounting bracket to the wall. Then connect the white fixture wires with the white cable wire. Join the bare grounding wires together, and attach them to the grounding screws. Join the black fixture wires to the red cable wire.

5 Attach the black and white wires from the three-wire cable to the second receptacle. Join the red wire from the three-wire cable to the white wire from the switch cable, and code it with black tape. Screw the black switch wire to the second brass receptacle screw.

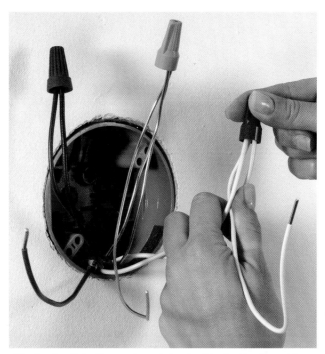

2 Connect the incoming power cable wires to the LINE side of the GFCI receptacle. Connect the wires that run from the receptacle to the fixture to the LOAD side of the receptacle.

3 In the light fixture box, join the black wire from the LOAD side of the GFCI receptacle to the black wire that runs to the other outlet with a wire connector. Join the grounding wires and add a white pigtail wire to the other two white wires.

6 Finish up the wiring for this installation by attaching the white and black wires to the switch. Make sure to code the white wire with black tape to indicate that it's now a hot wire.

WIRING FOR A DUAL-USE BOX

In this configuration a GFCI-protected outlet is always hot and shares a box with a switch that controls the light on the vanity. The black wire from the power source is attached to the brass screw of the outlet. A jumper wire connects the outlet and the switch.

9 tubs and showers

If you're planning a new full-size bathroom, the good news is that there is a vast array of bathtub and shower options on today's market. And what you select will affect your design and your budget. Updated technology is one factor that will boost the cost, both in terms of the price of the fixture and its installation. But if your aim is to create an at-home spa, a whirlpool tub or a steam-equipped shower is simply an investment in your dream. On the other hand, a standard tub or shower, without jets, may be all you desire. In either case, how can you be sure that the model you choose will meet your needs and hold up to daily use? Remember, cost does not necessarily reflect quality. In this chapter, you'll get a glimpse of what's out there and what you need to know about your options.

BATHTUB OPTIONS

Soakers; whirlpools; tubs for two; streamlined or sculpted models; classic claw-foot tubs; contour shaped, oval, square, rounded tubs; freestanding models; tubs set into platforms; tubs with neck rests, arm rests, TVs, and a host of therapeutic features—there are so many ways to tailor your bathing experience to your personal needs.

Before choosing a tub style, ask yourself what you want in a tub. Is it a long lingering hot soak, a therapeutic experience complete with massage, or just a frills-free bath? Whirlpool tubs are increasingly becoming standard in new homes, which is something to consider if you plan to sell your house someday. (See "Customized Bathing," on page 153 for more information on whirlpool features.)

Generally, modern bathtubs are made of one of three materials.

ABOVE A soaking tub does not require much floor space, but it lets you submerge your body to relax tight muscles.

Fiberglass. A lightweight and inexpensive material, fiberglass scratches easily and will show signs of wear after about a dozen years. Some fiberglass tubs come with an acrylic finish, which holds up longer against wear.

Solid Acrylic. A product in the mid-price range, acrylic is more durable than fiberglass and less prone to scratching. Whirlpool tubs are usually made of acrylic because the material can be shaped easily and it is lightweight, an important feature for large tubs that can put damaging stress on structural elements under the floor.

Cast Iron. A heavy, long-lasting material, porcelain-enamel-coated cast iron will last as long as the house stands. But because of its weight, the material is not recommended for a large soaking tub.

OPPOSITE TOP A deck around a tub allows you to place faucet handles where they are easiest to reach.

TOP LEFT Although reminiscent of an earlier time, a claw-foot tub, above, continues to grow in popularity.

LEFT Placing the tub on an angle allows the bather to enjoy outside views while bathing.

TUB SIZES

The most common size for a tub that backs up to a wall is 32 x 60 inches. Widths from 24 to 42 inches are generally available, and you can purchase a tub that's up to 72 inches long. Corner models come in at around 48 inches on the wall sides. A whirlpool tub can be as long as 84 inches. To properly size your tub, consider the amount of floor space that's available, your height, and the level of luxury you desire. When you visit a showroom, get into the tubs and try them out for size. Bigger may be better if you're tall, but you may feel uncomfortable in an oversized model if you're petite. If you're shopping for a whirlpool tub, make sure the jets are located where they will do you the most good. Check the head and arm rests for your comfort as well. If two people will use the tub, get in together to make sure that the model suits both of you. The inside width should be at least 42 inches.

Freestanding tubs require adequate clearance on all sides to look their best. Also, check the tub's dimensions against your doorways, hallways, and stairways to be sure that you can get it into the bathroom.

ABOVE A freestanding tub makes a dramatic design statement, but check clearances carefully before installing one.

BELOW A separate tub and shower provide design flexibility. Notice how the tub deck serves as a shower seat.

CUSTOMIZED BATHING

You can design your bathing experience to be many different things, thanks to today's bells and whistles, such as adjustable jets that let you choose between a deep-muscle therapy or something less invigorating. For an even gentler message, there is the air bath, which operates using warm-air jets. Some tubs come with both water and air that can be used separately or in combination and set to different strength levels to customize your bath massage even more.

An in-line heater that maintains the desired water temperature is one of today's most-popular features among a host of sybaritic amenities. Water bubblers can simulate the sound and sensation of river rapids, a babbling brook, or a cascading waterfall.

And would you believe that you can watch your favorite movie in surround sound while you soak? You can with a home theater that is built into the whirlpool tub. Lean back into a comfortable padded neck pillow (another amenity along with padded arm rests) and enjoy. For added drama, optional underwater lights enhance the mood.

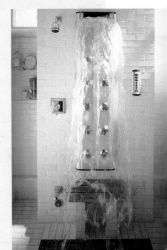

ABOVE The ultimate tub? This one features whirlpool jets, surround sound, and a plasma television.

RIGHT A shower tower can immerse you in a waterfall or provide a full-body massage.

BELOW The right tub in the right setting can transport you away from everyday cares.

INSTALLING A NEW TUB

project

Before moving the tub into the room, check your measurements to make sure it will fit. When satisfied, slide the tub in place, and check for level. Shim the tub if necessary; then make the drain connections. Install new tile or other wall covering, and add the faucet, or faucets, hardware. Install the tub spout, and seal around the entire tub with silicone caulk.

TOOLS & MATERIALS
▮ New bathtub unit & drain-waste-overflow kit
▮ 4-foot spirit level ▮ Shims
▮ Silicone caulk & caulking gun
▮ Locking pliers ▮ Standard pliers
▮ Screwdriver ▮ Hacksaw
▮ Adjustable wrench ▮ Measuring tape
▮ Galvanized deck screws

1 Make any necessary floor repairs; then slide the tub into place. Check the length and width for level, and shim as needed. Screw the tub flange to the wall framing.

TUB/SHOWER ANATOMY

Here is the plumbing system for a typical tub-and-shower combination. You'll need to have all of the plumbing roughed in before the tub is installed. The drain and overflow assembly are attached to the tub before it's set into position.

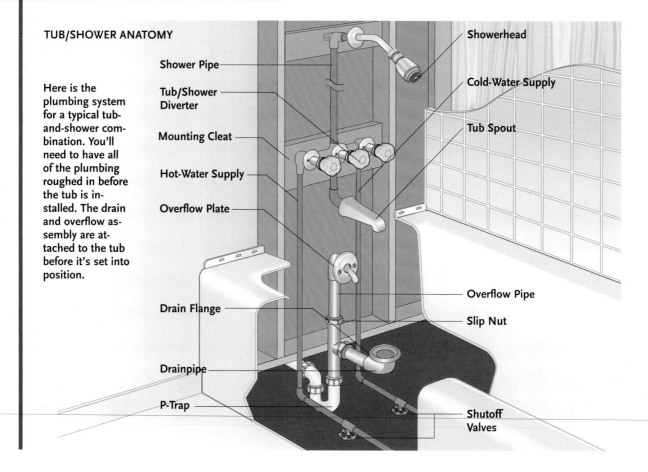

Shower Pipe
Tub/Shower Diverter
Mounting Cleat
Hot-Water Supply
Overflow Plate
Drain Flange
Drainpipe
P-Trap

Showerhead
Cold-Water Supply
Tub Spout
Overflow Pipe
Slip Nut
Shutoff Valves

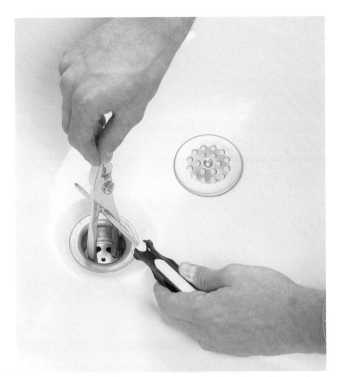

2 Center the drainpipe opening under the tub opening. Then spread plumber's putty around the bottom edge of the drain fitting, and thread it into the drainpipe, using pliers and a screwdriver.

3 Slide the tripwaste mechanism into the overflow tube, and adjust the linkage as necessary by turning the threaded rod. Then push the assembly into the tube, and attach the overflow plate.

4 Next, install standard stems, escutcheons, and handles for dual faucets and a diverter. In the case of a single-lever faucet (above), installation methods vary, so carefully follow the manufacturer's instructions.

5 Before screwing on the tub spout, measure the depth from the edge of the spout to the threaded fitting. Make sure the copper nipple is the correct length; then cover the adapter threads with pipe joint compound and attach the spout.

INSTALLING A SHOWER DOOR

project

If you're tired of living with the shortcomings of a shower curtain, consider installing a shower door. All that's required is to temporarily fit a base channel on the outside edge of the tub and two side channels on the bathroom walls. When satisfied with the fit, attach the base channel using silicone caulk and the side channels with caulk and screws. Add the top channel and the doors and you are done.

TOOLS & MATERIALS
- Door enclosure kit
- Power drill with $\frac{3}{16}$-inch bit (carbide-tipped, if wall is tiled)
- Screwdriver ▍ Hacksaw & miter box
- Spirit level ▍ Framing square
- Silicone caulk & caulking gun
- Masking tape

1 Begin by establishing the location of the bottom door track in the center of the outside tub wall. Tape the track in place, and carefully mark both sides of the track using a pencil.

3 Using a power drill with a carbide-tipped drill bit, bore the screw holes for the side tracks in the bathroom walls. Drill slowly to get a clean hole.

4 Turn over the base channel, and apply a bead of silicone caulk along both of its edges. Then carefully turn the track over, and press it down on the top of the tub wall between your pencil lines.

2 Hold one of the side channels against the wall so that it overlaps the base channel. Check it for plumb using a 4-foot level. Then mark the screw holes in the channels using a sharp pencil. Do the same thing with the other side channel.

5 Apply silicone caulk to the back of both side channels, and press them in place so that the channel holes align with the wall holes. Attach the channel using the screws that came in the door kit.

6 Attach the top channel to the two side channels; then test fit the doors. If any adjustment is required, loosen the channel screws and retighten them so that the channels are in the correct position.

INSTALLING A WHIRLPOOL TUB

Many whirlpool tubs are available with one or two finished sides. But most have four unfinished sides and are designed to fit in a site-built base. The base is not difficult to build and can look great if it's covered with tile as part of a larger tile job that includes the bathroom walls and floor. The most important thing to keep in mind is that these tubs, when filled with water, can be very heavy and you may need to strengthen your floor joists to accommodate the extra weight. Get advice from a structural engineer.

Begin by beefing up the floor (if necessary) and adding a support platform for the tub. Position the tub in its finished location, and shim any low spots. Install cement backer board to the walls above the tub, and lay out the platform walls on the floor. Build the walls, and check the fit; then nail them in place, and cover them with backer board. Build a pump-access hole, and install ceramic tile.

TOOLS & MATERIALS
- Whirlpool tub
- Pry bar
- ¾-inch subfloor-grade plywood
- Bolts & washers
- Waste & drain pipes
- 8d (2½-inch) nails or 3-inch drywall screws
- Power cable
- Wire connectors
- 2x4s or 2x6s for framing
- Junction box
- Receptacle box
- GFCI receptacle
- Sheet-metal shims
- Cement-based backer board
- 10d (3-inch) galvanized nails or 2-inch cement-board screws
- ½ or ¾-inch AC plywood (for access panel)

1 Usually installing a whirlpool tub means you have to tear up the old floor and beef up the floor joists. Once the framing is structurally sound, install the plumbing pipes, a new subfloor, and a plywood platform for the tub.

5 Build the knee walls that surround the tub, and push them into place. Check that the height of these walls is correct by sliding a piece of backer board and tile between the wall plate and the tub rim.

2 Slide the whirlpool onto the platform in its proper place. Then check it for level from side-to-side and end-to-end. If the tub is out of plumb, pry up the low spots and insert metal shims underneath.

3 If you plan to install tile, cover the walls around the tub with cement backer board. Drive screws into the studs every 6 in. in the middle of the panel and about every 4 in. around the perimeter of each piece.

4 Mark the perimeter of the tub on the subfloor using a 2-ft. level and a felt tip marker. Keep the level plumb, and check-and-mark every few inches.

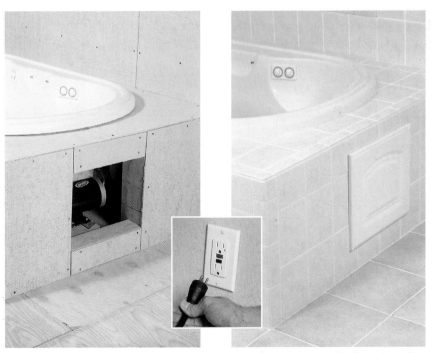

6 Install backer board on the surrounding platform frame using cement-board screws. When the platform is covered, drill the faucet holes in the top.

7 Build an access hole for servicing the whirlpool pump. Usually this is placed at the open end of the installation. Plug the pump into a GFCI receptacle, inset.

8 If you want to tile the tub enclosure, do it as part of a larger tile job that includes the bathroom walls and floor. This approach yields the most professional-looking results.

SHOWER OPTIONS

Showering used to be something you did when you were in a rush—hop in, soap up, rinse off. Today, it can still be the quick jump-start you need in the morning or much more. With jets and steam units, a shower now offers as much pampering as a long, lingering soak. In fact, in some households, the oversized and fully outfitted shower has replaced the tub entirely.

Before you decide on what kind of shower to include in your project, take a look at the amount of space you have. Although a luxury shower can be as highly prized as a a a sumptuous whirlpool tub, make sure it fits your lifestyle first, especially if you're sacrificing a bathtub for one.

Tub Showers

Showers combined with tubs save money and space, but not without trade-offs. Because bathtub bottoms are narrower and curved, tub showers are less safe and convenient than separate showers. Another drawback is the problem of keeping water from spraying outside the shower. Shower curtains often do a less than adequate job. Shower doors are better for keeping water inside the tub, but they take up room on the tub deck and they are harder to keep clean.

ABOVE Customize your shower to suit your needs. Even these small built-in shelves come in handy for holding showering supplies. The half-walls make a distinctive design statement.

LEFT Pamper yourself by installing multiple spray heads in your shower. This large shower features a useful bench and frosted-glass windows for privacy. Floor-to-ceiling glass walls and door add to the openness of the room.

OPPOSITE Shower designs are as varied as people's imaginations. The concrete tub next to a shuttered window, with an oversized, overhead spray head provides a unique showering experience.

Freestanding Showers

You can purchase a prefabricated freestanding shower, which is typically made of molded fiberglass or cast acrylic. These units come in widths of 32, 36, and 48 inches, and with a standard depth of 36 inches and height of 73 inches. Some units come as separate wall and floor components that are assembled on site. If you buy a one-piece model, make sure you can fit it through your house to its destination. Measure the widths of hallways and doorways and any points where you will have to turn a corner or negotiate stairs.

Don't let the concept of a prefabricated shower unit mislead you into thinking that this type is exclusively for the low-end market. Just visit any showroom and take a look at the features that are offered by high-end manufacturers of shower systems. You'll find multiple, adjustable, stationary, and handheld sprayers and showerheads, steam, body jets, and special effects such as waterfall and

rain heads, a remote control TV, and CD and stereo systems. You can preprogram your shower, too; at least one manufacturer allows up to three people to input different settings for water temperature and frequency of intervals between pulses from the jets.

A custom shower can be built to any size. This design flexibility carries over to the finishing materials for the shower floor and walls. You can combine any or all of the spectacular sprayer and showerhead options that have already been mentioned, as well as any number of body jets and a steam unit. Even with this freedom, you'll need an adequate space that is at least 30 inches wide and 36 inches deep.

Whatever type of shower you choose, it's wise to include a shower seat in your plans. (Some prefabricated units come with this feature.) In addition, you might install a light in the shower (one that is designated for use in a wet area), as well as a nook for holding soaps and shampoo.

LEFT Freestanding showers can be purchased as a complete unit or fabricated on site. The addition of a grab bar along the back wall increases the functionality of this site-built unit.

ABOVE Prefabricated showers do not have to be boring, as shown in this unusual design. But looks aren't everything, choose one that matches your needs.

SHOWERHEAD OPTIONS

Shower faucets fall into three categories:

▌ **Fixed sprays,** which are mounted on the wall or ceiling, can be fitted with more than the usual showerhead massage; you can also have a cascade of water delivered by a waterfall spout or a rain bar that lets you relax in a soft rain-like rinse. When installed on a vertical bar, you can adjust the height of the spray head.

▌ **Handheld sprays** are convenient devices for directing water where you need it; they are usually found in combination with fixed-spray heads. Pair a handheld spray with a stationary showerhead, and add a massager with as many as eight settings and a body brush, include a steam unit, and you've created a custom shower environment that rivals any spa.

▌ **Jet sprays** are like those used in whirlpool tubs. They are installed behind the shower walls. Set them to your desired intensity level, and enjoy a therapeutic massage.

TOP RIGHT Body-massage jets can turn an ordinary shower into a luxurious spa experience.

BOTTOM RIGHT Multiple showerheads provide versatility and let you customize a shower.

BELOW An adjustable showerhead lets you change the height or convert to a handheld spray.

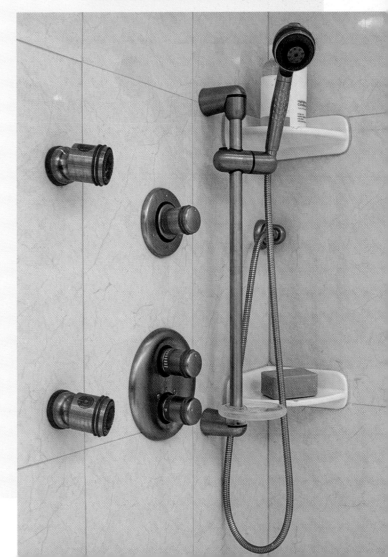

SHOWER PIPING

Replacing an existing shower won't require you to re-model the basic pipes, but installing a new one will mean baring the floor and wall that contain the water-supply and drainage pipes.

You can run hot- and cold-water lines through the floor, ceiling, or walls to reach the shower valve. Mount the valve about 48 inches above the floor. Use $\frac{1}{2}$-inch rigid copper tubing if you can make straight runs and $\frac{1}{2}$-inch flexible tubing if you need to snake the supply piping around difficult curves. Use 2-inch-diameter plastic pipe from the shower drain to the soil stack. Join elbows and T-fittings, as needed, with solvent cement. (See "Cutting and Joining Plastic Pipe," page 118.)

Code Requirements

Building codes usually require the floor drain to be at least 12 inches away from a wall. Just below the drain, place a P-trap, then a drainpipe that slopes at least $\frac{1}{4}$ inch per foot into the soil stack. If you are using $1\frac{1}{2}$-inch-diameter vent pipe, it should be within 42 inches of the P-trap. For 2-inch-diameter pipe, the maximum distance is 60 inches. The vent must rise vertically until it reaches the overflow level of the fixture it serves; then it can run horizontally or vertically through the roof. Because the vent can be a smaller diameter than the drain line, the connecting T- or Y-fitting needs to have a reduced opening on the vent side. After installing the drain, seal the joint between the lip of the drain flange and the shower floor with plumber's putty.

● CONSERVING WATER

Water-conserving showerheads—ones that deliver between $2\frac{1}{2}$ and 3 gallons per minute—are usually required by local plumbing codes. They come in a variety of styles and spray patterns; some have adjustable heads that deliver more than one spray pattern. Choose the showerhead that best fits your bathroom's design with the type of spray pattern you prefer.

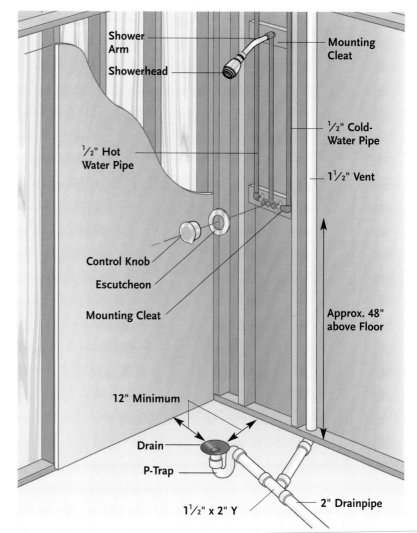

The rough-in plumbing for a shower stall includes hot- and cold-water supply lines and a drain connected to a P-trap. Codes typically require a separate vent (as shown) if the drain is more than 6 ft. from the soil stack.

REPLACING A SHOWERHEAD

There are a couple of good reasons to change a showerhead. The first is to save some water by installing a water-conserving head. Another is to install a massaging showerhead to help loosen stiff muscles. The job is easy. Just remove the head using adjustable pliers, and install a new one. Depending on the unit, you'll tighten either a collar nut or a retainer.

TOOLS & MATERIALS
▌ Duct tape (if needed)
▌ Adjustable pliers
▌ Standard pliers
▌ New showerhead
▌ New shower arm (if needed)
▌ Pipe joint compound or plumber's tape
▌ Adjustable wrench

1 To remove the showerhead, loosen the retainer or the collar nut using adjustable pliers. Turn the fitting counterclockwise, and keep a firm grip on the pliers so the jaws don't damage the fitting.

2 Sometimes a showerhead can't be loosened without turning the shower arm too. In these cases, wrap duct tape around the arm to prevent scratches, and hold the arm with another pair of pliers.

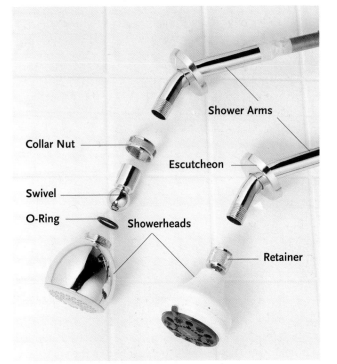

Collar Nut

Swivel

O-Ring

Showerheads

Shower Arms

Escutcheon

Retainer

3 Two types of showerheads dominate the marketplace. The one on the left has a collar nut that holds the head onto a swivel fitting. The one on the right is simpler. Its swiveling mechanism is inside the head.

INSTALLING A PREFAB SHOWER

Start by cutting the drain opening for the shower pan. Then prepare the walls for the shower sides, and drill a faucet hole in one side by following the manufacturer's instructions. Add a dry-mix mortar base to the floor; tip the shower into place; and attach it to the walls. Install the shower doors and faucet. To make the installation watertight, caulk the perimeter of the shower base and walls.

TOOLS & MATERIALS

- Shower stall kit ▪ Saber saw
- Hammer ▪ 12d (3¼-inch) common nails
- 1x3 furring strips ▪ 4-foot spirit level
- Power drill with screwdriver bit & hole saw
- Shower-pan liner ▪ Dry-set mortar
- Mason's trowel ▪ Mixing pan & bucket
- Silicone caulk & caulking gun ▪ Screwdriver

1 Begin by establishing the location of the shower drain on the floor. Push the base tightly against both walls, and trace the drain opening using a pencil or a felt marker.

3 Different shower units are attached to the walls in somewhat different ways. This model called for attaching furring strips to the walls, as shown, to provide a base for nailing the shower flange.

4 Temporarily place the side panels on the shower base, and push the assembly against the walls. Mark the location of the shower faucet. Then bore a hole for the faucet using a drill and a hole saw.

2 Start to cut the drain hole opening by drilling a ½-in. hole in the floor. Then slide a saber saw blade into this hole, and cut the perimeter of the drain opening. Working from below, install a shower trap and connect it to the plumbing waste system.

5 Cut a piece of shower pan liner to fit under the base of the shower, and tack it to the floor. Then cover it with a bed of dry-set mortar that is thick enough to fill the void between the floor and the underside of the base.

6 Attach the walls to the base; then tip this assembly onto the dry-mix mortar and against the room walls. Make sure to push the shower walls against the furring strips, and check the unit for level and plumb.

continued on next page

continued from previous page

7 This unit is attached to the wall furring with screws. The manufacturer's instructions will show where these should be located.

8 After attaching the shower assembly to the wall, begin installing the shower door. Start with the bottom track, followed by the side tracks, and finish up with the top track. Make sure all of these tracks are level or plumb.

10 Install the faucet escutcheon and handle according to the manufacturer's instructions. Also make the final drain connection by installing a drain fitting with plumber's putty.

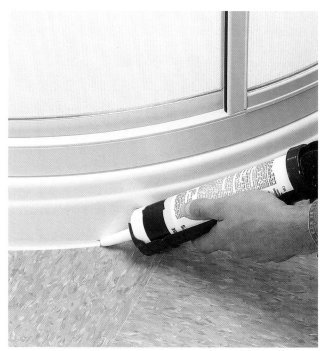

11 Caulk the shower pan where it meets the floor with silicone caulk. Smooth the bead using a plastic teaspoon dipped in water. Do this before it has a chance to glaze over, which is usually within 5 minutes.

9 Install the shower doors in the tracks, and check each for proper operation. Make any necessary adjustments to the tracks so the doors move smoothly. Attach any door handles or other hardware at this point.

12 Also caulk the sides and top of the shower with silicone caulk. Keep in mind that all caulk has to be maintained. Check it once or twice a year to make sure it hasn't cracked.

SHOWER DOORS

The simplest shower door is the curtain: a decorative plastic sheet suspended from a curtain rod. This is the best type of door for universal access; this way, the shower floor is continuous to the rest of the bathroom floor, with no metal threshold that can impede access.

Glass shower doors—most often smoked or scalloped for privacy—are the other popular type of shower enclosure. Pictured here are two kinds of glass shower doors. At left is a door pivoted off the threshold and top jamb by means of a hinge pin. The sliding door at right better suits wider showers. Follow the instructions provided with your kit to install the type of door you have.

SETTING A SHOWER PAN

If you want to build your own custom shower the easy way, get a ready-made shower pan for the floor, and then install the ceramic tile of your choice on the walls above. The best route to professional results is to make sure the walls and floor are level and square. Place the pan in position, and then mark and cut the drain hole in the floor. Install the drain spud and spud nut in the shower pan. You will also need to route your supply and waste lines to the shower location.

Pour a mortar bed for the pan; put the pan into the mortar; and level it in both directions. Attach the pan flange to the wall studs, and make the drain connection watertight by installing a drain gasket in the drain hole. Finish the job by installing cement backer board on the walls as a base for ceramic tile and grout.

TOOLS & MATERIALS
▌Shower pan
▌Framing square
▌2x4 lumber
▌Hammer ▌Nails
▌2x6s for blocking
▌Measuring tape
▌Saber saw
▌Dry-set mortar
▌Spirit level ▌Rubber mallet
▌Drill with screwdriver bit
▌Screws ▌Backer board

INSTALL THE PAN FIRST

YOU CAN INSTALL YOUR DRAIN PLUMBING BEFORE YOU HAVE YOUR SHOWER PAN BY USING THE MANUFACTURER'S PUBLISHED SPECS. BUT IT DOESN'T MAKE MUCH SENSE. SMALL DIFFERENCES IN PAN SIZE AND ROOM FRAMING CAN THROW OFF THE DRAIN AND PIPE ALIGNMENT.

1 Before installing any components, check the wall framing for square and plumb. Shim the studs as necessary to achieve flat, level, and square walls.

4 Mix and spread dry-mix mortar on the bath floor; then lower the shower pan into the mortar. Make sure that the drain holes align and that the pan is level in both directions.

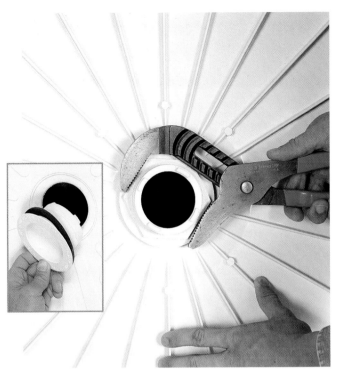

2 Slide the shower pan into place, and mark the drain hole opening on the floor. If you are replacing a shower, there will be drain plumbing already installed. Make sure it aligns properly with the new pan hole.

3 After running the new rough drain plumbing, install the drain spud in the pan from above (inset). Then from underneath the pan, thread the spud nut onto the spud. Tighten it using pliers.

5 Screw the flange on the shower pan to the wall studs. It's a good idea to predrill screw clearance holes to avoid the chance of cracking the fiberglass when you drive the screws.

6 In many shower pans, the final watertight connection between the drain spud and the drainpipe is formed with a flexible drain gasket. Carefully drive this in place using a rubber mallet. Or follow the manufacturer's directions.

7 Install cement backer board over the pan flange and wall studs. Use corrosion-resistant screws, and seal and tape the seams between boards. Finish up by installing the ceramic tile.

INSTALLING A MORTAR SHOWER FLOOR

Creating a custom shower starts with installing a mortar-bed shower floor to provide a watertight installation. The first step is to build the enclosure with a curb where the entrance of the shower will be. Then line the enclosure with a waterproof membrane, and install the drain assembly. Pour the mortar floor in two steps, and when the second layer is dry, spread thinset mortar and install floor tile.

TOOLS & MATERIALS
- Hammer ▮ Nails ▮ Measuring tape
- Utility knife ▮ Saw ▮ Spirit level
- Screws ▮ Trowel and float ▮ Drill
- Combination wrench ▮ Staple gun
- Reinforcing mesh ▮ Butyl caulk
- Thickset and thinset mortar
- Shower pan liner ▮ Shower drain assembly
- Exterior grade plywood ▮ 2x4s and 2x6s

SLOPING A FLOOR

IN A SHOWER, THE GOAL IS TO MAKE THE FLOOR SMOOTH AS IT FORMS A SHALLOW CONE AROUND THE DRAIN. WHY SMOOTH? IF THE SURFACE ISN'T SMOOTH THEN THE FLOOR TILE YOU LAY WON'T BE SMOOTH.

TO ACCOMPLISH THIS HOLD ONE END OF A STRAIGHTEDGE AGAINST THE DRAIN ASSEMBLY AND THE OTHER END NEAR THE TOP EDGE OF THE FLOOR PAN. MOVE THE STRAIGHTEDGE AROUND THE DRAIN LIKE THE HOUR HAND OF A CLOCK GOING AROUND THE FACE. APPLY LIGHT PRESSURE AND REMOVE ONLY A BIT OF MORTAR WITH EACH ROTATION. WHEN THE ENTIRE CONE IS FORMED AT THE SAME SLOPE AND ITS SURFACE IS SMOOTH, REMOVE THE STRAIGHTEDGE AND LIGHTLY FLOAT THE SURFACE.

1 Install another layer of subfloor plywood over the existing floor inside the shower enclosure framing. Then connect the lower drain assembly to the drain piping below the floor. Build a curb across the front of the enclosure and between the wall studs.

5 Reinforce the mortar base with metal mesh. Embed the mesh in the mortar; bend it up about 1 in. around the edges; and staple it in place. Carefully fit it around the drain fitting.

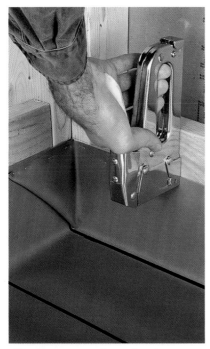

2 Measure and cut the shower liner to size, and push into the enclosure. Fold over extra material at the corners, and attach using staples driven only through the top edge.

3 Spread clear butyl caulk around the drain bolts. Then slide the top half of the drain over the bottom half, and tighten the bolts.

4 Mark lines on the perimeter of the enclosure to indicate the finished top of the mortar bed. Then fill the enclosure with about half this amount of mortar and trowel it smooth.

6 Mix the rest of the mortar to a consistency of wet sand, and trowel it over the mesh. Use a long float to do the final smoothing. The top lip of the drain fitting should stand above the surface of the mortar.

7 Once the mortar has cured according to the manufacturer's specifications, spread a layer of thinset mortar onto the floor, and install ceramic floor tiles. This finished floor should slope to the drain.

TILING A SHOWER ENCLOSURE

project

Once the shower floor is tiled, cover it with a piece of scrap plywood to keep it from getting damaged when you are working on the walls. Start by marking the vertical centerline of the shower's most visible wall. Then establish a horizontal base line, and install temporary support boards near the bottom of the walls. Spread thinset mortar on the walls and start installing full tiles. Then cut all the partial tiles and fill the gaps. Finish up by spreading grout between all the tiles and cleaning up any excess grout. Buff the surface with a clean cloth.

TOOLS & MATERIALS
- Measuring tape ▮ Chalk-line box
- 4-foot spirit level ▮ Framing square
- Power drill with screwdriver bit
- Notched trowel ▮ Masking tape
- Float ▮ Snap cutter or wet saw
- Sponge or squeegee
- 2-inch drywall screws
- 1x4 lumber for battens
- Ceramic tile ▮ Tile spacers ▮ Grout
- Accessories ▮ Thinset adhesive

smart tip

GROUT VERSUS CAULK

USING GROUT IS A GREAT WAY TO SEAL THE SEAMS BETWEEN TILES. BOTH ARE MASONRY PRODUCTS, SO THEIR BOND IS COMPATIBLE. UNFORTUNATELY, GROUT ISN'T ESPECIALLY FLEXIBLE, SO IT'S NOT A GOOD CHOICE IN PLACES THAT MOVE. THIS IS WHY THE SEALANT OF CHOICE FOR WHERE WALLS MEET A SHOWER FLOOR IS SILICONE CAULK. ONCE ALL THE TILE IS INSTALLED AND GROUTED, FILL THE SPACE BETWEEN THE BOTTOM OF THE WALLS AND THE TOP OF THE FLOOR WITH CLEAR SILICONE.

1 Slide a scrap piece of plywood over the shower floor to protect the floor tile; then divide the largest visible wall in half, and snap a vertical chalk line down the middle. Red chalk usually shows up better than standard blue chalk.

5 Start tiling by placing a full tile next to the vertical reference line and on top of a 1x4. Use plastic spacers to maintain the proper grout seams between tiles. Continue installing tiles until there are no more full tiles in the section. Make sure the tiles are completely embedded in the adhesive.

2 The next step is to establish the high point of the floor perimeter. Use a level to do this job, and mark the floor plywood at the high point. Measure up from this mark the height of a single wall tile.

3 Snap a horizontal chalk line on each wall at the height of the reference mark. Screw 1x4s under these lines to act as temporary support members for the wall tiles.

4 Use a notched trowel to spread thinset mortar adhesive on the first wall. Spread this material up to your reference lines and along the inside corner of the walls.

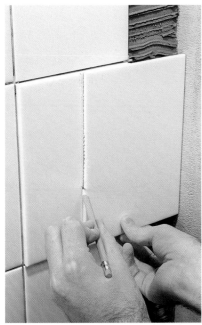

6 To mark the corner tiles, place a new full tile on the last full tile in a course. Put another full tile against the adjacent wall, and mark the cut line of the first tile.

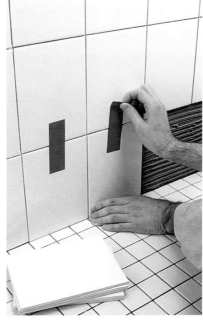

7 Remove the 1x4s at the bottom of the walls, and spread adhesive for the bottom row of tiles. Press full tiles into place, and hold them temporarily with masking tape.

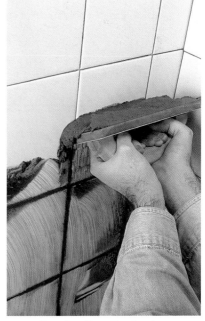

8 After the tile adhesive has set, spread grout across the wall using a rubber float. Firmly press it into the seams between the tiles. Remove the haze that forms using a clean cloth.

INSTALLING AN ANTI-SCALD SHOWER CONTROL

project

If you are tired of getting surprised by bursts of hot or cold water, it might be time to install an anti-scald control valve to keep the water temperature from changing abruptly. Start by shutting off the water to the existing shower valves. Then remove the tile and drywall around the valve. Use a torch to disassemble the existing piping, or cut it out with a hacksaw. Solder the new valve in place.

TOOLS & MATERIALS
- Adjustable pliers
- Adjustable wrench
- Reciprocating saw or keyhole saw
- Hacksaw with metal-cutting blade or tubing cutter ▮ Pry bar
- Propane torch ▮ Drop cloth
- Sponge & bucket ▮ Work gloves
- New tubing, pipe nipples & couplings as needed ▮ Anti-scald valve
- Flux ▮ Solder

caution

LEAD-BASED SOLDER

THE EPA HAS BANNED LEAD-BASED SOLDER FOR RESIDENTIAL PLUMBING SYSTEMS BECAUSE SMALL AMOUNTS OF THE LEAD WERE FOUND TO LEACH INTO HOME WATER SYSTEMS. LEAD-BASED SOLDER WAS THE INDUSTRY STANDARD AS RECENTLY AS THE LATE 1980s. THIS MEANS THAT YOU MAY STILL HAVE A ROLL OR TWO HANGING AROUND THE HOUSE. THE MAKE-UP OF THE SOLDER IS CLEARLY PRINTED ON THE PRODUCT. THE MOST COMMON TYPE WAS A 50-50 MIXTURE OF TIN AND LEAD. DON'T USE THIS SOLDER. BUY THE NEWER LEAD-FREE PRODUCTS AT HARDWARE STORES AND HOME CENTERS.

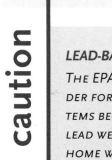

1 Shut off the water supply lines to the shower or tub and open the drain plugs so the water inside falls into a bucket. If there aren't any shutoff valves installed in your system, then turn off the water at your water meter and drain the plumbing system, usually into the basement laundry sink.

2 To replace the existing shower control, open up the wall around the valves. Use a flat pry bar, and wear gloves and eye protection because ceramic tile can shatter and fly when it breaks. Repairing the tile later is very difficult. The best approach is to replace the shower control only when you plan to install new tile.

ANTI-SCALD SHOWER CONTROL

To install an anti-scald shower control, join pipe and fittings to the new valve to make an arrangement similar to the one shown in this photograph.

Female Adapter

Temporary Cap

Male Adapter

Coupling

3 One way to remove the old control valve is to heat the joints with a torch until the solder melts and the pipe and fittings can be pulled apart. When you do this, protect the drywall in back with a piece of aluminum flashing. Another approach is to cut the old plumbing out with a hacksaw, and install new pipes and fittings.

4 Cut all the pipe nipples to size, and assemble them and the fittings to check everything for fit. Then disassemble the parts; clean all the joints using emery cloth or steel wool; and coat the mating parts with flux. Reassemble everything, and solder the joints using a torch and lead-free solder.

tub and shower options

ABOVE AND BELOW Standard-size bathtubs are available with offset faucet locations and whirlpool jets, above. Ceramic tile provides design flexibility when designing and building a custom shower, below.

ABOVE AND BELOW Place tub faucets where they are easiest to reach from both inside and outside of the tub, above. Multiple shower-heads, below, provide a relaxing massage.

CLOCKWISE FROM ABOVE LEFT
Custom showers allow for a number of different amenities. The corner unit shown above left includes built-in seating. Prebuilt showers, above, can include a variety of spray heads for a custom feel. The right tub surround, left, can create a custom look.

smart tip

VAPOR BARRIERS

IF YOU REPLACE THE DRYWALL ON ANY EXTERIOR WALLS, MAKE SURE THAT THE WALL INSULATION IS COVERED WITH A POLYETHYLENE VAPOR BARRIER BEFORE YOU REINSTALL DRYWALL. OVERLAP SEAMS BY 6 INCHES.

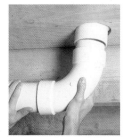

10 toilets

Toilets are elegant mechanical devices. The whole design is based on the fact that water stored at a certain height has enough potential energy to drive the whole mechanism. No electricity is required. It works best, of course, if you have pressurized water supplying the tank. The tank simply fills faster, so the recovery time between flushes is faster. But if you don't have pressurized water, everything still works fine if you take a bucket of rainwater and pour it down the bowl. This doesn't mean that toilets haven't changed over the years. Newer models use much less water than older designs. Residential units with pressure-assist features are gaining in popularity. And today's toilets look different from older models. They are sleeker and come in more colors, and some are designed to be part of a bathroom suite of fixtures.

TOILETS AND BIDETS

Toilets come in a great variety of styles, shapes, and colors—though colors other than white usually cost more. Vitreous china still prevails as the most common material.

You can choose between toilets that contain the tank and base in a single molded unit and those that have a separate tank. The most common type puts the tank directly behind the base. Another version, which raises the tank high on the wall, is available for people who want a Victorian look.

When selecting a toilet for a small room, it will help to know basic toilet sizes. Tank widths vary from 20 to 24 inches. Toilets with the tank mounted high on the wall are around 15 inches wide. Toilets project out from the wall 26 to 30 inches, requiring a minimum floor-area and room depth of 44 and 48 inches, respectively. Scaled-down toilets—even toilets that fit into a corner—are available for tiny apartment bathrooms or small powder rooms, such as those tucked under a stairwell.

BELOW This traditional toilet fits the design scheme of the room, and it is equipped with low-flush technology.

CORNER TOILETS

If you have to accommodate the cramped space of an extremely small bathroom where a conventional toilet will get in the way, you can use a corner toilet. This kind of toilet has a wedged-shaped tank to fit an inside corner and free up some floor space. The rough-in for this toilet is centered $12\frac{1}{2}$ inches from the rough framing of each of the walls that form the corner. A corner toilet is plumbed as you would any other toilet.

Low-Flush Toilets

Regardless of its color or style, you want a toilet that will function dependably and quietly. Another factor to consider is water conservation. Toilets used to require 5 to 7 gallons for each flush, making them the largest single daily user of household water. But with water becoming scarce in many parts of the United States, conservation has become a top concern. The federal government enacted a national standard that limits the water used by residential toilets made in the United States after January 1, 1992, to 1.6 gallons per flush (gpf). Manufacturers are meeting the challenge with improved versions of standard gravity toilets and new designs that use air pressure. Water-conserving toilets cost slightly more than the older 5-gallon units, but the money you save in water use (and for well users, electricity and septic maintenance) will eventually make up for the difference.

Gravity Toilets. The traditional gravity toilet has been improved to reduce the water required for flushing. Taller and narrower tanks, steeper bowls, and smaller water spots (the water surface in the bowl) account for most of the improved design. While users report general satisfaction with 1.6-gpf models, 1-gpf models sometimes require more than a single flush to clear the bowl.

Pressure-Assisted Toilets. Some toilets use the water pressure in the line to compress air. The compressed air then works with a small amount of water to empty the bowl. One model draws as little as one-half gallon per flush, but it costs two to three times more than the standard gravity-operated toilet. In more recent toilet design, a small pump pushes water through the toilet. You can set the amount of flush water at either 1 or 1.6 gpf with the press of a button. This unit's list price makes it the most expensive of all low-flush toilets.

Vacuum-Flush Toilets. Two internal chambers create a vacuum that is released, forcing water into the bowl and through the trap in this kind of toilet.

Bidets

A bidet is used for personal hygiene. It looks like a toilet without the tank or lid. Water is supplied by a sprayer mounted on the back wall or bottom of the bowl. Bidets have been standard in European countries for decades, and only recently have made much of an appearance in American bathrooms. Now they are made by all major fixture manufacturers in the same colors and styles as other bathroom fixtures. Like a lavatory, a bidet requires a hot- and cold-water supply line and a drain. You should allow at least 30 inches of space in length and width in your plan.

TOP Sleek low-profile toilets have a modern look that fits well with contemporary-designed rooms.

MIDDLE An elongated design helps this toilet fit into the narrow space next to the vanity.

BOTTOM The bidet—shown at right with matching toilet—is becoming increasingly common in many homes.

MOVING A TOILET

The first step in moving any toilet is to visit your local building department. They will tell you how far from the main stack a toilet can be before it needs a separate vent. This distance is usually 6 feet. If you can stay within the code limit, moving a toilet will be much easier. If you do need a vent, the building inspector can tell you the proper size and location of the vent.

TOOLS & MATERIALS
▌Measuring tape ▌Framing square
▌Hacksaw with carbide-tipped blade
▌New water-supply pipes, pipe nipples
  & couplings as needed ▌Shutoff valve
▌Threaded compression fitting
▌Closet flange ▌Coupling nut & compression ring (for chromed copper pipes)

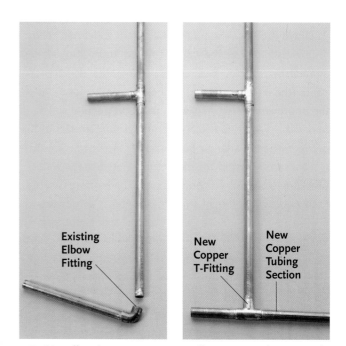

Existing Elbow Fitting

New Copper T-Fitting

New Copper Tubing Section

1 Usually when you move a toilet, you need to extend the cold-water supply line to reach the new location. A good place to make this change is at a 90-deg. elbow. Just loosen the joint using a propane torch; then solder a T-fitting and a new section of pipe where the elbow was before.

4 Use a framing square to establish the location of the toilet drain hole. In first floor bathrooms, you can generally get access to the plumbing waste lines from the basement. But bathrooms on other floors usually require tearing up the floor, modifying the waste pipes, and installing a new floor.

5 Using a framing square, measure the distance from the center of the toilet's drain hole to the back of the toilet base. Then mark the drain hole and the back of base on the floor, and place the toilet on the floor to align with these marks.

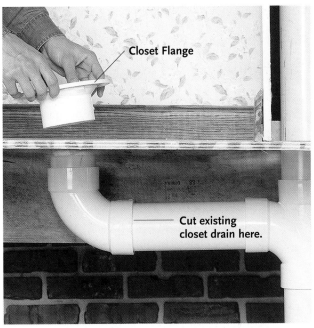

Closet Flange

Cut existing closet drain here.

2 Join the toilet-supply tubing to the cold-water supply line using a shutoff valve. This valve is mounted on the pipe using a compression fitting. Slide the nut onto the pipe, followed by the compression ferrule. Then push the valve on the pipe, and tighten the nut until the ferrule is compressed against the valve.

3 The toilet is joined to the plumbing waste system by bolts that hold the toilet base to the closet flange. This flange is glued to a waste pipe, which carries material to the main plumbing stack. To extend this pipe, first cut off the elbow attached to the flange.

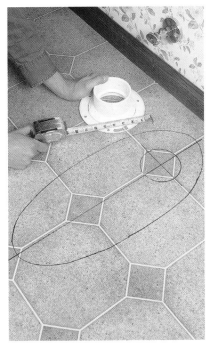

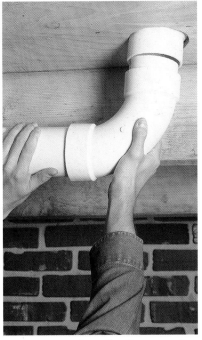

6 Measure the outside diameter of the flange, and mark the floor to match, using the middle of the drain hole as the centerline. Align the flange with these marks and trace it.

7 Drill a blade-entry hole through the floor. Then use a saber saw or a keyhole saw to cut the outline of the toilet flange. Insert the flange, and screw it to the floor.

8 Connect the toilet flange to the plumbing stack with an elbow and 3½-in. pipe. Test-fit the parts first. Once you're satisfied, clean and glue the parts together.

INSTALLING A TOILET

project

There are two basic types of toilets: two-piece units, which have a base and a tank, and single-piece units in which the tank is part of the base. The single-piece models are less complicated to install because you don't have to deal with mounting the tank. But these units are heavier and harder to move around. The two-piece units are generally less expensive.

TOOLS & MATERIALS
- Adjustable wrench ▮ Spirit level
- Silicone caulk & caulking gun
- New Toilet ▮ Wax ring seal
- Plumber's putty ▮ Spud washer
- Washers & nuts
- Braided stainless-steel riser or chromed copper riser

1 Begin installing a new toilet by gluing a toilet flange into the waste line. Make sure that the flange is aligned so the bolts that hold the toilet are on the sides of the flange. Screw the flange tightly to the floor. Push a rag into the hole to keep sewer gas from entering the room.

3 Lower the toilet onto the flange so the holes in the base of the toilet fall directly over the flange bolts. Gently rock the toilet from side-to-side and front-to-back until it sits firmly on the floor. Install washers over the bolts, and tighten the bolt nuts against these washers.

4 If your toilet has a separate tank, like this unit, first install a spud washer on the top of the base to act as a seal between the base and the tank. Then lower the tank into place, and fasten it to the base by tightening nuts on the tank bolts.

2 The toilet is sealed to the waste system with a wax ring mounted on a plastic cone. To install it, remove the rag and lower the ring onto the toilet flange. The cone goes directly in the flange hole, and the flange bolts push through the wax.

5 Connect the water supply line to the tank, and test the toilet by flushing it a few times. Look for leaks around the supply line, around the base, and between the tank and base. If everything is dry, finish up by applying a bead of silicone caulk where the base meets the floor.

TOILETS UNDER PRESSURE

In 1992, the Department of Energy mandated low-volume, 1.6-gallon toilets as a water-conservation measure. But a nationwide survey conducted by the National Association of Home Builders found that roughly four out of five builders and homeowners experienced problems with low-flush units. Most builders surveyed said that they receive more call-backs on low-flush toilets than on anything else. Here are three common complaints: multiple flushes are needed to clear the bowl, residue remains even after multiple flushes, and they clog easily. New low-flush units work better than the first models, but many builders and owners still have to call in plumbers. To deal with the problems, most people revert to double flushing, which defeats much of the water-conservation potential of the system.

If you have a choice, there's a better way. Pressurized toilets (pictured below) have a secondary container inside that uses the pressure of water coming into the main tank to compress air and give each flush a pressure assist to push out wastes. This hybrid design is roughly twice the cost of gravity units. While the flush mechanism is different, the outside appearance of the pressure-tank toilets is the same as the standard-flush units. And the flush noise—though it sounds a bit different—is not louder.

187

TROUBLESHOOTING TOILET PROBLEMS

Now that you know how traditional toilets are supposed to work, it's time to learn how and why they may not work and what to do when they don't. Keep in mind that poorly maintained toilets may display more than one symptom.

Mineral-Clogged Toilet

The toilet does not appear clogged, because water doesn't rise unusually high in the bowl, but it flushes sluggishly, and the bowl doesn't stay clean for long.

These symptoms suggest that the toilet bowl's rim holes—and possibly the siphon jet hole—are clogged with calcified minerals from hard water or with bacteria. To make sure, watch the water as it passes through the bowl. Open rim holes should send lots of water coursing diagonally across the sides of the bowl. If the water slides straight down, that may be a sign that the rim holes are partially clogged, either by bacteria or calcification. Dark, vertical stains beneath some of the holes suggest bacteria. Clogged siphon jets are almost always caused by bacteria.

How will you know whether blockages are made of mineral deposits or bacteria? Bacteria accumulations are soft and dark, ranging from orange to black. Mineral deposits are hard, scaly, and usually light in color.

Bacteria. To remove bacteria, not just in the bowl but in the bowl's rim and rim holes, pour a mixture of 1 part household bleach and 10 parts water directly into the tank's overflow tube, following steps 1–3 on the facing page.

Mineral Deposits. To remove calcified minerals left by hard water, you'll need slightly different tools. Instead of bleach, pour vinegar into the overflow tube, and let stand for at least 30 minutes. Vinegar dissolves and loosens mineral deposits, allowing you to break and scrape thick accumulations that may have built up around the rim holes. Vinegar seems to work better when it's heated. Don't boil it, just heat it to shower temperature, about 104 degrees F.

After letting the vinegar stand, ream each hole thoroughly. On heavily clogged holes, use Allen wrenches as reaming tools. Start with a small wrench, and use larger ones as you gradually unclog the hole. Remember that porcelain chips easily, so work carefully, and use a pocket mirror to check your work. This problem is a good indication that you might need to install a water softener.

Even though toilets are simple devices that can work for years without trouble, they do have a couple of weak points. Both are involved in how the flush water is dispersed throughout the bowl. The water that cleans the sides comes from holes in the underside of the bowl rim. The water that forces the waste in the bottom of the bowl past the trap and into the waste line comes primarily from the siphon jet. Both the rim holes and jet can become partially clogged, which results in sluggish performance.

TOOLS & MATERIALS
▍ Measuring cup
▍ Bleach solution
▍ Insulated wire ▍ Allen wrenches
▍ Pocket mirror (if necessary)

smart tip

CLEANING RIM HOLES

USE A POCKET MIRROR AND ALLEN WRENCH TO REAM MINERAL-CLOGGED HOLES AROUND THE UNDERSIDE OF THE RIM.

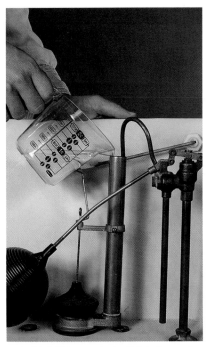

1 To kill bacteria buildup in and under the toilet bowl's rim, pour a bleach solution (1 part bleach to 10 parts water) directly into the overflow tube.

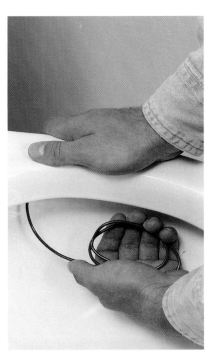

2 Clear bacteria from the rim holes using a short length of insulated electrical wire. Try approaching the hole from several angles.

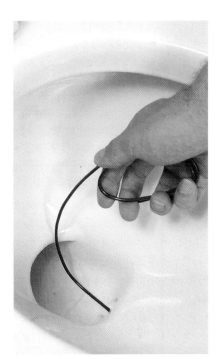

3 Clean bacteria from the siphon jet (the hole opposite the trap), using a piece of insulated electrical wire. A dark opening usually indicates the presence of bacteria.

FIXING A SLOW TOILET

Your toilet seems sluggish. It once flushed vigorously, but now the water seems to move slowly through its cycle, often rising high in the bowl before passing through the trap. You also notice large bubbles rising out of the trap during the flush. Sometimes the bowl even seems to double flush.

These are classic symptoms of a partially blocked trap. An obstruction, such as a toy, comb, cotton swab, and the like, has made its way to the top of the trap and lodged in the opening. Paper then begins to accumulate on the obstruction, further closing the opening. In many cases, enough of the trap remains open to keep the toilet working, but in time, partial clogs become complete clogs.

To clear a blockage, start with a toilet plunger, forcing the cup forward and pulling it back with equal pressure. If a plunger doesn't clear the clog, try a closet auger. If the closet auger fails, bail out the bowl with a paper cup or other small container, and place a pocket mirror in the outlet. Shine a flashlight onto the mirror, bouncing light to the top of the trap. The mirror should allow you to see the obstruction. When you know what and where it is, you should be able to pull it into the bowl by using a piece of wire. In rare cases, you may need to remove the toilet and work from the other side. To remove the toilet, just reverse the directions for installing one that were shown on pages 186–187.

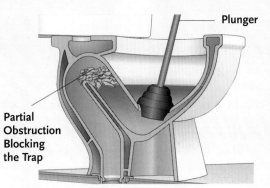

Plunger

Partial Obstruction Blocking the Trap

REPAIRING A RUNNING TOILET

project

A running toilet is not one of the big aggravations in life. It is one of the small ones, but it's still aggravating. If you are tired of going back to jiggle the handle, to say nothing of wasting all the water that goes down the drain unnecessarily, just take a few minutes and a screwdriver to make a quick adjustment. Turn off the water, and flush to empty the tank. If you have a tank flapper, just shorten the lift chain. If you have a tank ball, adjust the wire guide bracket from side-to-side.

TOOLS & MATERIALS
∎ Screwdriver

1 If your toilet has a flapper and its chain lift is too long, this will cause the toilet to run until you wiggle the flush handle. To fix this, lift the chain from the flush lever hook and reconnect it so that it has less slack. It should have no more than 1 in. of sideways deflection when pushed lightly with your finger.

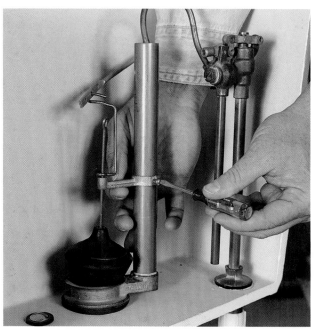

2 A running toilet can also be caused by a lift wire guide that is out of alignment. This can prevent the tank ball from hitting dead center on the flush valve seat, which stops the water flow to the toilet bowl. To adjust this, loosen the guide set screw and turn the bracket until the ball falls in the right spot.

3 Old overflow tubes can break when other toilet tank parts are being repaired. If this happens to you, just remove the broken tube; pry out any remaining threads in the flush valve; and install a new brass tube. Coat the threads with pipe joint compound before installing it.

REPAIRING A SLOW-FILLING TOILET

project

If your toilet flushes okay but refills slowly, sometimes with a hissing sound, you probably have sediment on the diaphragm in your ballcock fill valve. Sediment often finds its way into the valve as a result of work being done elsewhere, such as a new toilet being installed in another part of the house or utility work being done on a nearby water main. Cleaning the diaphragm solves the problem but sometimes it takes a couple of tries to remove all of the particles.

TOOLS & MATERIALS
▌ Screwdriver
▌ Tweezers

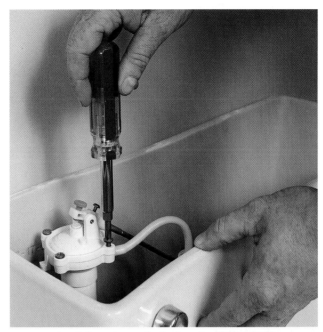

1 To check for grit on the ballcock valve's diaphragm, take off the tank cover and remove the screws on the top of the ballcock. Gently lift off the cover and the float ball that is attached to it.

2 Once the cover is off, take out the plunger from the center hole, and lift up the diaphragm gasket to look for sand or other kinds of sediment or debris.

3 If you find any sediment, remove it using tweezers. When everything is clean, reassemble the valve, and use the toilet for a few days. If it still fills slowly, repeat the process until all the sediment is gone. It often takes a couple of tries to get it completely clean.

FIXING A STUCK SEAT

This is a common problem when an old toilet seat has brass bolts molded into the seat hinge. When you attempt to loosen the corroded fastening nuts, they stick tight, causing the bolt heads to break loose within their molded sockets. No matter what you do, the bolts just spin. The only way to deal with this situation is to saw through the bolts, just under the seat. To keep from marring the toilet's

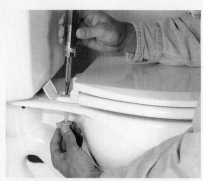

Tighten the new seat bolt using a screwdriver, and snap the hinged cover in place.

china surface, place a double thickness of duct tape on the bowl, all around the bolts. Remove the blade from a hacksaw; lay it flat against the bottom of the seat; and cut straight through the bolts.

With the old seat removed, position the new one, and insert the bolts through the seat and deck holes. Tighten the nuts. The plastic bolts on new seats will never corrode.

REPLACING A FLUSH HANDLE

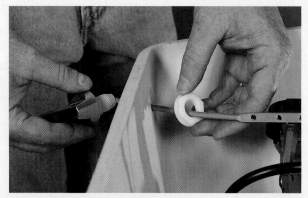

Remove the nut from the old lever, and pull the lever through the tank hole.

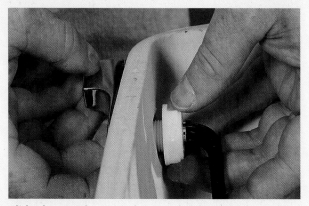

Slide the new lever in place, and tighten the nut. The nut has left-hand threads.

If you press down on the flush lever handle and it sticks, this usually means that the lever is heavily corroded. If on the other hand, the lever is very loose, it's probably broken. In either case a repair is required.

You may be able to free a sticking lever using a few drops of penetrating oil, but replacement is a good idea, especially considering how little a new one costs. Old lever handles also begin shedding their chrome or brass plating and look ugly.

There's nothing difficult about this repair, but in this case knowledge works better than leverage: you should know that the hex nut holding a flush-lever assembly to the tank uses left-hand threads. (That's right, the threads are backward.) To loosen this nut, turn it clockwise rather than the usual counterclockwise. If the nut is too corroded to break free, cut the assembly apart using a hacksaw.

Your new lever and handle will likely come in one piece, with the fastening nut the only other component. The lever may be metal or plastic, while the handle will probably be chrome- or brass-plated metal. Snake the lever through the tank hole; then slide the nut over the lever, and screw it onto its threads.

Finally, connect the flapper chain or lift wire for the tank ball.

REPAIRING A LEAKING BASE

project

Water near the base of a toilet is often the result of condensation dripping from the toilet tank. It can also mean a failed wax ring seal. But because replacing a wax ring is difficult, investigate other causes first. For example, the closet flange bolts may have loosened over time, and their nuts may need to be tightened to bring the base solidly against the floor. Or the water-supply-tube joints, at the shutoff valve or the tank-fill valve, are leaking. Tighten these connections.

TOOLS & MATERIALS
▐ Adjustable wrenches
▐ Groove-joint pliers
▐ Sponge
▐ Pipe joint compound

1 A leaking base can often be repaired by simply tightening the closet bolts. Use an adjustable wrench, and work in half-turn increments, alternating from side to side. Don't tighten the nuts more than two full turns.

2 Water around the toilet base can also come from a loose water-supply tube. To tighten the tube, back-hold the shutoff valve with one adjustable wrench and turn the nut that holds the tube to the valve with another adjustable wrench.

3 Leaks can also occur around the tank's fill valve. Usually just tightening the coupling nut on the end of the water-supply tube will stop the leak. Use groove-joint pliers for the job, and stop turning if you hear the nut squeak.

11 vanities and storage

Among the most common complaints that homeowners express about their existing bathrooms is that there isn't enough storage space. The problem becomes acute when two or more people share one bathroom. If you're lucky, you may have a large layout with room for a spacious linen closet and generous cabinetry. But when that's not the case, make smarter use of the space you do have. It pays to be creative. In addition to installing a vanity and a medicine cabinet, create storage pockets in the wall near the shower and the sink. If there is too little floor space for cabinetry or the cabinets you have won't hold all of your stuff, add wall shelving to accommodate everything from extra toilet tissue to shampoo, soap, and towels. In a pinch, fit the back of the bathroom door with hooks and bars for towels and robes.

THE VANITY
AND OTHER CABINETRY

Like fixtures and fittings, a vanity can make an important statement about how the new space will look, as well as how it will function. A vanity brings style into a bathroom while providing an area for grooming and storing toiletries and other sundries. Today there are numerous creative ways to approach the vanity. It can be a custom design or a stock piece. Look at kitchen cabinets, too. Some of these cabinets, such as pantry units, are interchangeable with bathroom storage pieces. Style-wise, you might be surprised by the sophistication offered by some manufacturers, even in the budget category.

Just as in the kitchen, cabinetry in the bathroom now features fine-furniture detailing. A variety of designs and finishes suits many decors, from modern to traditional. Inside, optional organizing systems make better use of storage space, allowing you to keep grooming and cleaning products handy and neat. A mirror and a medicine cabinet to match or coordinate with a vanity cabinet are optional.

Whether you shop for a vanity and other cabinetry or plan to build them to your specifications, give it as much consideration as you would cabinetry for the kitchen. Top-of-the-line solid-wood construction may be too expensive for most budgets; however, a sturdy plywood frame combined with dovetail and mortise-and-tenon joinery is excellent. If you buy stock cabinets, make sure that the interior is well finished and the shelves and drawers are not flimsy.

RIGHT As when selecting kitchen cabinets, estimate your storage needs before buying bath cabinetry. The bath at right contains plenty of storage options.

OPPOSITE TOP Matching vanities help tie double-lav bathrooms together visually. Single countertops as shown here provide needed storage and counter space.

OPPOSITE BOTTOM Adapting furniture designed for other rooms is a popular option. Tops should be waterproof, and the insides must accommodate plumbing.

INSTALLING A NEW VANITY

If you want a truly custom vanity cabinet and have experience in cabinetmaking, consider designing and making your own (which is beyond the scope of this chapter). If you'd prefer to keep it simple, however, check out the selection of prefabricated units available from your building-supply or kitchen-and-bath store. Prefab units usually have post-formed tops: particleboard that's been factory-laminated and often includes a built-in backsplash. All vanities come as base-only units, a base with an integral sink-countertop, or a base with a countertop for a separate sink. The steps shown here describe how to install a prefab vanity cabinet with a post-formed countertop, complete with backsplash. (See page 220 for instructions on installing a new sink into a laminated or post-formed countertop.)

TOOLS & MATERIALS
- Saber saw ▪ Straightedge ▪ Wood plane
- Power drill-driver ▪ Adjustable wrenches
- Silicone caulk and caulking gun ▪ Clamps
- Vanity unit ▪ Countertop ▪ Masking tape
- 2½-inch wood screws ▪ Shims
- 1¼-inch wood screws ▪ Paint or sealer
- Wood glue or construction adhesive

INSTALLING A VANITY ISN'T A HARD JOB. THE ONLY REAL PROBLEM IS HOOKING UP THE WATER SUPPLY LINES SO THEY ARE LEAK FREE. OTHERWISE, YOUR NEW VANITY CAN SUSTAIN QUITE A BIT OF DAMAGE IN JUST A FEW WEEKS. TEST THE CONNECTIONS AFTER YOU TURN ON THE WATER. AND CHECK THEM AGAIN IN A COUPLE OF DAYS TO MAKE SURE THEY ARE STILL DRY.

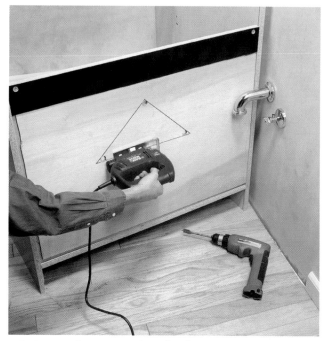

1 Locate the proper place for the vanity; then mark a triangle on the back of the cabinet to provide clearance for the supply and waste lines. Drill blade-entry holes at all three corners, and cut out the waste using a saber saw.

4 Stock countertops usually have to be cut to length to fit a vanity. Do this job with a saber or circular saw. For best results, cut from the underside of the countertop, clamping a metal straightedge in place to act as a guide.

2 Push the vanity against the wall, and check it for level from front-to-back and side-to-side. Slide wood shims under the low points to lift up the cabinet. If a section is too high, scribe it to the floor; then trim off the extra stock using a circular saw or a hand plane.

3 Attach the vanity to the wall by driving screws through the back of the cabinet into the wall studs. Wall studs almost always fall on 16 in. centers. So once you find one stud, measure 16 in. along the wall to find another.

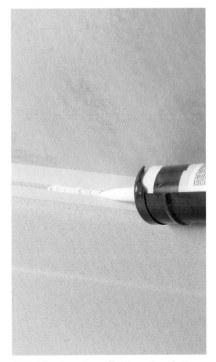

5 Once the top is cut to length, the ends need to be covered with end-cap pieces. Use wood glue to attach these strips, and hold them until dry with masking tape.

6 Place the counter on top of the vanity cabinet, and push it tight against the wall. Attach it by driving screws from underneath up into the bottom of the top.

7 The last installation step is to caulk the joint between the top of the backsplash and the wall. Use silicone caulk for best results.

MAKING A LAMINATE VANITY TOP

Plastic laminate is a durable, affordable, and attractive vanity top finish material. It's available in solid colors, patterns, and metallic-coated sheets, to name just a few design options. Working with it requires some special skills. But compared with other counter options, such as natural stone or solid-surfacing material, building a laminate vanity top is pretty straightforward.

TOOLS & MATERIALS

- Basic carpentry tools ■ Laminate roller
- Contact cement and brush ■ Laminate
- $\frac{3}{4}$-inch plywood and cement backer board (optional) ■ $1\frac{1}{2}$-inch screws
- Brown wrapping paper or lattice strips
- Router with carbide flush-trimming bit and roller-guided bevel bit

1 Start by cutting the laminate for the top edges. You can rough-cut these pieces using a sharp utility knife. Just use it with a metal straightedge to score the back of the sheet.

3 Glue laminate pieces to the top substrate using contact cement. Spread the adhesive on both mating surfaces; allow it to dry a bit; and then press the parts together. Use a disposable brush, and wear gloves, eye protection, and a respirator to avoid contact with the fumes.

4 Once the cement has set properly, carefully align the edge laminate and push it in place. Roll it smooth using a laminate roller, and trim all the edges using a router and a flush-trimming bit.

2 Next, position the scored line along the edge of the vanity top, and hold it with a metal straightedge clamped in place. Snap the laminate along the score line with a quick turn of your wrists.

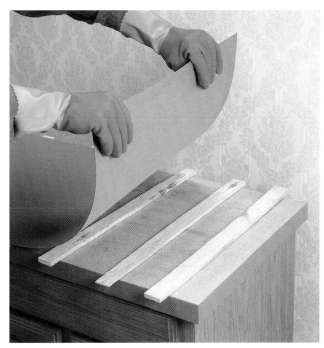

5 Place lattice strips or thick dowels on the counter, and lower the laminate onto them. Make sure the sheet overhangs on all sides. Pull out the strips one at a time; press down on the sheet; and roll it smooth.

CUTTING AND TRIMMING LAMINATE

Laminate can be tricky to work with because of its hardness. You need this kind of durability on countertops, but the brittle sheets chip unless cut with very sharp tools. Laminate countertops and edgings are installed with a slight overlap and then trimmed to a fine joint with a router. To avoid exposing dark substrate material under the color surface of inexpensive laminate, use slightly more expensive solid-color laminate. If your router bit does not have a ball-bearing guide, friction from the high-speed rotation is likely to scorch the laminate. If you push the router fast enough to avoid scorching, the joint is more likely to chip. It takes practice.

caution

USE CONTACT CEMENT ONLY IN WELL-VENTILATED AREAS. EXPOSURE TO ITS FUMES CAN IRRITATE YOUR NOSE, THROAT, AND LUNGS. A GOOD WAY TO LIMIT YOUR EXPOSURE TO THE FUMES IS TO OPEN WINDOWS ON OPPOSITE SIDES OF THE ROOM AND INSTALL A WINDOW FAN IN ONE OF THE WINDOWS. THIS SHOULD DRAW ENOUGH AIR THROUGH TO CARRY THE FUMES AWAY. ALSO, WEAR A RESPIRATOR, NOT JUST A DUST MASK, TO AVOID BREATHING IN THE FUMES.

TILING A VANITY TOP

project

Once your vanity top substrate is prepared, take the time to dry fit the tile. Lay out all the field tile, and check for satisfactory appearance. Usually starting with a full tile at the front of the counter and cutting the tiles along the wall will look best. These partial tiles will almost always be covered by soap dishes, tissue boxes, and other things. It's also a good idea to use full tiles alongside the sink perimeter if possible.

Once all the tiles are installed, you should add a backsplash to the wall to protect it from moisture damage. Some people omit the backsplash on vanity tops, but most use a ceramic tile treatment that consists of a single row of tile. (See "Tiling A Backsplash," on page page 204.)

TOOLS & MATERIALS
- Tile snap cutter or wet saw
- Chalk-line box ▌Notched trowel
- Putty knife ▌Float
- Clean rag or squeegee
- Grout ▌Thinset adhesive
- Ceramic field and edging tile
- Fiberglass mesh tape (optional)
- Plastic tile spacers (optional)

smart tip

HIDING CUT TILES

IF YOUR VANITY TOPS REQUIRE A ROW OF CUT TILES, THE LOGICAL PLACE TO USE THEM IS ALONG THE BACK EDGE OF THE TOP, WHERE THEY'LL BE LESS NOTICEABLE. ONCE THESE TILES ARE CUT, MAKE SURE THAT YOU PUT THE CUT EDGE AGAINST THE WALL, INSTEAD OF NEXT TO THE LAST ROW OF FULL FIELD TILES. THIS WAY THE BACKSPLASH WILL COVER THE CUT EDGE.

1 Start the tile layout by holding an edge tile to the side of the substrate and marking the back of the tile on the top. Do this at both ends of each section of the vanity top.

4 Starting at the chalk lines, lay the field tiles using small plastic spacers between the tiles. Periodically check the surface of the tiles to make sure each is lying flat. High spots can be pushed down using gentle hand pressure.

2 Snap chalk lines between the edge tile marks. These lines will show through the tile adhesive once it's spread, so you'll have a straight line to follow when installing the tiles. Red colored chalk tends to be more visible than blue chalk.

3 Brush off, or vacuum, all dust and other debris from the vanity top. Then spread thinset adhesive over the backer board using a notched trowel. Spread the adhesive in sections that you can comfortably finish before it sets. Read the product label for the specified setting time.

5 After all the full tiles have been set, begin marking the partial tiles for cutting. Hold the partial tile over a full tile, and mark the length. Cut the tile using a tile cutter.

6 Apply adhesive to the edge of the vanity top with a notched trowel. Then cover the back of the trim tile with adhesive using a putty knife.

7 Install plastic spacers on the field tiles, and then press the edge tiles against the top. Make sure to align the grout joints; then slightly wiggle the tile to embed it completely.

TILING A BACKSPLASH

First establish the design of the backsplash. Do you want to use trim tiles, decorative tiles, or the same field tiles you used on the vanity top? Draw your layout on the wall; then mask off adjacent surfaces to protect them from damage. Next, spread thinset adhesive onto the wall, and press the tile into the adhesive. Grout the joints; remove the masking material; and clean the tile.

TOOLS & MATERIALS
- Snap cutter or wet saw
- Chalk-line box ▮ Notched trowel
- Putty knife ▮ Float
- Clean rag or squeegee
- Grout ▮ Thinset adhesive
- Ceramic field, cove, and edging tile

1 Determine your backsplash layout, and mark the perimeter on the wall. Then use a notched trowel to spread thinset mortar within the layout lines. Work carefully to avoid smearing the adhesive on adjacent surfaces.

2 Align each backsplash tile with the vanity top tiles; then press it into the adhesive. Maintain uniform grout lines between wall tiles and between the wall tiles and the top tiles.

3 Cap tiles are held in place with thinset and grout. They provide a substantial finished look to any backsplash. For something more subdued, use standard tile with a bull nose on one side. Install these tiles so that the bullnose faces up.

SINKS

Many bathroom vanity tops are made of solid-surface material and have integral sinks—the sink and the counter are cast in one seamless piece. Small half-baths (which don't need much room for storage) usually have freestanding pedestal sinks. With other types of vanities—such as ceramic tile or the post-formed laminate described in "Installing a New Vanity," on page 198—you install a separate sink in an opening in the countertop. These sinks are held in place with clips or an adhesive applied under their rims.

Use the following guidelines for installing a sink into a vanity countertop. (If you must cut a hole in the countertop, it's usually easier to make the cutout before securing the countertop to the base cabinet.)

For Solid-Surface Countertops

If the sink is not an integral part of the countertop, you can mount a self-rimming sink into the cutout. Order the countertop piece with the cutout already made, if possible. However, if you need to cut it yourself, mark the cutout; drill a pilot hole along the line; and cut the opening using a saber saw equipped with a carbide-tipped blade. Install the sink into the cutout as described in "Installing a Sink in a Laminate Countertop," page 220.

For Tiled Countertops

There are three ways you can install a new sink in a tile countertop:

▌ **Over the tile** by dropping the sink into the opening after tiling the countertop. Set the sink into a bead of caulk, and secure it with clips installed from below.

▌ **Under the tiled surface** by routing out a recess for the rim in the countertop. This allows you to set an unrimmed sink flush with the untiled surface. Install the sink in the countertop following the manufacturer's instructions before setting the tile. Then install bullnose trim tile over the edge of the sink.

▌ **Flush with the tile** by installing a self-rimming sink in the cutout before tiling. Lay a bead of caulk, and then install tile up to the sink's edge.

SETTING A SINK IN A TILED COUNTERTOP

A sink set in a tiled countertop can be installed on a bead of silicone caulk set over the tile, left. If you want the tile to overlap the sink, rout out a notch or recess in the substrate so that the sink's edge is flush with the untiled surface, center. For a sink with a rimmed edge, you can install the sink first and then tile up to the rim of the sink (right).

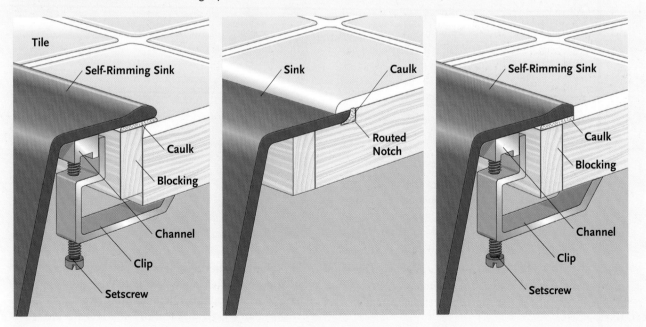

INSTALLING A MEDICINE CABINET

You can purchase an attractive medicine cabinet that can be wall-mounted or recessed into a wall between the studs. From ultracontemporary visions in glass and lights to designs that make bold architectural statements, there is a wide selection of stock units from which to choose, and they come in all price points. If you hate to wait for the exhaust fan to do its job, and your budget permits it, buy a medicine cabinet that contains a defogger for the mirror. Consider investing in a model that that will span the width of your vanity or beyond if wall space allows. Make sure that it is large enough to neatly hold everyone's toothbrush, a can of shaving cream, your deodorant, and first-aid supplies. Also look for an extra-deep interior where you can store extra rolls of toilet tissue and a blow dryer if there's no other place in the bathroom for these items. Some medicine cabinets have special pockets and racks for items such as toothbrushes and disposable shavers.

Other features to look for in a medicine cabinet include built-in lighting, swing-out mirrors, and three-way mirrored doors. A medicine cabinet with a separate compartment that can be locked is a wise investment when there are young children in the house.

TOOLS & MATERIALS
- Magnetic stud finder
- Pencil or masking tape
- Power drill-driver with screwdriver bit, $\frac{1}{4}$-inch drill bit, and $\frac{3}{4}$-inch spade bit
- Keyhole saw ▮ Drywall taping knife
- Sandpaper ▮ Paintbrush ▮ Hammer
- Cabinet ▮ Drywall ▮ Drywall tape
- Joint compound ▮ Paint ▮ 2x4s
- $3\frac{1}{2}$-inch-long L-clips
- Screws or nails for cabinet
- 3d ($1\frac{1}{4}$-inch) and 6d (2-inch) nails

1 Begin by laying out the position of the medicine cabinet on the wall. Mark the preferred height, usually about 72 in. off the floor; then make a level mark at this height using a level as a guide.

4 Mark the location of the studs on the back of the cabinet; then drill clearance holes through the back at these points. Have a helper hold the cabinet against the wall while you drive the mounting screws. These screws should extend at least $1\frac{1}{2}$ in. into the studs.

2 Surface-mounted cabinets must be screwed to the wall studs. Find the studs using an inexpensive magnetic stud finder, or lightly tap a hammer head across the wall and listen for a change in sound. Mark the location of any studs on the wall.

3 Another way to locate studs is to drill a series of small holes across the wall in the area that will be covered by the cabinet. When the bit hits wood, you'll know you've found a stud.

5 To install a recessed cabinet, first mark its outline on the wall, then drill a blade-access hole in each corner. Cut out the drywall between these holes using a keyhole saw.

6 Remove the waste drywall; measure the distance between the studs; and cut two 2x4 blocks to this size. Nail them in place with L-clips or right-angle mending plates.

7 Slide the cabinet into the opening, and screw the sides to the wall studs. Make sure the cabinet is both level and square in the opening.

INSTALLING A WIDE CABINET

A medicine cabinet is a great place to store the odds and ends that clutter our bathrooms. But the standard 14-inch-wide cabinet, designed to fit between wall studs, doesn't hold very much. This is why so many people are adding either bigger medicine cabinets or separate cabinets elsewhere in the room. Because space is almost always a premium in bathrooms, both types of cabinets are designed to be recessed into the wall. This makes very good use of space but does complicate the job. You'll have to cut out one or more studs to make the cabinet fit. We show this process for a partition wall that doesn't carry any structural weight. If your wall is load-bearing, like an outside wall or a wall that supports ceiling joists, the opening needs to be reinforced, which is a job best left to a carpenter.

TOOLS & MATERIALS

▮ Magnetic stud finder ▮ Wood chisel
▮ Utility or keyhole saw ▮ Backsaw
▮ Wood plane ▮ Rasp ▮ Drywall taping knife
▮ Sandpaper ▮ Paintbrush
▮ Power drill-driver with screwdriver bit
  and ¾-inch spade bit
▮ Cabinet ▮ Drywall ▮ Drywall tape
▮ Joint compound ▮ Paint ▮ 2x4s
▮ Screws or nails for cabinet
▮ 3½-inch-long L-clips ▮ 3d, 6d, 8d,
  and 10d (1¼-inch to 3-inch) nails

HIDDEN WIRES AND PIPES

EVERY BATHROOM WALL HAS A GOOD CHANCE OF HIDING WIRES AND PIPES. THE ONLY GOOD WAY FOR MOST OF US TO FIND WHERE THEY ARE IS TO OPEN UP THE WALL. DRILL ACCESS HOLES, AND CUT DRYWALL CAREFULLY TO AVOID HURTING THESE MATERIALS.

1 Determine the side-to-side location of the cabinet; then measure up from the floor 72 in. to mark the height of the cabinet. Using a level as a guide, mark a level cut line for the top of the cabinet on the wall.

4 Frame the opening with 2x4 blocks cut to fit between the studs. Nail these blocks directly into the cut studs, and toe nail them into the uncut studs on both sides. If the cabinet is smaller than the opening, close down the opening with a trimmer stud nailed to small blocks on the sill and the header framing (inset).

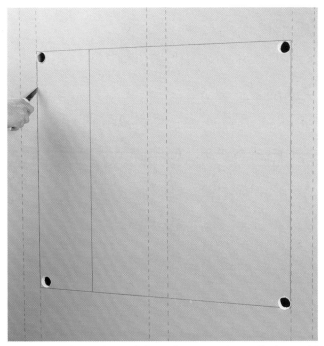

2 Draw the outline of the cabinet on the wall; then add 1½ in. to the top and the bottom of the outline for new framing. Next, drill an access hole at each corner, and carefully cut the drywall between the holes using a keyhole saw. If you hit anything, put the saw aside and use a utility knife to cut the drywall.

3 Once the drywall is removed, the wall framing is exposed and you can see how many studs have to be cut for the cabinet to fit. In this case, only one stud needed cutting. To make the cuts, use a backsaw or a reciprocating saw.

5 Nail drywall pieces to the part of the wall that won't be covered by the cabinet. Then finish all the seams with paper tape and joint compound.

6 When the joint compound is dry, sand it smooth with 120-grit sandpaper. Remove the dust, and apply a coat of primer. Then paint the patch to match the rest of the wall.

7 Slide the cabinet into the opening, and attach it to the surrounding framing with screws. Make sure the cabinet is square and level before driving the screws.

BELOW Surface-mounted cabinets can make a bold design statement. This cabinet provides mirrors on three sides.

RIGHT Choose a medicine cabinet that contributes to the design of the room. Note how this cabinet complements the reproduction sink and wainscoting.

OPPOSITE Drawer storage is great for holding towels, wash cloths, and personal grooming supplies. Shallow drawers are great for small appliances.

smart tip

GIVE YOUR BATHROOM A BREAK

BATHROOMS ACCOMPLISH MORE PER SQUARE FOOT THAN ANY OTHER ROOM IN THE HOUSE. BECAUSE OF THIS, IT'S HARD TO BELIEVE THAT SO MANY BATHROOMS ARE SO SMALL. ONE WAY TO MAKE YOUR BATHROOM WORK BETTER IS TO TRANSFER SOME RESPONSIBILITIES TO OTHER ROOMS. IF THE KIDS NEED TO BRUSH THEIR TEETH BEFORE HEADING OUT TO SCHOOL, WHY NOT DO IT AT THE KITCHEN SINK? WHY NOT KEEP MEDICINE IN A LOCKED KITCHEN CABINET, TOWELS IN A BEDROOM DRAWER, OR DANGEROUS CLEANING PRODUCTS IN A PLASTIC BOX ON A CLOSET SHELF?

CREATING A STORAGE SYSTEM

Clutter happens. The neat, well-organized vanity top that looked just right on Sunday night can be positively besieged by Wednesday morning: hair brushes piled on top of toothpaste tubes and rubber bands tangled in colored combs. If you are going to the trouble and expense of creating a new bathroom, you'll want to keep it looking attractive and functioning smoothly. That takes organization. Here's a list of items commonly stored in the bathroom and how to store them safely and efficiently.

Medicines

There are a few things to remember when planning storage for your medicines. Store medicines where you'll find them quickly and easily. Some medicines need to be taken every day, so they must be stored where adults can get at them but where children cannot. If you can't effectively store medicines in a bathroom cabinet where they will be out of the reach of small children, consider another location, such as in a high kitchen cabinet. To be really safe, install a childproof latch or even a lock on the medicine cabinet—but be sure you can open it quickly in emergencies.

FAR LEFT Drawers help keep you organized. Assign specific items to each drawer.

LEFT Open shelves make great display areas, but plan necessary storage first.

OPPOSITE Counter-to-ceiling cabinets provide storage and help divide double-sink layouts into separate areas.

Dental-Care Accessories

Locate toothbrushes and toothpaste within easy reach of the sink. A squeezed tube of paste and a couple of wet brushes left on the countertop look unsightly, however, and they are unsanitary. Make room inside the medicine cabinet for them. If you can't do that, install a receptacle for them or keep them to the rear or side of a vanity top. Electric toothbrushes and waterpicks are becoming increasingly popular. They need a place near an outlet protected with a ground-fault circuit interrupter (GFCI) for their chargers. Keep cords for the chargers neat and out of the way.

Shaving Gear

Keep shaving gear near the sink but out of sight (and out of the reach of children). The lower shelves of a medicine cabinet with doors fills this need nicely, as does a bin or tub under a vanity or in a vanity drawer.

If you use an electric shaver, you need a way to locate it near a GFCI-protected outlet and a mirror. For maximum convenience, you might keep the razor plugged into the outlet, hung on a nearby hook or sitting on a narrow

shelf. But because cords tend to get in the way of other activities in a cramped space and outlets usually have to be shared with other appliances, a shallow drawer below the vanity might be better.

First Aid

Every house should be equipped with basic first-aid items, and the bathroom is a logical site to store them because administering first aid usually requires ample clean water. When your child is screaming with a cut hand, the last thing you want is to have to grope around for that long-missing box of bandages or bottle of disinfectant. The answer is to locate everything in one easy-to-reach place. Designate one drawer for first-aid items, and be sure nothing else ends up in that drawer. Besides the convenience of having all your gear in one place, you will be able to pull the whole drawer out and move it to the site of the patient, if necessary.

Personal Grooming Accessories

You can relieve bathroom gridlock by providing space outside the bathroom for grooming routines not requiring water, such as makeup application and hair-drying. In addition, a dressing table with several shallow drawers in an adjacent area or bedroom can do much to unclutter the bathroom. Those items that need to be used near a water source can be handily squirreled away in shallow drawers in a vanity near the sink. If you choose to use a hair dryer in the bathroom, store it near a GFCI-protected outlet. A deep drawer in a vanity cabinet is a good place.

ABOVE Sliding shoji screens allow you to keep storage items out of sight but add a distinctive design touch.

TOP RIGHT Use baskets under freestanding sinks to hold towels and other bathroom supplies.

RIGHT Hampers are often overlooked during planning but always missed when not included.

RIGHT Using dead space effectively is the key to good storage planning. The simple shelves can hold everything from towels to soaps to extra toothbrushes.

You need two kinds of storage for wet-grooming items. Items you use every day need to be within easy reach. Store infrequently used items in a cabinet or on a shelf. Soap is most convenient in a soap dish or pump bottle at the side or rear of the sink. Built-in shelves and soap dishes or hanging bags and plastic-coated racks can give you easy access to items used in the shower or bathtub.

Towels and Washcloths

Place towels and wash-cloths within easy reach of every sink, bidet, shower, and tub. Plan towel racks with a separate towel bar for each member of the house-hold (for better harmony) and a few additional bars for guests. Fresh towels and washcloths stored on open shelves or in bins in the bathroom can become part of the room decor, or you may want to store them in an adjacent linen cabinet in or near the bathroom.

Most bathrooms don't provide space for dirty wash-cloths and towels. A bathroom hamper is one solution; a hamper bin built into the vanity is another. You can also retrofit a wire-basket hamper into a vanity cabinet. Look for one in the organizing section of a home center.

Cleaning and Maintenance Supplies

The odd-shaped space below the sink in a vanity cabinet is ideal for storing cleaning supplies, an advantage that freestanding sinks don't offer. Fit one side of the cabinet with adjustable shelves for small items; keep the other side open for tall items such as scrub brushes and plungers. Consider rollout trays or pullout bins for large vanity cabinets. Check on other optional storage features that can customize a unit and put items easily within reach. If you have small children, be sure to install a child-proof latch on any cabinet that houses potentially danger-ous cleaning chemicals.

12 sinks and faucets

One of the first things you'll notice when you start poring through bathroom catalogs and product literature is the vast number of fixtures and accessories available today. Gone are the days of the purely utilitarian bathroom furnished with three white fixtures jammed in side by side. Now you can add or remodel a bathroom with a variety of colors, a multitude of styles, and a host of amenities. The products you select for your new bathroom will affect both your design and your budget. Factors that influence the cost of new fixtures include updated technology and type of finish. The more advanced the device, the more you'll pay for it. Likewise, the fancier the finish, the higher the price tag. Before you make your choices, do a little research. Shop around, visit designer showrooms, read a few reviews, and always ask questions.

SINKS

Sinks are often called lavatories or basins by the industry. But if it walks like a sink and talks like a sink, it probably is one. Sinks come as ovals, rectangles, circles, and other shapes. Manufacturers have gone to great lengths to give sinks appeal by sculpting their forms, but the simpler shapes are both more practical to use and easier to keep clean. Sizes vary from a 12 x 18-inch rectangle to a 33-inch-diameter oval.

Sinks used to be made either of glazed vitreous china or porcelain. These sinks' finishes proved impervious to water, mold, and mildew; they dulled only after years of abrasion. Modern innovations in fiberglass, acrylic, metal, and glass open endless possibilities for shapes, colors, and patterns but are much more susceptible to scratches. Fortunately, manufacturers have created many products to keep these sinks looking like new.

Freestanding Sinks

A good place to begin your sink selection is to decide whether you want a freestanding fixture or one built into a countertop. Freestanding sinks—including those designed specifically to go in corners—can be mounted either directly on the wall or on legs or pedestals. Freestanding sinks are available in colors, shapes, and sizes to suit any taste. They come with flat tops or raised backsplashes that meet the wall. If you choose a freestanding sink, be sure you allow enough space in your design. Wall-mounted units will look and feel cramped if they abut a wall or other fixture with minimal clearance at the sides. While you can stuff a pedestal sink into a space as narrow as 22 inches, it will look better with generous open space on each side. Also keep in mind that you're losing under-sink storage with a freestanding sink, which may affect the rest of your bathroom layout.

ABOVE Above-counter sinks, above, are available in a variety of materials, including metal.

RIGHT Create drama by choosing an unusual installation method, such as this cantilevered design.

the countertop). Under-mounted sinks are installed from below, creating a sleek look; however, the edges of the countertop must be able to withstand moisture. Molded solid-surface countertops, stone, and ceramic tile work well for this kind of application. However, plastic laminate, which has a seam at the edge, will not hold up.

The way the sink is mounted in the countertop has both aesthetic and practical consequences. The exposed edge of a self-rimming sink sits atop the vanity surface. Though attractive, the edge prevents water splashed onto the counter from draining into the sink. Metal rims overcome this drawback by aligning the edge of the sink with the countertop, but the metal trim usually creates a less-elegant

Vanity-Mounted Sinks

Vanity-mounted sinks became popular when bathrooms shrank to the tiny size that marked much of the housing built after World War II. For extra storage, the space under the fixture was enclosed in a cabinet; any extra space above could be used to hold accessories such as drinking glasses, toothpaste, or soap. Combination vanities and sinks may not be much wider than the sink, or they may be as wide as the room. If you are stuck with a bathroom measuring 50 square feet or less, a vanity-mounted sink may be the only way to get enough storage space.

Sinks mounted on a countertop are self-rimming (where the bowl forms its own seal) or rimmed (where the bowl is installed with a metal trim piece to join it to

TOP LEFT
Freestanding and pedestal sinks come in both traditional and modern designs.

LEFT Under-mounted sinks look best with solid-surfacing or stone countertops.

BOTTOM LEFT
Self-rimming sinks are easy to install and work well with most countertop materials.

look than the self-rimming model. Sinks mounted below tile, solid-surfacing material, or stone countertops provide a pleasing separation between countertop and sink.

Integral Sinks

One-piece sink/countertop units are molded from a single material, such as solid-surfacing material or faux stone. There are no seams with this type of sink. The look is seamless, sleek, and sculptural. Many of these units contain preformed backsplashes, built-in soap dishes, and other useful design features.

INSTALLING A SINK IN A LAMINATE VANITY TOP

Most bathroom sinks are either self-rimming or metal-rimmed models. The basic difference between the two is how each is attached to the vanity top. Self-rimming units rest on top of the counter and are kept from moving by metal clips that are installed from underneath or by a generous bead of adhesive caulk. Metal-rimmed units, on the other hand, are attached to the underside of a metal rim, and the metal rim is attached to the counter. The drawings below show the difference between the two.

These days the self-rimming type is more common. It is the type installed here. In many contemporary bathrooms, the sink of choice is more often an above-counter model (see opposite page), which works as well as the other sinks, but has a much more distinctive look.

TOOLS & MATERIALS
- Saber saw ▌Adjustable wrench
- Screwdriver ▌Utility knife
- Power drill-driver with ⅜-inch bit
- Silicone caulk and caulking gun
- 2x4s for bracing ▌8d finishing nails
- Colored wood filler ▌Hammer ▌Nail set
- Sink and laminate countertop

BELOW Self-rimming sinks are set in caulk and held with clips. Rimmed sinks, on the other hand, are supported by metal rims that are set in sealant. The sink is pushed up against the rim from below and is held by a clip.

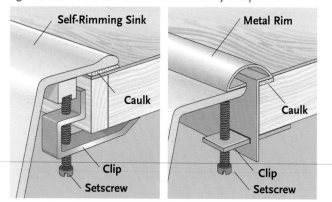

Self-Rimming Sink — Caulk — Clip — Setscrew

Metal Rim — Caulk — Clip — Setscrew

1 Mark the centerline of the sink location on the vanity top. Then mark the centerline of the sink on the underside of its rim. Turn the sink over, and place it on the countertop so that the two marks line up. Then trace around the perimeter of the sink.

4 Cut the sink opening with a saber saw. Make sure to use a sharp blade and hold the saw firmly against the vanity top. If the saw bounces up and down when you are cutting, this can mar the surface. If you can't keep the base from bouncing, cover it with duct tape to prevent any damage.

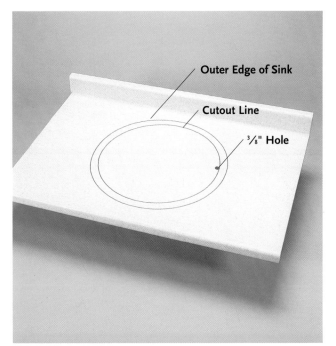

2 Consult the installation instructions that came with your sink to establish how far inside the traced line the cut line should fall. Mark this cut line; then drill a blade-entry hole through the countertop on the inside edge of the cut line.

3 Provide extra support for a heavy sink by installing a 2x4 brace on both sides on the sink opening. Attach them with screws driven through the cabinet framing and into the ends of the braces. On the finished side of the cabinet, use finishing nails; set their heads; and fill the holes with colored wood filler.

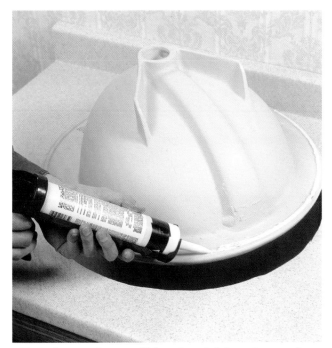

5 Before putting a self-rimming sink into the opening, apply a generous bead of silicone caulk to the underside of the sink rim. Then turn the sink over and lower it into place. If the sink needs clips, install them now. Let the caulk dry, and clean up any caulk squeeze out.

ABOVE-COUNTER SINKS

For an arresting—and easily installed—addition to your bathroom, consider an above-counter, sometimes called a vessel, sink. An above-counter sink is one step beyond a self-rimming sink—it's designed to sit on top of the counter rather than down inside it. A sink intended as a vessel sink must have finished surfaces both inside and out. These sinks are available in cast iron, ceramic, and even translucent glass. They are plumbed the same as any sink, but remember that your faucet must be tall enough to curve over the top of the sink's edge.

221

INSTALLING A PEDESTAL SINK

Pedestal sinks are popular because they look great in just about any bathroom. But installing one is harder than it looks. This is because, in most cases, the sink is not supported by the pedestal. Instead it hangs on the wall. To provide adequate support for this job, you must install solid wood blocking between the wall studs before you can install the sink.

TOOLS & MATERIALS
- Power drill-driver with bits ▮ Level
- Socket wrench ▮ Groove-joint pliers
- Basin wrench ▮ Open-end wrenches
- Sink and pedestal ▮ 2x4 supports
- Lag screws and washers

1 Determine the sink position on the wall. Then remove the drywall in that area, and install blocking to support the sink. Reinstall and finish the drywall; then touch up the paint. Support the sink on the pedestal with scrap 2x4s. Mark the exact location of the sink and the pedestal.

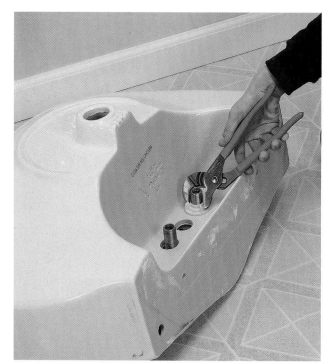

3 It's much easier to install the faucet and the drain assembly before any sink is mounted on the wall. But this is especially true of a pedestal sink, which is hard to work on when the pedestal is in the way. Use groove-joint pliers to tighten the faucet nuts.

4 Put the sink back on the pedestal, and push both against the wall. Slide the lag screws through the mounting holes on the back of the sink, and tighten the bolts. Make sure the sink is level before completely tightening the bolts.

WALL-MOUNTED STORAGE FIXTURES

A PEDESTAL SINK REPLACES A VANITY, REDUCING THE AMOUNT OF STORAGE YOU HAVE IN THE ROOM. PLAN TO STORE THE THINGS THAT USUALLY ACCUMULATE ON A VANITY TOP, SUCH AS SOAP, TOOTHBRUSHES, AND DRINKING GLASSES ELSEWHERE. A GLASS SHELF INSTALLED JUST ABOVE THE SINK HELPS.

BELOW Pedestal sinks are available in a variety of styles. When buying the sink and pedestal, make sure to match the sink to the correct pedestal. Just as with two-piece toilets, the fixture's carton will list which pedestals match the sink you want.

2 Remove the sink and pedestal. Then bore pilot holes for the lag screws that hold the sink in place. Some models require you to install a hanger bracket on the lag screws and to hang the sink from the bracket.

5 Once the sink is attached to the wall, hook up the waste line by connecting the sink tailpiece to the P-trap that goes into the wall. Then hook the faucet to the water supply lines using chrome supply tubes and compression fittings.

FAUCETS

Today's faucet technology promises more control over your water and improved reliability. You can preset water temperature or purchase a faucet that comes with a pressure-balancing anti-scald feature. Plus, you can say goodbye to the tortuous drips and leaks of yesteryear's models.

For quality, inquire about the materials, especially the valving. Better choices are solid brass or a brass-base metal, which are corrosion-resistant. The cheapest faucets may cost less up front, but the savings aren't worth what you'll be sacrificing in the long run. Inexpensive compression-valve faucets work by means of a stem that moves up and down to open and close the water valve. Naturally, this action wears the washer at the base of the stem and causes the faucet to leak. Many new models come with washerless valves. There are a few different types available, with ceramic-disc and cartridge models the most popular. They last longer and are less prone to leaks than compression valves.

Real Lookers

Besides the innards of a faucet, fashion-forward homeowners are concerned with the looks of a faucet. Luckily, you can find faucets to coordinate with any decor, from contemporary chic to reproduction designs.

BELOW Cross-handle faucets may harken back to an earlier time, but their valving system can be strictly up to date.

TOP LEFT Wall-mounted faucets make a design statement that can't be matched with sink-mounted faucets.

BELOW Lever handles are a good choice for people who have trouble turning other types of handles.

BOTTOM LEFT Match gooseneck spouts with a deep bowl to prevent unnecessary splashing.

BOTTOM RIGHT Dark matte finishes are becoming a popular option for bathroom faucets.

Handle styles may include everything from wrist blades and levers (including single-lever versions once reserved only for kitchens) to cross handles and knobs. Levers and wrist blades have a contemporary appeal. While cross handles are nostalgic and charming, they can be difficult to grasp for the elderly, the disabled, or the very young. Levers and wrist blades make more sense in these cases.

Some faucets are hands-free, but whatever the style, a faucet needs a spout. Like handles, today's spout styles are handsome. Some are geometric and sleek; others are curvaceous. If you choose one of the arc styles, consider the sink's depth. If the faucet is a tall gooseneck style, you'll need a deep bowl sink to prevent splashing. A slightly arched or standard spout is more suited to a shallow bowl.

225

The most exciting part of the faucet is the finish, and there are many. Chrome is still a popular choice. From a maintenance standpoint, brushed chrome is more care-free than the polished version because it doesn't show water spots as readily. Brass is always a contender. As with chrome, it will require more upkeep in the polished form. When you shop, inquire about the improved coatings that are applied to the higher-end metals to make them spot-, scratch-, and wear-resistant.

Nickel, pewter, and copper are highly fashionable today, coming in polished, brushed, or matte finishes as well. Matte black is another look that you'll see in design centers and showrooms, too, along with gold-plated, enamel, and porcelain finishes.

ABOVE Widespread faucets appear to be made of sepa-rate spout and valves.

RIGHT This unique center-set faucet complements the under-mount sink installation.

Types of Sets

They are so good-looking that you could think of faucets as jewelry for your bathroom, and like gems, you can set them in several ways.

Center Set. A center-set faucet has two separate valves (one for hot and one for cold) and a spout that are all connected in one unit.

Widespread. A widespread set features a spout with one valve for hot water and another valve for cold water. The valves appear to be completely separate pieces.

Single Lever. A single-lever faucet set has a spout and a single lever in one piece for one-hand control.

If you visit a showroom or design center, be sure to check out the various mounting styles, too. Depending on your design, you can set faucets onto the deck of the sink, into the countertop, or even into the backsplash—the wall behind the sink.

Other Fittings

Don't forget to coordinate your sink's fittings with those on the tub and shower and with any other hardware in the room: towel bars, grab bars, and cabinet and door handles and knobs. You can often find sets, but you can also mix and match as long as you select the same finish for all of the hardware to maintain a coordinated look.

ABOVE This elegant faucet makes an emphatic design statement. This is one type of center-set faucet.

BELOW LEFT Single-lever faucets generally complement the design of modern or contemporary baths.

BELOW RIGHT Match sink faucets to the faucets used on tubs and showers to unify the bathroom design.

faucet options

TOP LEFT Lavatories designed for tight spaces won't force you to compromise on design.

ABOVE Above-counter lavs create a distinctive style.

LEFT The dramatic lav and faucet commands attention.

BELOW These faucets create a unified look.

OPPOSITE This bathroom has matching faucets and lavs but distinctive counter and cabinet treatments.

INSTALLING A ONE-PIECE FAUCET

Bathroom faucets are pretty simple. Most are one-piece devices with either two separate handles for hot and cold water or a single handle, much like a typical kitchen faucet. Some units use better materials than others and as a result cost more. But there isn't too much variation in how they are installed. They either have flexible copper supply tubes (photo 2) or standard tailpieces (photo 3).

TOOLS & MATERIALS
- Adjustable wrench ▮ Tubing bender (optional) ▮ Clean rag
- Silicone caulk & caulking gun
- New faucet
- Braided stainless-steel risers (if chromed copper supply tubing not included with faucet)

1 Take off the old faucet by removing the water supply lines and unthreading the mounting nuts on the faucet tailpieces. Then slide a putty knife between the faucet and the sink and gently pry off the faucet. Clean any remaining caulk from the sink using the putty knife.

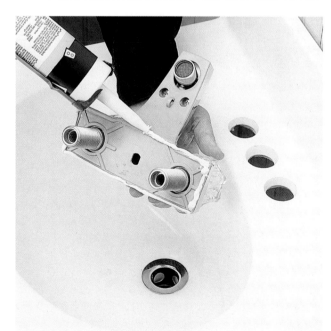

3 On faucets that don't have a gasket, run a bead of silicone caulk or plumber's putty around the perimeter of the base. Then press the faucet into the sink holes, and let the caulk or putty dry. Cut away any excess caulk or putty that squeezed out around the base using a sharp utility knife.

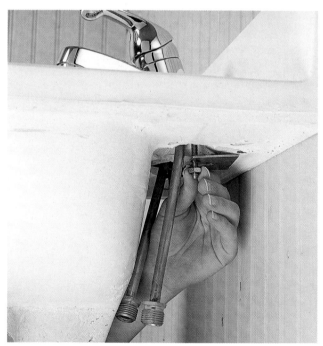

4 If the new faucet has pre-attached copper supply tubes, it won't have threaded tailpieces. Instead the faucet will have two threaded bolts that get fitted with washers and nuts. To secure the faucet, just tighten the nuts on these bolts using an adjustable wrench.

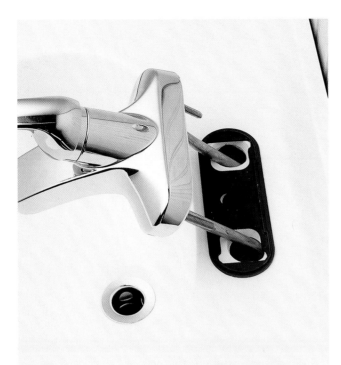

2 New faucets usually have a gasket that must be installed between the faucet and the sink to prevent water from leaking around the base of the unit. Put the gasket over the holes, and lower the faucet onto the gasket.

5 The best way to join the faucet's copper supply tubes to the shutoff valves on the wall is to use braided stainless-steel risers. Use an adjustable wrench to tighten both of the compression fittings on each riser.

● BENDING TUBING

If your faucet has flexible copper (or chromed copper) supply tubing pre-attached to it, you may need to bend the tubing slightly to reach from the faucet to the shutoff valve. To do this, you'll need to use a tubing bender, which looks like a pipe made from concentric rings. You just insert the flexible tubing into the sleeve, and bend it slowly into shape by hand. This tool will minimize the crimping that often occurs when you bend flexible tubing with only your hands.

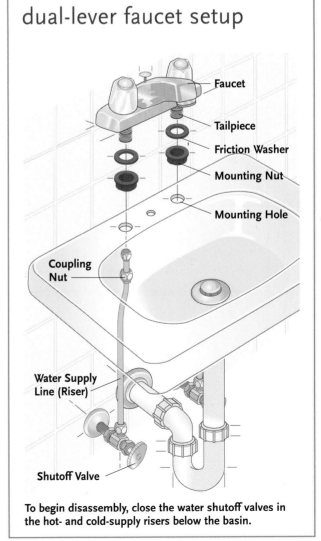

dual-lever faucet setup

- Faucet
- Tailpiece
- Friction Washer
- Mounting Nut
- Mounting Hole
- Coupling Nut
- Water Supply Line (Riser)
- Shutoff Valve

To begin disassembly, close the water shutoff valves in the hot- and cold-supply risers below the basin.

REPLACING A SEAT WASHER

It's easy to tell when a faucet washer is worn out: the faucet leaks. It's just that simple. And while you may be able to stop the leak for a short time by tightening the handle excessively, you shouldn't do this. It can result in damaging the faucet valve seat and possibly the whole faucet. The better approach is to take a few minutes and replace the washer. If you have an assortment of replacement washers on hand, the job is easy and can usually be wrapped up in less than a half hour.

TOOLS & MATERIALS
▪ Utility Knife ▪ Screwdriver
▪ Handle puller ▪ Adjustable wrench
▪ Repair kit

REMOVING STUCK HANDLES

IF YOU CAN'T EASILY BREAK THE FAUCET HANDLE LOOSE FROM THE VALVE STEM BY PRYING IT UP WITH A SCREWDRIVER, DON'T PRY HARDER. YOU CAN BREAK THE HANDLE, WHICH IN MOST CASES MEANS YOU'D HAVE TO REPLACE THE ENTIRE FAUCET ASSEMBLY. A BETTER APPROACH IS TO USE A SIMPLE HANDLE PULLER. THESE TOOLS ARE VERY EASY TO USE. JUST REMOVE THE HANDLE SCREW; SLIDE THE TWO PRONGS OF THE PULLER UNDER THE LIP OF THE HANDLE; AND TIGHTEN THE CENTER BOLT SO THAT IT BEARS AGAINST THE VALVE STEM WHERE THE HANDLE SCREW USUALLY GOES. THE HANDLE WILL POP OFF AND YOU'LL SEE ALL THE SOAP AND/OR MINERAL DEPOSITS THAT WERE HOLDING IT IN PLACE. CLEAN THE HANDLE AND STEM BEFORE REPLACING THE HANDLE.

1 Start work by turning off the water to the sink faucet at the shutoff valves. Then remove the faucet handles. Many of these handles have plastic covers, called index caps, protecting the handle screws. Remove these caps by prying them up using a utility knife blade.

5 When the stem is out, the valve seat washer on the bottom of the stem is exposed. It's held in place by a brass screw. To remove the washer, back out the washer screw (inset). Push the screwdriver firmly into the screw to reduce the chances of stripping out the screw head.

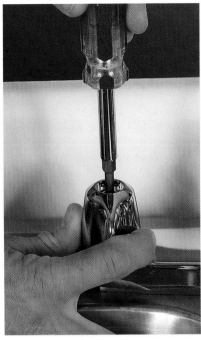

2 Remove the handle screws with a screwdriver. Press down firmly on the screw so that when you turn it you reduce the chances of stripping the screw head.

3 Once the screw is removed, pry off the handle by sliding a screwdriver blade between the handle and the faucet base. If you can't pry it off, use a handle puller.

4 Use an adjustable wrench to loosen the valve stem bonnet nut. Then unthread and remove the entire stem assembly.

6 Choose a new washer to match the size and shape of the worn washer. Make sure it fits tightly inside the retainer rim. Then slide a screw through the washer and install both together in the bottom of the valve stem.

7 Once the washer is screwed securely to the stem, coat the washer and the stem threads with heat-proof grease. Then reinstall the stem; replace the handle; and finish up by replacing the index caps.

Repairing Worn Stem Packing

When you rotate a faucet stem up into the "On" position, water rushes past the seat and into the spout. It also rises against the top of the stem, where it is held in check by an O-ring or, in older faucets and valves, a soft filler material called packing string. The packing is compressed between the stem and packing or bonnet nut, and the packing seal is completed with a cone-shaped leather or graphite washer.

When O-rings are used, the stem will usually not have a separate packing washer; rather, the O-ring fits between the stem and a brass sleeve, or stem nut, and is held in place by the bonnet nut. (See "Replacing O-Ring Packing Seals," on page 236.) In some faucets, the stem nut replaces the bonnet nut entirely. On faucets and valves where stem nuts have male threads, a thin nylon or composition washer seals between the nut and the faucet to keep water from passing by.

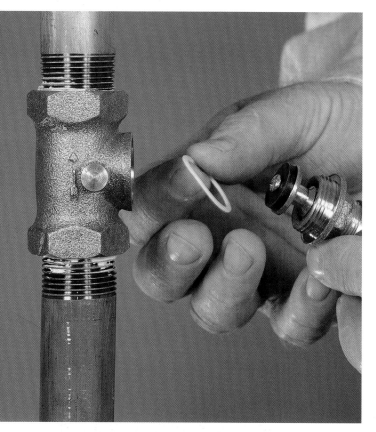

ABOVE Modern shutoff valves have flat nylon washers to seal the stem against the fitting body.

● SIMPLE FIXES

When dealing with valves and faucets that have separate packing nuts, try tightening the nut about one-half turn. This will usually compress the existing packing material enough to stop the leak. Several threads showing beneath the nut are a good indication that additional tightening will help. While you may need to remove the faucet handle to get to this kind of packing nut, you won't need to turn the water system off. Just tighten the nut until the leak stops.

If the leak persists, turn off the water at the shut-off valves, undo the nut, and raise it enough to clear the threads. Wrap packing string around the stem, just above the old packing washer, and retighten the nut. The added material will compress the old packing enough to create a new seal. While packing string works in most cases and will save your having to find a perfectly matched replacement washer, don't overdo it. Two turns around the stem are usually plenty.

smart tip

DEALING WITH DAMAGED FAUCET STEMS

AS YOU MIGHT GUESS, NOT ALL COMPRESSION-FAUCET REPAIRS GO SMOOTHLY. IN SOME CASES, THE RETAINING RIM THAT KEEPS THE SEAT WASHER CENTERED ON THE END OF THE STEM WILL HAVE CRUMBLED. IN OTHERS, THE STEM OR THREADS MAY HAVE BEEN DAMAGED PREVIOUSLY. IF YOU FIND A DAMAGED, BENT, OR BADLY WORN STEM, YOU MAY BE ABLE TO REPLACE IT. PLUMBING SPECIALTY COMPANIES MAKE REPLACEMENT STEMS FOR MANY OLDER FAUCETS. TAKE YOUR DAMAGED FAUCET STEM TO A WELL-STOCKED PLUMBING OUTLET OR TO A PLUMBER WHO SPECIALIZES IN SERVICE WORK. CHANCES ARE, YOU'LL BE ABLE TO BUY A NEW STEM. IF NOT, IT'S TIME FOR A NEW FAUCET.

REPAIRING A FAUCET PACKING WASHER

Older faucets, without O-rings to keep water from passing between the faucet body and valve stem, are sealed with graphite packing washers. These fit over the valve stem and are compressed by a bonnet nut. If water starts to leak around the valve stem, first try tightening the bonnet nut. If this doesn't work, replace the packing washer. And it's a good idea to add some faucet packing string above the washer for a little added leak protection.

TOOLS & MATERIALS
▌ Screwdriver
▌ Adjustable wrench
▌ Packing materials

1 If a faucet starts to leak near the top of the valve stem, try to tighten the bonnet nut to compress the packing washer. But if this doesn't stop the leak, shut off the water to the faucet and remove the handle and bonnet nut.

2 Remove the old graphite packing washer by prying it off using a flat-blade screwdriver. Clean any debris or soap buildup from the valve stem, and slide a new washer onto the stem.

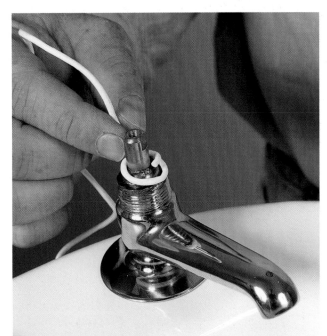

3 Make sure the packing washer is pushed down tightly against the valve. Then wrap a couple of turns of packing string around the valve stem, just above the washer. Slide the bonnet nut over the stem, and carefully tighten it in place to compress the string against the washer. Reinstall the faucet handle.

REPLACING O-RING PACKING SEALS

To deal with O-ring stem leaks, shut off the water and drain the faucet or valve. Then remove the handle, and loosen the stem nut. Lift the stem from the port, and pull the nut from the stem. (See the photo at right.) Roll or cut the old ring from the stem, and slide an exact replacement in place. If the old O-ring was seated in a groove in the stem, make sure the new ring seats as well. Lubricate the O-ring lightly with plumber's grease. (See the photo far right.) Then press the stem nut back over the stem. As always with O-rings, try to find one that is made or at least recommended by the faucet manufacturer.

Although you won't usually need to, it's a good idea to replace the flat washer as a preventive measure, especially if one is included in the O-

ring kit. If you find that the flat washer is leaking and don't have a replacement, you may be able to fortify the old washer with a thin layer of nonstick plumber's pipe-thread sealing tape. It works best if you

stretch the tape around the washer, lapping it in the direction of the nut's rotation. Drop the washer into the recessed rim of the port, tighten the nut, replace the handle, and turn the water back on.

Expose the O-ring by lifting the bonnet nut from the faucet stem.

Roll a new O-ring onto the stem, and lubricate it using plumber's grease.

compression faucet repair supplies

Besides basic tools like wrenches and screwdrivers, you may need some special materials to make a successful repair of a compression faucet. Common repair materials include washers, heat-proof plumber's grease, stem packing, bonnet nuts, and packing washers.

Stem Packing

Seat Washer

Seat-Washer Screw

Seat Washer

Packing Washers

Heat-Proof Plumbers Grease

Correcting Aerator Problems

If a sudden drop in pressure occurs at only one faucet or the water doesn't seem to flow properly, the aerator may be clogged.

All kitchen- and bathroom-sink faucets have spout attachments called aerators. As the name implies, an aerator mixes air into the flow from the spout and keeps the water from spiraling out at an angle or with too much force. Aerators also contain sediment screens. The screens hold a little water after you shut the faucet off, so with hard water they're prone to calcification, but the most common problem is sediment, usually from a line repair or a sandy well. When sediment is caught in an aerator, it shows as a pressure drop. If only one faucet in your home exhibits a pressure drop, suspect a clogged aerator. If all faucets seem to lose pressure, you have a system problem.

Clearing Sediment and Mineral Buildup. Sediment can be easily cleaned from an aerator. Just grip the aerator with your fingers or with padded pliers, and unscrew it from the faucet. Carefully remove the various screens and disks, and lay them out in order of removal. Use a paper clip to poke through each hole in the plastic disk, and backflush the metal screens. Reassemble the components, and install the aerator. If this doesn't correct the problem, throw the old one out and buy a new one.

If a white crusty buildup from calcification is the problem, remove the aerator and soak it in warm vinegar for an hour or so. If the aerator holes and screens remain partially plugged, poke at them using a paper clip.

Repairing an Older Ceramic-Disk Faucet

If sediment in the faucet is not the culprit, you can often stop a leak in an older ceramic-disk unit by increasing tension on the disk. Pry off the index cap, and remove the screw and handle. You'll see a chrome cap concealing the ceramic water-control mechanism. Remove the cap. This will reveal a large plastic adjustment nut with a series of holes around its rim. The holes correspond to holes in the faucet body. Using large pliers, rotate the nut clockwise until the next set of holes aligns. Replace the cap and handle, and test your work. If the faucet still leaks, advance the nut one more hole. Continue until the leak stops or the nut feels too tight to move. If these quick-fix methods don't help, it's time to replace the cartridge.

Shut off the water; remove any decorative cap and the handle from the faucet; and back the adjustment nut out of the faucet. Remove the screws that hold the old disk in place, and install an exact replacement. Thread the adjustment nut back into the faucet until its alignment is roughly the same as it was when you first opened the faucet. Test your work. If the faucet drips, continue tightening the adjustment nut, one hole at a time.

LEFT Mineral-encrusted aerators are easy to unscrew from the faucet spout for cleaning or replacement.

RIGHT Soak the scaled-over aerator parts in vinegar, and clear the screens using a straightened paper clip.

REPAIRING A SINGLE-HANDLE CARTRIDGE FAUCET

project

If you need to repair a cartridge faucet, don't worry about valve stem washers and O-rings. Just install a new cartridge and you're done. The hardest part of the job is making sure you get the right cartridge. So the best approach is to remove your existing one; take it to a well-stocked hardware store, home center, or a plumbing-supply house; and buy an exact replacement. That way you will be sure to get the right part. Take it home and put it in.

TOOLS & MATERIALS
- Utility knife
- Allen wrench
- Screwdriver
- Groove-joint pliers
- New cartridge

smart tip
GETTING RID OF A FAUCET SPRAYER

IF THE FAUCET SPRAY ATTACHMENT DOESN'T WORK PROPERLY AND YOU'D RATHER BE RID OF IT ENTIRELY, YOU CAN REMOVE IT AND IN THE PROCESS FREE UP THE SINK DECK HOLE FOR A SOAP DISPENSER OR HOT-WATER DISPENSER. YOU'LL HAVE TO CLOSE OFF THE FAUCET DIVERTER NIPPLE UNDER THE SINK WITH A THREADED CAP, HOWEVER. (SOME NIPPLES ARE THREADED INSIDE AS WELL, SO YOU CAN BUY A THREADED PLUG TO CLOSE IT OFF INSTEAD.) TO ELIMINATE THE HOSE SPRAY, REMOVE IT; APPLY PIPE JOINT COMPOUND TO THE FAUCET NIPPLE THREADS; AND TIGHTEN THE PLUG OR CAP ONTO THE NIPPLE.

1 To repair a cartridge faucet, begin by turning off the water. Then tip the faucet handle back, and remove the decorative index plug using the point of a utility knife blade. Behind the plug is an Allen screw that must be removed to free the handle.

2 Once the handle is removed, you'll find a metal covering plate that holds the cartridge in place. Remove the screw that holds the cover, and pull the cover off.

• WATCH THE SLEEVE

Many single-handle cartridge sink and tub-shower faucets require an extra step before you can remove the retaining clip that holds the cartridge in place. With the handle off the faucet, you may see a stainless-steel sleeve installed over the cartridge and column. This sleeve is partly decorative, but it also keeps the clip from backing out. Pull the sleeve from the column; remove the clip; and replace the cartridge. Then reinstall the clip followed by the sleeve and the handle. As is the case with many single-handle cartridge faucets, reversed hot and cold sides can be corrected by taking apart the faucet and by rotating the stem 180 degrees.

With single-handle cartridge faucets, you might find stem sleeves that you must remove before you can reach the retainer.

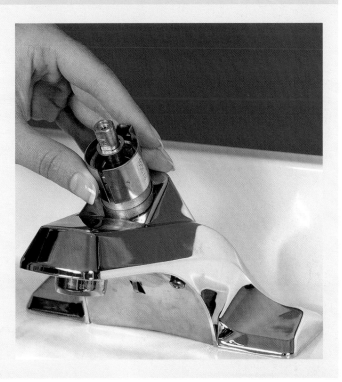

3 Beneath the cover is a plastic ring that must be removed by turning it counterclockwise. Once this ring is removed, a nylon nut and the cartridge retaining clip will be accessible.

4 Pull out the U-shaped clip at the back of the assembly to free the nut and cartridge. Then remove the nut using groove-joint pliers, and set it aside.

5 Grab the top of the cartridge using pliers, and wiggle it back-and-forth as you pull up. If it won't budge, buy a cartridge extraction tool at a local plumbing supply house.

13 finishing touches

This is the home stretch of the remodeling process. The plumbing and wiring are in place, and all of the major fixtures have been installed. It is now time to apply the finishes that will make the new bathroom truly your own, a reflection of your taste and style.

In this chapter, you'll learn to install resilient flooring and ceramic tile, today's most practical and beautiful flooring options. If your tastes run more toward natural stone tiles, follow the directions for installing ceramic tile, but use a mortar designed for stone.

You will also learn how to install radiant heat in the floor. And, finally, we will give you tips on prepping and painting the walls, one of the last steps in the process.

FLOORING LAYOUT

Before planning a layout for new flooring, you will have to make sure that the floor is reasonably square.

Is the Room Square?

In small rooms, such as most bathrooms, you can check the squareness using a framing square positioned at each corner of the room, or by using the 3-4-5 triangle method: measure 3 feet along one wall, at floor level; then measure along the other wall 4 feet. If the distance between these two points is 5 feet, then the walls are square. For larger rooms, use a multiple of the 3-4-5 triangle (such as 6-8-10 or 12-16-20).

If the walls are less than ¼ inch out of square in 10 feet, it will probably not be noticeable. If they are more than ¼ inch out of square, the condition will be visible along at least one wall, and you'll need to make angled cuts. Try to plan the layout so that the angled tiles are positioned along the least noticeable wall.

Making Working Lines

Once you've established the pattern and flooring material, you can snap the working lines used to guide the installation on the underlayment.

If you're installing any kind of tile flooring, plan the layout so that a narrow row of cut tiles does not end up in a visually conspicuous place, such as at a doorway. Often, the best plan is to adjust the centerline so that cut tiles at opposite sides of the room will be the same size. If you start by laying a full row of tiles along one wall or if you start laying tiles from the centerline, you can end up with a narrow row of partial tiles along one or both walls.

To correct this, shift the original centerline, or working line, a sufficient distance to give you wider cut tiles at both walls. Also, try to center the tiles across large openings, such as archways, or beneath focal points, such as picture windows or fireplaces.

Working Lines for a Square Layout. If the room is relatively square, snap a chalk line along the length of the area down the center of the room. Then snap a second chalk line across the width of the room so that each chalk line crosses in the center of the room. Check the cross with a framing square to make sure that the intersection forms a 90-degree angle.

Working Lines for a Diagonal Layout. When laying tiles diagonally, a second set of working lines is required. You'll need to snap a chalk line at exactly 45 degrees from your vertical and horizontal working lines; you can't just snap a line from the center point to the corner.

From the center point, measure out an equal distance along any two of the lines, and drive a nail at these points, marked A and B on the drawing at left. Hook the end of a measuring tape to each of the nails, and hold a pencil against the measuring tape at a distance equal to that between the nails and center point. Use the measuring tape and pencil as a compass to scribe two sets of arcs on the floor. These arcs will intersect at point C.

Snap a diagonal chalk line between the center intersection and point C. Repeat the process for rest of the room.

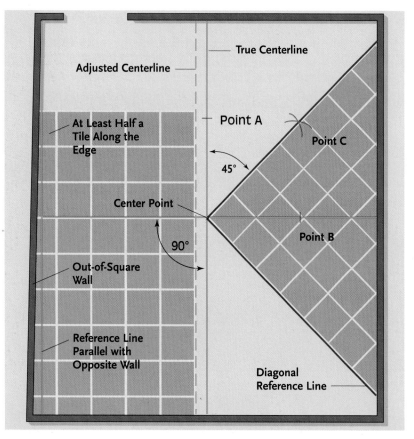

True Centerline

Adjusted Centerline

At Least Half a Tile Along the Edge

Point A

Point C

45°

Center Point

Point B

90°

Out-of-Square Wall

Reference Line Parallel with Opposite Wall

Diagonal Reference Line

ABOVE Carefully snapping chalk layout lines before you begin to install the flooring will help you to make a balanced, symmetrical layout. The blue lines indicate the lines for a standard layout; the red lines for a diagonal layout.

CHECKING A ROOM FOR SQUARE

project

The biggest problem with an out-of-square room is not knowing about it. If you're in the dark, then you can't exercise any of the many strategies to hide the problem. One of the best is simply to identify the least visible wall and use that to absorb all the trouble. A good candidate is the bathroom wall that falls behind the toilet and the vanity. Another is along the tub. You can install the tub so it's square to the room and fur out the wall behind the tub.

TOOLS & MATERIALS
▍ Measuring tape ▍ Chalk-line box
▍ 4-foot spirit level ▍ String
▍ Long 2x4
▍ 3 scrap blocks, all ¾ inch thick

1 The best way to check a room for square is to use a 3-4-5 right triangle. Measure from the corner along one wall to the 3-ft. point and mark the floor. Do the same with the other wall, but mark the floor at 4 ft. If the diagonal distance between these two marks is 5 ft., the room is square.

2 Level is another room characteristic you should check. Do this by placing a 4-ft. level on a long 2x4. If the floor is more than ½ in. out of level in 10 ft. it will be noticeable where the wall meets the floor. Because of this, it's a good idea to avoid using tile on the floor and the walls.

3 Also check the walls for straightness. Do this by running a string between same-sized blocks nailed to both ends of the wall. Then run a third block, of the same thickness, between the string and the wall, and mark where the wall isn't parallel with the string.

VINYL FLOOR TILE

Installing vinyl or resilient floor tiles is fairly simple and requires only a few tools. For professional results, you'll need to plan the layout and prepare the substrate properly. Keep in mind that most resilient floor tiles come in 12-inch squares. Trim strips in various accent colors are available in ¼- to 6-inch widths. When ordering, figure the areas in square feet to be covered (length times width) and add 5 to 10 percent for waste.

Start with the Right Base

When you pick out a resilient flooring material, check the manufacturer's instructions for acceptable substrates. (See "Underlayments to Avoid," below.)

Plywood that bears the stamp "Underlayment Grade" is the best choice for resilient flooring. Only use material that is ¼ inch thick, or thicker. Lauan, a tropical hardwood, is also used. But make sure you get Type 1 with exterior-grade glue.

Wood strip flooring will serve as underlayment only if it is completely smooth, dry, free of wax, and has all joints filled.

Old resilient tile, sheet flooring, and linoleum should be clean, free of wax, and tightly adhered with no curled edges or bubbles.

Ceramic tile must be clean and free of wax. Joints should be grouted full and leveled.

Concrete must be smooth and dry. Fill the cracks and dimples with a latex underlayment compound.

smart tip

UNDERLAYMENTS TO AVOID

ALWAYS CHECK WITH THE MANUFACTURER WHEN SELECTING AN UNDERLAYMENT MATERIAL. TWO THAT MOST MANUFACTURERS REJECT:

▌ *PARTICLEBOARD BECAUSE IT SWELLS GREATLY WHEN WET. IF YOU HAVE PARTICLEBOARD ON THE FLOOR NOW, REMOVE IT OR COVER IT WITH UNDERLAYMENT-GRADE PLYWOOD.*

▌ *HARDBOARD BECAUSE SOME TILE MANUFACTURERS DO NOT CONSIDER IT A SUITABLE UNDERLAYMENT FOR THEIR PRODUCTS.*

project

LAYING VINYL FLOOR TILE

Vinyl floor tiles come in two basic types. The tiles that are laid in adhesive, as shown here, and the self-sticking tiles that come with protective paper on their sticky side. To lay these tiles, you just peel off the paper and press the tile down onto the floor. While there's no question that self-sticking tiles are easier to install, the traditional type provides a more durable installation.

TOOLS & MATERIALS
▌ Framing square ▌ Chalk-line box
▌ Measuring tape ▌ Utility knife
▌ Rolling pin or floor roller
▌ Notched trowel (notch size as specified by adhesive manufacturer)
▌ Resilient tiles ▌ Adhesive ▌ Solvent

3 Carefully lower each tile into place to avoid smearing the adhesive. Press the tile down with your hands; then roll it smooth with a kitchen rolling pin or floor roller. If any adhesive squeezes up between tiles, wipe it up immediately with the solvent specified on the product container.

1 After marking work lines on the floor, lay out the tiles dry to make sure your installation plans are correct. Place the tile against the work lines in all four directions.

2 Check the adhesive container to find out how long the adhesive can be exposed before it starts to dry. Then plan to install an area that you can comfortably get done in this period. Spread the adhesive in this area, using a notched trowel held at a 45-deg. angle.

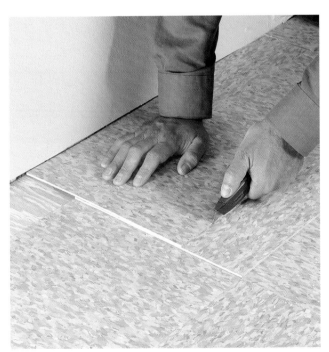

4 To cut a border tile, place a new full tile over the last full tile that has been installed. Then take another full tile and butt it against the wall. Cut along the edge of the top tile that is farthest away from the wall.

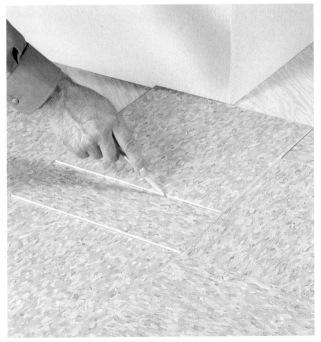

5 To cut around an outside corner, mark one side of the tile using the same technique that's explained in step 4. Then lift the tile and butt it against the other side of the corner, and mark it in the same way. Remove the tile, and cut it on a flat surface, such as a piece of scrap plywood.

CERAMIC FLOOR TILE

Ceramic and stone floor tiles are installed much the same way as vinyl tile, described on page 244. But there are differences, and it's the differences that make tiling more difficult than setting a vinyl floor. Tile is set in thinset adhesive, and cutting tiles is more difficult than trimming vinyl products. (See "Cutting Tiles," opposite page.) You must also grout the spaces between tiles, a step that takes some time and practice to get right. However, the results are well worth the extra effort and will provide a durable, long-lasting floor.

You can start your tile installation in a corner or from the center of the floor, using chalk lines as described on page 242. In either case, it is best to lay out the tiles in a dry run. Use tile spacers to indicate the width of the grout joint; if using mesh-backed tile sheets, you don't have to worry about joint spacing. Try to lay out the tiles to avoid narrow pieces of tile (less than 1 inch) abutting a wall. If this happens, adjust the layout.

If the corners in the room are not square or if you must install cut tiles around the perimeter of the room, make guide strips by temporarily nailing 1x2 or 1x4 battens to the underlayment. If you are tiling to concrete, weigh down the ends of the guides with heavy weights, such as a few stacked bricks. Place a strip parallel with each of two adjacent walls, with their leading edges positioned on the first joint line. Begin your installation here and then go back and fill in the space between the first full row of tiles and the wall by cutting each tile to fit.

To make sure that the strips are at right angles, use the 3-4-5 method. Measure 3 units (3 feet, if the room is big enough) from the corner along the guideline (or strip), and mark the spot. Measure out 4 units (4 feet) along the long guide line, and mark the spot. Now measure the diagonal between the two points. If the diagonal measures 5 units (5 feet), then the two guides are at right angles. If not, adjust the lines (or strips) as necessary.

Laying a Threshold

The transition from the tiled bathroom floor to an adjacent floor of a different material, and possibly different height, is made with a saddle, or threshold. Choose from among the following: trim pieces of tile that come with a molded edge, solid-surface material (cultured marble), metal, or hardwood.

Apply adhesive to the floor and bottom of the saddle. Then screw or nail the saddle in place. Conceal the screw or nailheads with putty or plugs. Allow space between the saddle and tile for a grout joint.

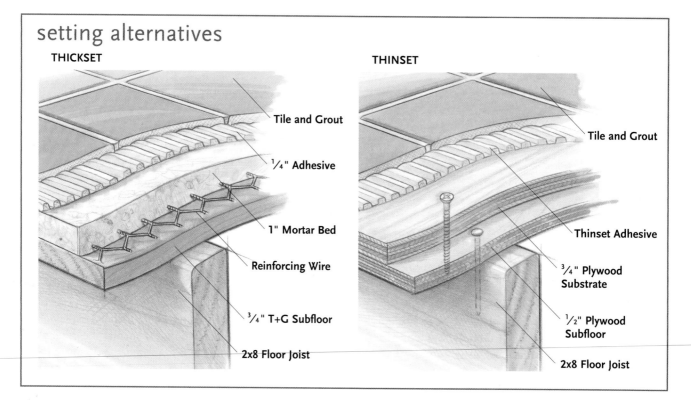

setting alternatives

THICKSET

- Tile and Grout
- 1/4" Adhesive
- 1" Mortar Bed
- Reinforcing Wire
- 3/4" T+G Subfloor
- 2x8 Floor Joist

THINSET

- Tile and Grout
- Thinset Adhesive
- 3/4" Plywood Substrate
- 1/2" Plywood Subfloor
- 2x8 Floor Joist

basic tile shapes and patterns

The basic floor tile measures 12 x 12 in. with a $\frac{1}{8}$- to $\frac{1}{4}$-in. grout joint.

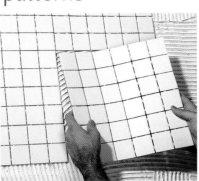

Sheet-mounted tile will look like individual mosaic tiles when installed.

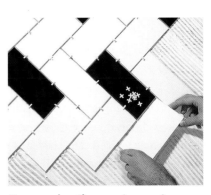

Rectangular tiles can be used to create basket-weave patterns.

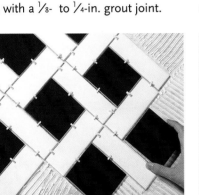

Combining different shapes allows you to create a variety of patterns.

Hexagon-shaped tiles create an interlocked pattern.

Multicolor and multisize tiles are available in sheets.

● CUTTING TILES

A snap cutter consists of a metal frame that holds the tile in position, a carbide blade or wheel to score the tile, and a lever to snap the tile along the score line. You can buy or rent snap cutters, but many tile dealers loan these tools to their customers for the duration of the project. If you do buy or rent one, make sure that it can handle the tiles with which you will be working. Some models will not cut thick, unglazed quarry tiles or pavers.

Tile nippers take small bites out of tiles. They are good for cutting out curves and other irregular shapes to fit tiles around pipes or openings. The cuts will not be as smooth as cuts produced by the other tools, so plan on hiding the edges of these tiles under molding or some other type of trim.

A wet saw is a step up from both the tile nippers and the snap cutter. This rental tool is a stationary circular saw with a water-cooled carbide-grit blade. Don't use this tool on floor tiles coated with a slip-resistant abrasive grit because the grit will dull the blade.

LAYING CERAMIC FLOOR TILE

project

Ceramic floor tiles come in a wide variety of different shapes and colors. One of the primary differences is whether the tile is glazed or unglazed. The unglazed type that we show here is a common choice for both bathrooms and kitchens. The reason is simple: most unglazed tiles provide better traction in wet conditions. To protect them from staining, apply a sealer every year or two.

TOOLS & MATERIALS
▌Rubber float ▌Notched trowel ▌Pail
▌Sponge ▌Soft cloths ▌Hammer
▌Tile cutter ▌Tile nippers ▌Small brush
▌Jointing tool or toothbrush
▌Roller and pan ▌Tiles ▌Grout
▌Adhesive ▌Solvent ▌Sealant
▌12-inch piece of 2x4 wrapped with carpet

1 Begin by laying out the floor and snapping chalk lines to guide your work. Then spread only as much adhesive as you can cover with tile before it dries. The container will specify the open time of the adhesive inside. Use a notched trowel held at a 45-deg. angle.

4 After the tile adhesive has cured, clean out the grout joints between all the tiles using a soft broom or a shop vac. Then mix the grout, and spread it into the joints using a float tool. Make sure the grout completely fills all the joints.

5 To remove the excess grout, drag the rubber float across the joints at a 45-deg. angle. Do not press too hard because this can pull grout out of the joint and require you to apply a second coat.

2 Press individual tiles into the adhesive, giving each a slight twist to make sure the back of the tile is completely covered with adhesive. Keep tiles and grout lines aligned as you work.

3 Make sure all the tiles are embedded completely in the adhesive by tapping them with a padded board and a hammer. Use the block every couple of courses, and make sure the block spans several tiles every time you strike it.

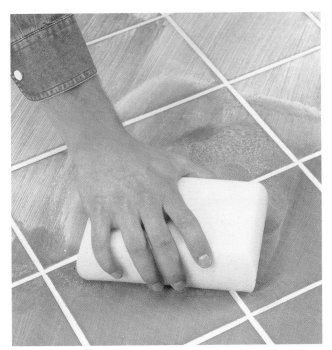

6 Clean off any remaining grout using a sponge and clean water. Work in a circular motion, and clean the sponge frequently. Also, change the water as soon as it becomes completely cloudy. When the tiles are as clean as you can make them, let the surface dry. Then buff the tiles with a clean, soft cloth.

7 Seal unglazed tiles and grout with a transparent sealer. Use a roller to apply it, according to the manufacturer's instructions printed on the product container. Diagonal strokes force the sealer into the grout joints better. If your tiles are glazed, apply sealer only to the grout with a brush.

INSTALLING RADIANT FLOOR HEATING

project

Ceramic tile and other masonry flooring products are elegant and durable, although they often feel cold even at comfortable room temperatures. Radiant floor heating systems are an effective and economical method of removing the chill from ceramic, marble, or stone-type floors. Installed between the subfloor and the finished flooring material, these cables will heat the floor to a comfortably warm temperature with a minimal use of electricity.

There are a number of these products on the market, but in general they consist of an insulated, flexible resistance-type heating element with attached electrical leads. The product shown here has these conductors contained in a fabric material. This fabric keeps the conductors spaced properly. Once the conductors are attached to the floor, you simply tile over them.

Keep in mind that you need to test these heating cables before putting them in place. You don't want to install a whole system, including the finished floor, only to find that it doesn't work. The instructions that come with the product you buy will explain the testing procedure.

TOOLS & MATERIALS
▌Radiant heating kit and controls
▌Long-nose pliers
▌Notched trowel
▌Ceramic tile or other suitable finished flooring
▌Sponge
▌Digital multimeter
▌Insulated screwdrivers
▌Thinset tile adhesive
▌Duct tape
▌Scissors
▌Tile grout
▌Grout float

1 Determine where you want radiant heat. There's no need to cover the entire floor, just the areas where you commonly walk or stand in bare feet. Cover this part of the floor with thinset mortar; let it dry; and install the fabric and cable over the thinset.

4 Mount an outlet box on the side of a stud, and bring a power cable into the box. Bring the power wires from the heating mat, through rigid conduit, into the other side of the box. Join the like-colored wires with wire connectors.

2 Locate the best spot for the temperature sensor by following the instructions that come with the radiant-heating components. Use duct tape to hold the sensor cable in place on the heating pad. Make sure the cable falls between the heating elements.

3 Spread a layer of thinset adhesive over the heating pad, and start laying tiles. Don't cover the entire floor with adhesive. Spread only as much as you can comfortably cover with tile before the thinset dries. Consult the product container for drying times. When all the tiles are laid and dry, grout the joints.

5 Once the power hook-ups are done, install the temperature sensor cables to special terminals on the controller thermostat. Follow the product instructions for the specific unit you are installing.

smart tip
RADIANT HEAT OPTIONS

THERE'S NO DOUBT THAT A RADIANT-HEATED BATHROOM FLOOR FEELS GREAT FIRST THING IN THE MORNING. LUXURY IS, AFTER ALL, LUXURIOUS. BUT IF YOUR REMODELING JOB DOESN'T INCLUDE REPLACING THE FLOOR, YOU CAN STILL TAKE THE CHILL OFF WITHOUT A LOT OF WORK. IN DRY CLIMATES, CARPETING IS A GOOD CHOICE, ESPECIALLY A SHORT PILE TYPE THAT DRIES OUT EASILY. IN MORE HUMID AREAS, AREA RUGS WITH SLIP-RESISTANT BACKINGS ARE A GOOD CHOICE. OR YOU CAN GO TO A CARPET STORE; PICK A REMNANT THAT YOU LIKE; HAVE IT CUT TO SIZE TO FIT THE ROOM WITH A BORDER OF ONE TO TWO FEET; AND PUT IT DOWN OVER A WATER RESISTANT PAD. PERIODICALLY HANGING THE RUG AND PAD OUTSIDE WILL DISCOURAGE MOLD AND ODORS. AND YOU CAN ALWAYS HAVE THEM CLEANED BY PROFESSIONAL CARPET CLEANERS.

flooring options

LEFT Some laminate flooring is designed for wet locations.

RIGHT Ceramic tile offers a variety of design options.

BELOW Marble tiles add a touch of elegance to any bathroom design.

RIGHT Stone offers the opportunity to create unique designs, such as the restful ambiance of this room

BELOW RIGHT New protective finishing materials make wood floor use in bathrooms possible.

MOLDING AND TRIMWORK

Besides the added beauty it brings to your bathroom, molding can conceal the gaps between cabinets and walls or ceilings and hide nailholes, screw holes, and other blemishes that are inevitable in construction. If the original bathroom contained intricate moldings that you want to keep, remove them carefully and reinstall them later.

Starting at the end of a wall, coax the existing molding away from the wall using a pry bar. Pry as close to the nails as possible, and use a thin scrap of wood behind the pry bar to protect the wall. After you've pried part of the trim away from the wall, move to the next nail. Continue this process until you gradually pry away the entire length of material. If a strip of molding won't come loose, drive the nails through the piece with a nail set. It's much easier to patch these holes later than to fix broken trim.

If you plan on installing new molding, you do not need to be careful with the old wood, but you should protect the surface of the drywall around the molding. Trying to get some leverage with the pry bar placed between wall studs can lead to large holes in the drywall.

UPGRADING BASE MOLDING

To replace vinyl cove molding with real wood, first remove the vinyl. Insert a pry bar or screwdriver into the corner to peel a small section back. Once it is free and you can grip the vinyl, pull back as you work the pry bar behind the molding. Use a hand scraper to remove the old adhesive. Don't use chemical adhesive removers.

Attach the new molding to wall studs with finishing nails. Set the nails, and fill the holes with putty. You can install a simple one-piece molding or build up the profile with a decorative top bead and quarter-round installed along the floor.

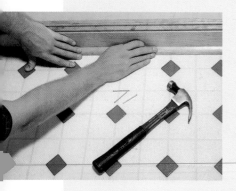

MAKING A COPED JOINT

project

The hardest part of cutting coped joints is getting used to working with a coping saw. Its thin, narrow blade makes it easy to follow a curved cut line. But it also makes it harder to achieve a smooth cut. Getting used to the saw just takes a little time. Most people who use these saws regularly, install the blade so the teeth point toward the handle, so the cutting takes place on the pull stroke.

TOOLS & MATERIALS
▌ Molding ▌ Backsaw ▌ Combination square
▌ Miter box or power miter saw
▌ Coping saw ▌ Utility knife or small chisel
▌ Round file and half-round files
▌ Power drill-driver and $\frac{1}{16}$-inch bit
▌ Hammer and nail set ▌ Glue ▌ Sandpaper

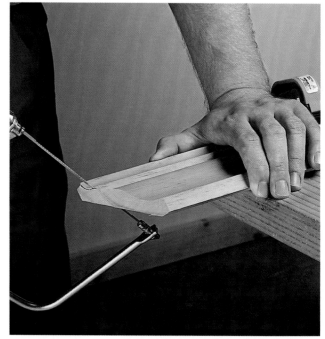

3 Use a coping saw to cut the molding profile along the mitered edge. Tip the saw toward the back of the board at about a 50-deg. angle, and follow the line formed by the miter and the outside surface of the board.

1 Start installing the ceiling molding by pushing a full size piece into one corner. Nail the bottom edge into the wall studs and the top edge into the ceiling joists or blocking above. Set the nailheads below the surface and fill the depressions with wood putty.

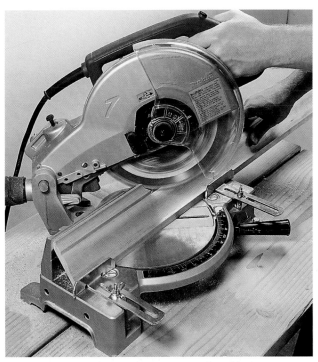

2 The first step in coping a piece of molding is to miter one end. Note how the board is installed in the miter box at a 45-deg. angle between the bottom and the fence.

4 Once the coped cut is complete, use an assortment of files and rasps to clean up the cut. Test fit the coped cut periodically to check your progress. The first couple of joints will take a while, but later ones will move faster as your techniques improve.

5 When you are satisfied with the fit, spread glue on the coped cut, and push the coped board in place next to the uncoped board. Make sure the joint is tight; then nail the coped board to the wall and ceiling; set the nailheads; fill the depressions with putty; and sand the filler smooth.

PREPARING DRYWALL FOR PAINTING

project

Paint is the most economical finish for bathroom walls, ceilings, and trim. It's also the easiest to apply. And there's no shortage of color choices and finish options. For the best results, the surfaces have to be properly prepared. And don't forget one of the basic rules of a good paint job: the higher the gloss, the more any imperfections will show.

TOOLS & MATERIALS
- Hammer ▮ Nail set
- Sandpaper ▮ Paintbrush
- Power drill-driver with screwdriver bit
- 6- and 12-inch-wide drywall taping knives
- Primer ▮ Joint compound
- Drywall screws or drywall nails

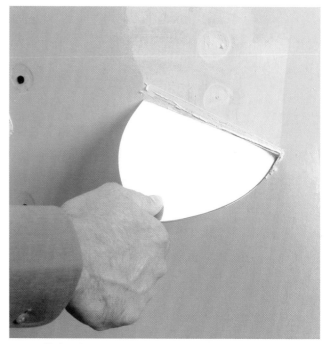

1 Fill the depressions over all exposed nail and screw heads with joint compound. Also fill any other dents or holes that may have occurred during the remodeling process. Try to apply the compound so it's as smooth as possible to reduce the amount of sanding that will be required later.

2 Once the joint compound is dry, sand it smooth to the surrounding surfaces with 100- to 150-grit sandpaper. Brush or vacuum the sanding dust off the surface. If there are still voids in the compound, apply more compound; let it dry; and sand it smooth.

3 The last step in paint preparation is to spot-prime all the joint compound with latex primer. Seal any mildew-stained areas with white-pigmented shellac.

PREPARING PLASTER FOR PAINTING

project

Traditional plaster isn't installed in many new homes these days, but there are still a lot of old houses that have this premium finish. Serious plaster problems, such as big sagging sections of ceiling, are better left to an experienced plasterer. But smaller troubles, such as cracks in otherwise sound plaster, are easy to fix and require just a couple of common tools.

TOOLS & MATERIALS
- Utility knife or can opener
- 6- and 12-inch-wide drywall knives
- Fiberglass mesh drywall tape
- Patching plaster

1 To fix small plaster cracks, first clean out the crack and slightly undercut both sides using a sharp tool, such as a utility knife or a can opener. Brush any dust out of the crack; then fill it with patching plaster. When the plaster is dry, sand it smooth to the surrounding surface.

2 Fix wider cracks by cleaning them out first and then filling them with patching plaster. Let the plaster dry, and sand it smooth. Then cover the crack with self-sticking fiberglass mesh tape. Flatten the tape with your fingertips.

3 Cover the mesh tape with two or three coats of patching plaster. Feather the edges of each coat away from the tape to make a gradual transition to the rest of the wall. Sand each coat smooth before adding another.

257

PREPARING WOODWORK FOR PAINTING

project

The way you prepare wood trim for painting depends on the condition of the trim. If you are reusing old trim boards that have nicked or deeply scratched paint, you'll have to carefully sand the boards and try to feather the edges of any damage so it won't be so apparent when the boards are painted. If you are working on new boards, proceed as shown in these photos.

TOOLS & MATERIALS
▌ Hammer and nail set
▌ Putty knife
▌ Narrow paint brush
▌ Wood filler
▌ Primer
▌ Caulk and caulking gun

● SORTING OUT WOOD FINISHES

Wood/Finish	Undercoat
Bare wood, penetrating oil	Penetrating oil; one or more coats
Bare wood, clear finish	Stain (if desired); two coats clear surface finish
Bare wood, paint finish	Latex wood primer or white shellac
Painted wood, paint finish	Spot-prime filled areas with latex wood primer or white shellac

1 Set all nailheads below the surface of the trim boards with a hammer and nail set. Fill the depressions above the set nails with wood filler. If you plan to use a clear finish, chose a colored filler that matches the wood. If you plan to paint, any type of wood filler can be used.

2 Once all the nailholes are filled, caulk all the joints between the trim boards and the walls and ceilings. Use latex caulk and try to apply a smooth bead. Finish the caulk by running a wet finger over the bead.

3 After the caulking is done, apply a latex or alkyd primer. Use smooth brush strokes to achieve the best surface. After the primer is dry, lightly sand any rough areas. Then wipe up the dust, and apply a top coat of paint.

PAINTING WALLS AND CEILINGS

For best results on new surfaces, use one coat of primer and two coats of paint. And before beginning work, protect wall or ceiling light fixtures with plastic trash bags and the floor with drop cloths. The typical painting sequence is to start with the ceiling, followed by the walls, and finishing up with the trim. But if you are painting all the surfaces the same color, do the trim before the walls.

TOOLS & MATERIALS
▌ Screwdriver ▌ Roller pan
▌ Paint shield ▌ Razor blade
▌ 1½- or 2-inch sash brush
▌ Roller with ¼-inch nap cover
▌ Masking tape (if necessary)
▌ Roller handle extension (optional)
▌ Wall and ceiling paint ▌ Drop cloths

For bathroom surfaces, choose paint with a high sheen. Gloss and semigloss paints resist moisture and are easier to clean than more porous flat or eggshell paints, making them good choices for bathroom walls, ceilings and woodwork. Because oil-based paints are being phased out by antipollution legislation, the steps below apply to water-based latex paints.

You can paint intricate surfaces, such as wood trim or cabinets, and small wall areas using only a brush. If the project extends to larger walls or ceilings, you'll save time and effort by using a roller.

Preparing and Priming

The key to a successful paint job is what lies below the paint. Paints with a gloss or semigloss sheen reveal imperfections more than flat or eggshell paints, so begin with a good substrate. Wash previously painted surfaces with phosphate-free trisodium and water. If stains or marks remain after washing, brush white-pigmented shellac over them. To remove any adhesive that clings after stripping off an old wallcovering, brush on wallpaper remover solvent. Make repairs as shown on pages 256-257. Also, temporarily remove all switch and outlet covers.

1 It only takes a few minutes to remove the cover plates from electrical switch and receptacle boxes. But it makes the painting go much faster with less aggravation. Just be sure to turn off the power to all the circuits before taking off the covers.

2 Begin painting your bathroom by trimming around the ceiling with a sash brush. Don't worry if the paint overlaps the walls. It's easier to paint a finished trim line on a wall than on the ceiling.

continued on next page

continued from previous page

3 A roller is the best tool for painting a ceiling. It distributes the paint evenly over a large area and it's much quicker than a brush. If you'd like to roll the ceiling by standing on the floor, just use an extension on the roller.

4 When the ceiling paint is dry, start with the walls by cutting in a trim line along the ceiling. Use a sash brush and try to maintain smooth strokes. Keep in mind that the finished line doesn't have to be perfect. It may look rough when you are working just a foot away. But from the floor it will look much better.

PAINTING WOODWORK

To get a clean job, remove any knobs from doors and cabinets before painting. Unless you need to paint large surfaces, use a small sash brush ($1\frac{1}{2}$ to 2 inches wide) to paint all wood. Paint the edges of doors first, ending with the larger surfaces. It is a good idea to work from the inside out. For example, on a raised-panel door, paint the panels first and then the rails and stiles; on windows, paint the muntins and then the sash frame. Use a paint shield while painting baseboards.

When painting a window sash, don't worry about applying painter's tape to the glass. Allow the paint to cover about $\frac{1}{16}$ inch of glass to help seal the juncture between the glazing and the wood. Don't worry if too much paint slops over onto the glass. Go back after the paint dries, and scrape any spills off the glass with a razor blade. Protect tile surfaces with painter's tape.

5 Once you paint the wall perimeter and around any windows and doors, start on the center of the wall. Use a roller and apply the paint in a zigzag motion. Finish off the section with strokes that are straight up and down.

INSTALLING A GRAB BAR

project

Grab bars are great safety devices for old and young alike. It always good to have a little help when moving around on a wet floor in your bare feet. But grab bars need strong support so that they can do their job safely and reliably. This means either attaching directly to the wall studs (which isn't always practical) or using heavy-duty anchors of toggle bolts.

TOOLS & MATERIALS
▌ Power drill-driver with carbide tipped bit
▌ Grab bar and fasteners
▌ Hollow-wall anchors or toggle bolts
▌ Screwdriver
▌ Masking tape
▌ 4-foot level

1 Locate the wall studs behind the ceramic tile over the tub or in the shower. Apply masking tape to the surface of the tile; trace the grab bar mounting holes on the tile; and drill the fastener holes with a carbide drill bit.

2 If you don't have studs located where you need them for the grab bar, mount it where you want it using heavy-duty hollow-wall fasteners or toggle bolts. Drill the holes to match the size specified on the product package. Then install the bolts on the grab bar first, and push the fasteners into the holes.

3 Tighten the wall fasteners using a screwdriver so that when you apply force to the grab bar it doesn't move. But don't overtighten them because this could lead to cracked tiles. Finish up by sliding escutcheons over the mounting plates on both ends of the grab bar.

This list of manufacturers and associations is meant to be a general guide to additional industry and product-related sources. It is not intended as a listing of products and manufacturers represented by the photographs in this book.

American Society of Interior Designers (ASID)
608 Massachusetts Ave., NE
Washington, DC 20002
Phone: 202-546-3480
www.asid.org
ASID, a nonprofit organization, represents interior design professionals and provides designer referrals.

American Olean/Dal-Tile
7834 C.F. Hawn Frwy.
Dallas, TX 75217
Phone: 214-398-1411
www.americanolean.com
American Olean, a division of Dal-Tile, manufactures floor and wall tile, including glazed and mosaic tiles. Its Web site offers consumer information.

Ann Sacks Tile & Stone
8120 NE 33rd Dr.
Portland, OR 97211
Phone: 800-278-8453
www.annsacks.com
Ann Sacks Tile and Stone, a division of the Kohler Company, manufactures a broad line of ceramic and stone tile, including terra-cotta and mosaics.

BainUltra (also known as Ultra Bath)
956 chemin Olivier
Saint-Nicolas, QC
Canada G7A 2N1
Phone: 800-463-2187
www.ultrabaths.com
BainUltra manufactures luxury bathtubs with massage features.

Bathease, Inc.
3815 Darston St.
Palm Harbor, FL 34685-3119
Phone: 888-747-7845
www.bathease.com
Bathease manufactures bathroom products for handicapped persons, including a flat-bottomed bathtub with a watertight door for safe access.

Center for Universal Design
N.C. State University
College of Design
Campus Box 7701
Raleigh, NC 27695-7701
www.design.ncsu.edu
The Center for Universal Design (College of Design) promotes design that accommodates people with ranges of physical ability.

Ceramic Tile Institute of America, Inc.
12061 W. Jefferson Blvd.
Culver City, CA 90230-6219
Phone: 310-574-7800
www.ctioa.org
The Ceramic Tile Institute of America, a membership trade organization, promotes the tile industry.

Grohe
241 Covington Dr.
Bloomingdale, IL 60108
Phone: 800-444-7643
www.grohe.com
Grohe manufactures bathroom and kitchen faucets, sinks, and shower systems. Its Web site provides an online product catalog.

Jacuzzi Whirlpool Bath
2121 N. California Blvd.
Walnut Creek, CA 94596
Phone: 800-288-4002
www.jacuzzi.com
Jacuzzi manufactures luxury tubs and showers for the home, as well as accessories.

Kohler Co.
444 Highland Dr.
Kohler, WI 53044
Phone: 800-456-4537
www.kohlerco.com
Kohler, a major manufacturer of bath and kitchen fixtures, offers a variety of toilets, bidets, lavs, tubs, and accessories.

Mannington Mills, Inc.
75 Mannington Mills Rd.
Salem, NJ 08079
Phone: 800-241-2262
www.mannington.com
Mannington, a manufacturer of residential and commercial floors, offers resilient, laminate, hardwood, and porcelain tile flooring.

Moen, Inc.
25300 Al Moen Dr.
North Olmstead, OH 44070
Phone: 800-289-6636
www.moen.com
Moen manufactures faucets and accessories for the bath and shower. Its Web site offers helpful consumer information including a product showcase.

National Association of Home Builders (NAHB)
1201 15th St., NW
Washington, DC 20005
Phone: 800-368-5242
www.nahb.org
NAHB, a trade association, promotes housing policies and offers consumers information on housing trends.

National Association of the Remodeling Industry (NARI)
780 Lee St., Ste. 200
Des Plaines, IL 60016
Phone: 800-611-6274
www.nari.org
NARI is a professional organization for contractors, remodelers, and designers. Its Web site offers consumer and membership information.

National Kitchen and Bath Association (NKBA)
687 Willow Grove St.
Hackettstown, NJ 07840
Phone: 800-843-6522
www.nkba.org
NKBA, a national trade organization, provides remodeling information and a designer referral service for consumers.

Springs Global, Inc.
P. O. Box 70
Fort Mill, SC 29716

Phone: 888-926-7888
www.springs.com
Springs Industries manufactures window treatments and hardware, including shades, shutters, and blinds, as well as bath accessories.

Sun Touch Floors
3131 W. Chestnut Expy.
Springfield, MO 65802
Phone: 888-432-8932
www.suntouch.net
Sun Touch Floors manufactures floor heating mats. Its product line includes both standard and underfloor mats, as well as accessories.

Thibaut Wallcoverings
480 Frelinghuysen Ave.
Newark, NJ 07114
Phone: 800-223-0704
www.thibautdesign.com
Thibaut Wallcoverings, a manufacturer of residential wallcoverings, offers a variety of wallpaper and border styles for all rooms in the home.

Tile Council of America, Inc.
100 Clemson Research Blvd.
Anderson, SC 29625
Phone: 864-646-8453
www.tileusa.com

TCA, a membership association, is committed to improving the tile-installation industry. Its Web site offers literature on selecting and installing tile.

Velux America, Inc.
450 Old Brickyard Rd.
P.O. Box 5001
Greenwood, SC 29648
Phone: 800-888-3589
www.velux.com
Velux America manufactures skylights, roof windows, and solar-energy systems for the home.

Accent lighting   Spot lighting that focuses on decorative features.

Ampere (amp)   The unit describing the rate of electrical flow.

Anti-scald valve   Single-control fitting that contains a piston that automatically responds to changes in line water pressure to maintain water temperature.

Backsplash   The wall area behind a sink or countertop.

Barrier-free fixtures   Fixtures specifically designed for people who use wheelchairs or who have limited mobility.

Base plan   Scale drawing made by using the rough measurements of an existing room. A convenient scale for planning a bathroom is to use a $1/2$ inch to represent 1 foot.

Bearing wall   A wall that supports the floor or roof above it.

Bidet   A bowl-shaped bathroom fixture that supplies water for personal hygiene.

Blanket insulation   Flexible insulation, such as fiberglass or mineral wool, that comes packaged in long rolls.

Blocking   Small pieces of wood used to reinforce framing members.

Bridging   Lumber or metal installed in an X shape between floor joists to stabilize and position the joists.

Cable   One or more wires enclosed in protective plastic or metal sheathing.

Cement-based backer board   A rigid panel designed for use as a substrate for ceramic tile in wet areas.

Cleanout   A removable plug in a trap or drainpipe, which allows easy access for removing blockages.

Cleat   A piece of lumber fastened (for example, to a joist or post) as a support for other lumber.

Closet bend   A curved section of drain beneath the base of a toilet.

Closet flange   The rim of a closet bend used to attach the toilet drainpipe to the floor.

Code   Locally or nationally enforced mandates that regulate structural design, materials, plumbing, and electrical systems.

Double-glazed window   A window consisting of two panes of glass separated by a space that contains air or argon gas. The space provides most of the insulation.

Downlighting   A lighting technique that illuminates objects or areas from above.

Dry run   The process of arranging the tiles to check the layout before applying adhesive; usually tile spacers are used to indicate the width of the grout joints.

DWV   Drain-waste-vent: the system of pipes and fittings used to carry away wastewater.

End-of-run   Outlet or switch box at the end position of a circuit.

Escutcheon   A decorative plate that covers a hole in the wall in which the pipe stem or cartridge fits.

Fish tape   Flexible metal strip used to draw wires or cable through walls and conduit.

Fixed window   A window that cannot be opened. It is usually a decorative unit, such as a half-round or round window.

Fixture   Any fixed part of the structural design, such as a tub, bidet, toilet, or lavatory.

Flux   The material applied to the surface of copper pipes and fittings when soldering to assist in the cleaning and bonding process.

Full bath   A bathroom that contains a sink, toilet, tub, and shower.

Furring   Wood strips used to level parts of a ceiling, wall, or floor before adding the finish surface. Also used to secure panels of rigid insulation. Sometimes called strapping.

Ground   The connection between electrical circuits and equipment and the earth.

Ground-fault circuit interrupter (GFCI)   A circuit breaker or outlet that compares the amount of current entering a receptacle with the amount leaving. If there is a discrepancy of 0.005 volt, the GFCI breaks the circuit in $1/40$ of a second. GFCIs are required by the National Electrical Code in areas, such as bathrooms, that are subject to dampness.

Grounding screw   Terminal screw to which a bare or green grounding wire is connected.

Grout   A binder and filler applied in the joints between ceramic tile.

Half bath   A bathroom that contains only a toilet and a sink.

Hardboard   Manufactured pressed-wood panels; hardboard is rejected by some manufacturers as an acceptable substrate for resilient and tile floors.

Junction box   Electrical box in which all standard wiring splices and connections are made.

Lavatory (or Lav)   A fixed bowl or

basin with running water and a drainpipe that is used for washing.

Middle-of-run Electrical box with its outlets or switch lying between the power source and another box.

Nonbearing wall A wall that does not support the weight of areas above it.

On center A point of reference for measuring. For example, 16 inches on center means 16 inches from the center of one framing member to the center of the next.

Overflow An outlet positioned in a tub or sink that allows water to escape if a faucet is left open.

Particleboard Reconstituted wood particles that are bonded with resin under heat and pressure and made into panels. Particleboard has a tendency to swell when exposed to moisture.

Pedestal A stand-alone lavatory with a basin and a supporting column.

Pigtail Short piece of wire that connects an electrical device or component to a circuit.

Proportion The relationship of one object to another in terms of size.

Resilient flooring Thin floor coverings composed of materials such as vinyl, rubber, cork, or linoleum. Comes in a wide range of colors and patterns in both tile and sheet forms.

Rigid foam Insulating boards composed of polystyrene or polyisocyanurate that may be foil backed. Rigid insulation offers the highest R-value per inch of thickness.

Riser A supply pipe that extends vertically, carrying water, steam, or gas.

Roughing-in The installation of the water-supply and DWV pipes before the fixtures are in place.

Rubber float A flat, rubber-faced tool used to apply grout.

Sconce A light fixture that is mounted to a wall.

Sister joist A reinforcing joist added to the side of a cut or damaged joist for additional support.

Soil stack The main vertical pipe in a house that carries waste to the sewer or septic lines.

Spa An inground or aboveground tublike structure or vessel that is equipped with whirlpool jets.

Spud washer The large rubber ring placed over the drain hole of a two-piece toilet. The tank is placed over the spud washer.

Stops On doors, the trim on the jamb that keeps the door from swinging through; on windows, the trim that covers the inside face of the jamb.

Stub-out The end of a water-supply or DWV pipe extended through a wall or floor.

Stud Vertical member of a framed wall, usually 2×4s or 2×6s installed every 16 or 24 inches on center.

Subfloor The surface below a finished floor. In newer homes, the subfloor is usually made of sheet material such as plywood; in older homes the subfloor is usually made of individual boards.

Switch loop Installation in which a switch is at the end of a circuit with one incoming power cable, and the outgoing neutral wire becomes a hot wire to control a fixture.

Thickset A layer of mortar that is more than $1/2$ inch thick and is used as a base for ceramic tile.

Thinset Any cement-based or organic adhesive applied in a layer less than $1/2$ inch thick that is used for setting tile.

Three-quarter bath A bathroom that contains a toilet, sink, and shower.

Toenail To join boards together by nailing at an angle through the end of one and into the face of another.

Tongue-and-groove Boards milled with a protruding tongue on one edge and a slot on the other for a tight fit on flooring and paneling.

Trap A section of curved pipe that forms a seal against sewer gas when it is filled with water.

Tripwaste A lever-controlled bathtub drain stopper.

Universal Design Products and designs that are easy to use by people of all ages, heights, and physical abilities.

Vanity The countertop and cabinet that supports a sink.

Vent stack The main vertical vent pipe in the DWV system.

Volt The unit of electrical force.

Watt The unit of measurement of electrical power required or consumed by a fixture or appliance.

Wax ring A wax seal between the base of a toilet and the closet flange that prevents leaking.

Whirlpool A bathtub that includes motorized jets inside the walls of the tub.

Wire connector A small cap used for twisting two or more wires together.

index

Metric Equivalents

Length

1 inch	25.4mm
1 foot	0.3048m
1 yard	0.9144m
1 mile	1.61km

Area

1 square inch	645mm^2
1 square foot	0.0929m^2
1 square yard	0.8361m^2
1 acre	4046.86m^2
1 square mile	2.59km^2

Volume

1 cubic inch	16.3870cm^3
1 cubic foot	0.03m^3
1 cubic yard	0.77m^3

Common Lumber Equivalents

Sizes: Metric cross sections are so close to their U.S. sizes, as noted below, that for most purposes they may be considered equivalents.

Dimensional lumber	1 x 2	19 x 38mm
	1 x 4	19 x 89mm
	2 x 2	38 x 38mm
	2 x 4	38 x 89mm
	2 x 6	38 x 140mm
	2 x 8	38 x 184mm
	2 x 10	38 x 235mm
	2 x 12	38 x 286mm
Sheet sizes	4 x 8 ft.	1200 x 2400mm
	4 x 10 ft.	1200 x 3000mm
Sheet thicknesses	1/4 in.	6mm
	3/8 in.	9mm
	1/2 in.	12mm
	3/4 in.	19mm
Stud/joist spacing	16 in. o.c.	400mm o.c.
	24 in. o.c.	600mm o.c.

Capacity

1 fluid ounce	29.57mL
1 pint	473.18mL
1 quart	0.95L
1 gallon	3.79L

Weight

1 ounce	28.35g
1 pound	0.45kg

Temperature

Fahrenheit = Celsius x 1.8 + 32
Celsius = Fahrenheit - 32 x 5/9

Nail Size & Length

Penny Size	Nail Length
2d	1"
3d	1¼"
4d	1½ "
5d	1¾"
6d	2"
7d	2¼"
8d	2½"
9d	2¾"
10d	3"
12d	3¼"
16d	3½"

photo credits

Project sequences by Freeze Frame Studio except where noted.

page 1: Anne Gummerson, design: Gina Fitzsimmons, Fitzsimmons Design Associates **pages 2:–3** *both* Mark Lohman **page 6:** courtesy of Moen **pages 8–9:** Gray Crawford/Redcover.com **page 11:** Mark Samu, courtesy of Hearst Specials **pages 12–13:** *all* Mark Lohman **pages 14–15:** *top left* Jessie Walker; *center* Tria Giovan; *top right* Anne Gummerson, design: Brennan Architects; *bottom right* Jessie Walker; *bottom center* Anne Gummerson; *bottom left* Randall Perry **page 17:** www.davidduncanlivingston.com **page 21:** *top illustration* Ian Warpole **page 23:** *right* Clarke Barre **page 38:** *top* Ron Solomon; *center* Stickley Photo•Graphic; *bottom* George Ross **page 39:** www.davidduncanlivingston.com **page 40:** *top* Phillip H. Ennis Photography; *bottom* Tim Street-Porter/Beateworks.com **page 41:** courtesy of Jacuzzi **page 42:** Randall Perry **page 43:** George Ross **page 44:** *left* Stickley Photo•Graphic; *right* Maggie Cole, design: Lauren Muse **page 45:** *top* Peter Paige; *bottom* Lisa Masson **page 46:** *top* Elizabeth Whiting Associates; *bottom* Toillon/Inside/Beateworks.com **page 47:** Mark Samu, courtesy of Hearst Specials **page 48:** Ron Solomon **page 49:** melabee m miller, design: Elizabeth Gillin **pages 50–53:** *all illustrations* Glee Barre **page 54:** *top* courtesy of Moen; *center* courtesy of Kohler; *bottom* Eric Roth **page 55:** Eric Roth, architect: Ben Nutter **page 56:** *top right & bottom right* www.davidduncanlivingston.com; *bottom left* Wauman/Inside/Beateworks.com **page 57:** *top right* Philip Clayton-Thompson; *bottom right* Eric Roth; *bottom left* courtesy of Price Pfister **page 58:** *top* Eric Roth; *bottom* Jessie Walker **page 59:** *top* Phillip H. Ennis Photography, design: Andrew Chary & Associates; *bottom* courtesy of Kohler **page 60:** *top* Tria Giovan; *bottom* Mark Lohman **page 61:** Randall Perry **page 62:** Stickley Photo•Graphic **page 63:** *both* Mark Lohman **page 64:** *top right* Anne Gummerson; *center right* courtesy of Kohler; *left* Mark Samu **page 66:** Scott Darrance **page 67:** *top* www.davidduncanlivingston.com; *bottom* Phillip H. Ennis Photography **page 68:** *illustrations* Glee Barre **page 69:** *top* www.davidduncanlivingston.com;

bottom courtesy of Kohler **pages 70–73:** *illustrations* Glee Barre **page 74:** *top & bottom* courtesy of Seagull Lighting; *center* www.davidduncanlivingston.com **page 75:** Rob Melnychuk **page 76:** Beth Singer **page 77:** *left* Tria Giovan; *right* Mark Lohman **page 78:** Anne Gummerson **page 79:** *top* Jessie Walker; *bottom* www.davidduncanlivingston.com **page 80:** *top right* Mark Lohman; *bottom right* Rob Melnychuk; *top left* www.davidduncanlivingston.com **page 81:** *right* Tony Giammarino/Giammarino & Dworkin; *bottom left* Mark Lohman; *top right* Randall Perry **page 82:** Bill Geddes/Beateworks.com **page 83:** *top* Mark Lohman; *illustration* Glee Barre **pages 84–85:** *illustrations* Glee Barre **page 87:** www.davidduncanlivingston.com **page 94:** *right* courtesy Velux America; *bottom left* Phillip H. Ennis Photography; *top left* courtesy of Springs Window Fashions **page 95:** *top* Phillip H. Ennis Photography; *bottom both* Elizabeth Whiting Associates **page 100:** *bottom* www.davidduncanlivingston.com **page 102:** *top* Mark Lohman; *center* Tria Giovan; *bottom* Phillip H. Ennis Photography **page 103:** Joseph De Leo Photography **pages 104–105:** *both* www.davidduncanlivingston.com **page 106:** *left* Mark Lohman; *right* www.davidduncanlivingston.com **page 107:** *left* Tria Giovan; *right* www.davidduncanlivingston.com **page 108:** Todd Caverly **page 109:** Mark Lohman **page 110:** Phillip H. Ennis Photography **page 111:** *left* www.davidduncanlivingston.com; *right* Phillip H. Ennis Photography **page 113:** courtesy of Kohler **page 119:** *right all* Brian C. Nieves/CH **page 125:** Jessie Walker **page 142:** *bottom* courtesy of Lightology **pages 146–147:** *all* John Parsekian/CH **page 149:** www.davidduncanlivingston.com **page 150:** *top* Tria Giovan; *bottom* courtesy of Ann Sacks Tile Co. **page 151:** *top* Nancy Hill; *bottom* Philip Clayton-Thompson **page 152:** *top* Rob Melnychuk; *bottom* www.davidduncanlivingston.com **page 153:** *top* courtesy of Jacuzzi; *center & bottom* courtesy of Kohler **page 160:** *left* Tria Giovan; *right* Eric Roth **page 161:** Tim Street-Porter/Beateworks.com **page 162:** *left* Jessie Walker; *right* courtesy of Jacuzzi **page 163:** *top right & bottom right* Mark Samu;

bottom left courtesy of Kohler **page 178:** *top right* courtesy of Kohler; *bottom right* www.carolynbates.com; *bottom left* courtesy of Moen; *top left* courtesy of Moen **page 179:** *right* courtesy of Grohe; *bottom left* Elizabeth Whiting Associates; *top left* Mark Samu **page 180:** *bottom* Merle Henkenius **page 181:** Mark Lohman **page 182:** *left* www.davidduncanlivingston.com; *right* courtesy of Kohler **page 183:** *top* Jessie Walker; *center* Nancy Hill; *bottom* courtesy of Kohler **pages 188–193:** Merle Henkenius **page 195:** Beth Singer, design: Jeffrey King Interiors and Richard Ross Interiors, architect: Bryce, McCalpin & Palazzola Architects, builder: Ray Wallick **page 197:** *top right* Mark Lohman; *bottom right* Mark Samu; *left* Mark Lohman, design: Harte Brownlee & Assoc. **page 210:** *left* Phillip H. Ennis Photography; *right* Mark Samu, courtesy of Hearst Specials **page 211:** Phillip H. Ennis Photography **page 212:** *left* Mark Lohman; *right* Rob Melnychuk **page 213:** Mark Samu, courtesy of Hearst Specials **page 214:** *top right & bottom right* Tria Giovan; *left* melabee m miller, builder: Doyle Builders **page 215:** Mark Lohman **page 216:** *top & bottom* Merle Henkenius **page 217:** Anne Gummerson **page 218:** *left* www.davidduncanlivingston.com; *right* Rob Melnychuk **page 219:** *top* courtesy of Kohler; *center* Phillip H. Ennis Photography; *bottom* Mark Lohman **page 221:** *bottom right* courtesy of Kohler **page 223:** Phillip H. Ennis Photography **page 224:** Mark Lohman **page 225:** *top right & bottom right* Jessie Walker; *bottom left* Anne Gummerson; *top left* Tria Giovan **page 226:** *top* Mark Samu; *bottom* courtesy of Kohler **page 227:** *top* Rob Melnychuk; *bottom right* Tria Giovan; *bottom left* Anne Gummerson **page 228:** *top right* Mark Lohman; *bottom right* courtesy of Moen; *bottom left* Rob Melnychuk; *top left* courtesy of Kohler **page 229:** Phillip H. Ennis Photography **pages 232–239:** *all* Merle Henkenius **page 241:** Beth Singer **pages 250–251:** John Parsekian/CH **pages 252–253:** *top right* www.davidduncanlivingston.com; *bottom right & top center* Jessie Walker; *bottom left* Randall Perry; *top left* courtesy of Mannington Floors **page 263:** www.davidduncanlivingston.com

Have a home improvement, decorating, or gardening project? Look for these and other fine Creative Homeowner books wherever books are sold.

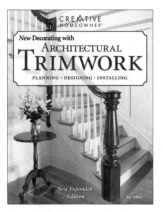

Transform a room with trimwork. Over 550 color photos and illustrations. 240 pp.; 8^1/$_2$"×10^7/$_8$"
BOOK #: 277500

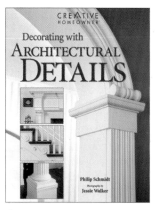

Covers design treatments such as moldings and window seats. 300+ color photos. 224 pp.; 8^1/$_2$"×10^7/$_8$"
BOOK #: 278225

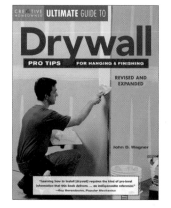

A complete guide, covering all aspects of drywall. Over 450 color photos. 160 pp.; 8^1/$_2$"×10^7/$_8$"
BOOK #: 278320

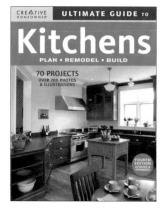

Includes step-by-step projects and over 700 photos and illustrations. 272 pp.; 8^1/$_2$"×10^7/$_8$"
BOOK#: 277071

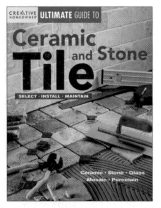

Complete DIY tile instruction. Over 550 color photos and illustrations. 224 pp.; 8^1/$_2$"×10^7/$_8$"
BOOK #: 277532

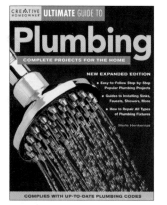

The complete manual for plumbing projects. Over 750 color photos and illustrations. 288 pp.; 8^1/$_2$"×10^7/$_8$"
BOOK#: 278200

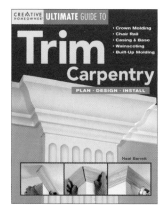

Add trimwork and molding to your home. Over 700 photos and illustrations. 208 pp.; 8^1/$_2$"×10^7/$_8$"
BOOK#: 277516

The ultimate home-improvement reference manual. Over 300 step-by-step projects. 608 pp.; 9"×10^7/$_8$"
BOOK#: 267870

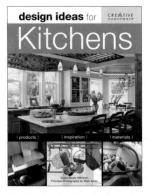

Design inspiration for creating a dream kitchen. Over 500 color photographs. 224 pp.; 8^1/$_2$"×10^7/$_8$"
BOOK #: 279415

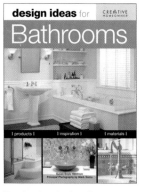

Design inspiration for creating a new bathroom. Over 500 color photos. 224 pp.; 8^1/$_2$"×10^7/$_8$"
BOOK #: 279268

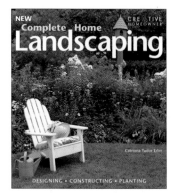

An impressive guide to garden design and plant selection. 950 color photos and illustrations. 384 pp.; 9"×10"
BOOK #: 274610

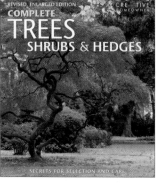

How to select and care for landscaping plants. More than 700 photos. 240 pp.; 9"×10"
BOOK #: 274222

For more information and to order direct, visit our Web site at www.creativehomeowner.com